RENÉ

WHO MADE SPANISH COOL WITH THEIR BILINGUAL POP MUSIC HITS

Best known for

"ANGELITO"

The "First Original Spanish-English Bilingual Hit on America's Top 40 charts" and the story behind the songwriting team who wrote and recorded this song, plus their second million-seller,

"LO MUCHO QUE TE QUIERO"

as well as many other hits

By Ramón R. Hernández and Saundra Ornelas

Copyright © by René Víctor Ornelas

ISBN: 979-8-864-14435-0

RENÉ Y RAMÓN
PUBLISHING

All rights reserved. No part of this book may be reproduced or transmitted in any form or by any means, electronic or mechanical, including photocopying, recording, or by an information storage, database, or retrieval system, without the prior written permission from the copyright owner. or in accordance with the provisions of the Copyright, Designs and Patents Act 1988 or under the terms of any license permitting limited copying issued by the Copyright Licensing Agency.

Cover photo/Graphics: Ramón Hernández Archives

Back cover graphics by Ramón Hernández

Inside images are credited to photographers and contributors beneath photograph, or on the edge of image

René Ornelas contact info:
reneloveslucy@gmail.com (210) 828-4444

Ramón Hernández contact info:
ramon.photog.hernandez@gmail.com (210) 803-1411

San Antonio, Texas

AUTOGRAPHS

[signature] *[signature]* *[signature]*

René Ornelas   René Herrera

[signature] *[signature]*

Juan Garza-Góngora   Juan Orfila

THE QUARTER NOTES

The 2nd, 3rd, 4th and 5th Second René's

[signature] *[signature]*

Jorge Ramírez   Marvin Palacios

[signature] *[signature]*

Mario Rivera   Richard Noriega Jr.

Immaculate Heart of Mary | Sacred Heart of Jesus

This book is dedicated to
The Blessed Virgin Mary
who always leads us
to her only son - Jesus Christ

INTRODUCTION

From the mid-1960s to the mid-1970s, no two Hispanic American singers, songwriters and composers did more for the Latinization of American music than René Víctor Ornelas Montemayor Garza de la Garza García Cantú Valle Madrigal Flores and his partner, René Ede Herrera. René Ornelas was the lead singer and René Herrera sang the harmony part under the stage name of René and René.

This is the artistic name by which they became known as for their million-seller hits, "Angelito" and "Lo Mucho Que Te Quiero." These were the two trailblazing compositions which contained their bilingual lyrics.

Their accomplishments have not been forgotten and this book will tell you the story behind their music. However, success did not come overnight, because this duo's musical journey began in 1954 when René Ornelas composed the song, "Please Come Home," the first song he wrote when he was in high school. Nevertheless, without the songwriting talents and determination of Ornelas and Herrera, the success of René and René would never have happened.

Best known for their bilingual hits, their compositions have been recorded by Vikki Carr ("No Te Vayas"), Trini López, José Feliciano, Sandler & Young, The Sandpipers, The Seven Days, and The Gauchos.

Instrumental versions of the René and René hit songs were also recorded by Herb Alpert and the Tijuana Brass, Lawrence Welk, Al Hirt, Peter Nero, Martin Denny, the 50 Guitars of Tommy Garrett, Ray Anthony, Steve Allen and Soulful Brass, Santo and Johnny, Lo Tampicos, Carlos Campos and the Matadors, the Banana Monkeys, and the Organ Masters; plus, many others.

In Texas, a soulful version of "Angelito" was recorded by Joe Jama with the Royal Jesters and by Roberto Zenteno and His Combo. In California, it was recorded by Joe Flores con sus Trovadores del Bravo.

In Mexico, the René and René hit songs were recorded by world famous artists such as Trio Los Panchos, Pedro Vargas, Toña La Negra, Marco Antonio Muñiz, Manolo Muñoz, Pedro "Pedrito" Fernández, Irma Serrano, Carlos Cuevas, Los Hermanos Rosario, Irene y Fidel, Los Abajeños, plus other bands, mariachis and vocalists. It was also recorded by Los Angeles in the mother country of Spain.

Los Traviezos del Norte recorded "Lo Mucho Que Te Quiero" with a *norteño* rhythm. Jessie Morales did it in *banda* style. Pepe Maldonado used a steel guitar and turned it into Tejano country. Then, Frankie y Los Matadores plus the Gilberto Sextet turned it into a *salsa* hit; El Medio Grupo, featuring Chacalón, gave it a cumbia beat.

Joel Sol rocked it, Anthony Arizaga turned it into a guitar instrumental while Tony Janak and his orchestra recorded it as a romantic instrumental with the English title of "The More I Love You."

In other parts of the world, Brazilian and Portuguese artists – such as Deny e Dino, Jovem Guarda, Jerry Adriani, and João Mineiro e Marciano - were recording "Lo Mucho Que Te Quiero" as "O Quanto Eu Te Quiero." All those versions are on YouTube.com. Add to this list the Israeli singer Aliza Kashi and Clive Sands in Holland.

Some Chicano/Tejano artists who recorded some of their other hits were Little Joe, Rocky Padilla, Sunny (Ozuna) of the Sunliners, The Royal Jesters, Laura Canales, Lisa Lopez, Grupo Mazz, Chito Gonzales and the Sun Rays, and also Mary, featuring Rabb Rodríguez on Rosina Records, and many, many others.

But giving credit where it's due, before René and René, the first Latino vocalist to have waxed a bilingual tune was Andy Russell (r.n. Andrés Rabago Pérez). And no, this internationally known crooner was not of Spanish, Italian or French origin. He was a Mexican American from Boyle Heights in East Los Angeles.

Notwithstanding, it was Gene Autry, an Anglo Saxon, that recorded a bilingual tune in 1940. That ditty was "Allá En El Rancho Grande,"written by Mexican songwriter Juan Díaz del Moral's in 1927 and recorded by Tito Guízar in 1936.

Russell's bilingual English/Spanish song was "Besame Mucho" ("Kiss Me Much") (Capitol 114-A); and it was this record that gave a then new Hollywood label named Capitol one of its first big hits in 1944. Meanwhile, Andy Russell continued to record and perform bilingual versions of Mexican standards in radio, television, and films.

Closer to home, Johnny Herrera was the first TexMex artist to record a bilingual song, when he waxed "Jealous Heart" as a bilingual country and western tune in 1949. The second Tejano artist to record a bilingual tune was Sonny Ace (r.n. Domingo Solís) and the Del-Sharps with the vocal backing of The Royal Jesters. It was "If My Teardrops Could Talk" (www.youtube.com/watch?v=eN7sRi6pDI8) in 1958.

Despite those "firsts," it was René Ornelas and Rene Herrera's "creative original compositions" that took bilingual tunes to a new level of popularity that spread from the United States to Central and South America plus Europe.

The bottom line is that Rene and Rene's compositions are crafted so well, the lyrics lend themselves to any language and their musical arrangements fit any music genre. That's why today the music of René and René continues to weather and withstand the test of time.

And now, here's the story behind the songwriting team and the other Rene's that followed - the story of how they came to be as we dug all the way back to the origin of the musical roots that preceded their birth as told by René Ornelas since René Herrera, the other half of this famous music history-making duo passed 15 years before this writer was able to conduct an in depth interview him.

Furthermore, in an effort to have more of Herrera's side of the story, I also visited with widow, Velia, twice; and followed up with numerous telephone calls to no avail. Therefore, my most profound apologies to his friends and fans who were hoping to know more of his story.

PROLOGUE

Many people want to write a book. Some of them have already started and they want to tell me all about it. I listen to them, and I always try to support and inspire them by giving them encouragement. But deep down inside, I know that most of them will never finish writing that book.

Most people like the idea of producing a book because it stimulates and excites their interest. They see themselves involved in that artistic, creative, and gifted process of writing a book. But the true, practical, down-to-earth, and sober reality is that creating a book is just very hard work - period!

When you first begin to develop the idea for your book, everything is amazing, fabulous, extraordinary and out of this world. But you know that doesn't last very long and then the hard work begins. As you continue in the process, you might feel a surge of inspiration. But if you write only when you get inspired, you'll never finish your book.

To write a book, you must have daily discipline; this means fortitude, training, drilling, willpower, self-control, and mental toughness, and you must work at it every day - even if some days all you do is read again what you wrote yesterday to keep it new, fresh, and up to date. You must have the discipline to write when you feel like it and also when you don't. A lot of people do not have this commitment, which is why many who have started writing a book will never finish it.

When most of us think of creating a book, we have a mental picture of an artist at work in an exciting, electrifying, and breathtaking situation, and without effort, he is rapidly composing page after page. As we have mentioned before, the truth is that this creative process is mostly very hard work. And we are still just talking about writing a book. We have not discussed writing a best seller or even a great book yet.

There is no guarantee that just because you are writing a book it will be a good one, much less a great or powerful book. But there is a better chance that if you do the necessary research and apply the required discipline – it will be a much better book.

In the case of this book, I have included some tidbits from my very early youth. Since my musically gifted father trained and guided me as a very young child to follow in his footsteps, the goal was to use my talents to the best of my ability. The lengthy career of René and René has been the largest and most important part of my life --- singing, writing songs, recording and performing on stage to thousands of my fans. So, I want to share all the fun I have had --- and still continue to have in my life. That is why I decided to write this book.

We are very confident and optimistic that you will enjoy and get a tremendous kick out of reading our book on René and René. You can be sure that we - (Ramón, Saundra, and René René) - worked extremely hard writing, researching, editing and re-editing until it was completed and we felt that it was ready for publication. Hope you enjoy the trip down memory lane with us.

René René Ornelas
"Lo Mucho Que Te Quiero"

Saundra Ornelas, René Ornelas and Ramón Roberto Hernández

CONTENTS

ONE........1912 – 1944, (Page 1): Mike Ornelas; René Ornelas and René Herrera become classmates.

TWO........1945 – 1948, (Page 10): Ornelas learns to play trumpet and discovers girls.

THREE.....1948 – 1950, (Page 15: Mike Ornelas and his Orchestra; René joins his father's band; René the future farmer.

FOUR........1950 – 1955, (Page 23): René records his first single; The Martinaires, The Casa Blanca Quintet, The Quarter Notes, Jack O'Toole, performing at the most famous venues

FIVE........1956 – 1963, (Page 33): The Quarter Notes become national recording artists. They join the Army and win the All-Army Entertainment contest. They complete their military stint, return to Laredo and disband.

SIX.........1964, (Page 46): Ornelas and Herrera unite to record "Angelito"

SEVEN.....1964 – 1966, (Page 52): Million-seller lands them on Dick Clark's "American Bandstand." They change record labels – to ARV International/Falcón

EIGHT......1967 – 1969, (Page 60): The story behind "Lo Mucho Que Te Quiero"

NINE.......1970 – 1974, (Page 74): Tommy Pharr, Fermín Dos Santos, Jorge Ramírez, Cupid, Saundra Sessions, the wedding, the honeymoon.

TEN.........1974 – 1977, (Page 86): The Brown Album; Ornelas records as René Ornelas and also as René(René; Marvin Palacios enters the picture

ELEVEN....1980 – 1982, (Page 95): Raúl Velásco, "Siempre En Domingo," Mario Rivera

TWELVE...1982 – 1986, (Page 105): René René Ornelas; "Hoy Amanecí Pensando En Ti;" Richard Noriega; the turning point,; Ramón Hernández; and the promotional tour

THIRTEEN ...1985 – 1999, (Page 115): "Vámonos A Cozumel," "Tequila," "Flashback," René goes Tejano, his music is influenced by La Isla del Coqui (Puerto Rico)

FOURTEEN...2000 – 2006, (Page 130): Catalina Records; René finds peace in the Lord; René writes and records Christian songs; his Christian ministry; René Herrera joins God's heavenly choir.

FIFTEEN.....2007 – 2017, (Page 139): Tejanos for Christ; Oldies But Goodies concert tours and music cruises; the high school class reunions; Andrew Dunbar shows up.

SIXTEEN.....2017 – 2020, (Page 149): René on the secret to a long and happy marriage; on politics vs. Christianity; he addresses the inevitable.

SEVENTEEN 2021 – 2022, (Page 156): Life after death

EIGHTEEN (Page 161): Art Laboe; René makes videos in California; René today, recapping the hits; where are they now?

(Page 171): Selected Discography, television appearances and awards

And now ....
the story begins

© Ramón Hernández Archives

CHAPTER ONE

WHAT'S IN A NAME?

No musician becomes a household name overnight; and when they do, it may be under a stage name totally unrelated to their real name, perhaps a combination of their first and last name, or they may succeed as a one-name artist.

An example in the first aforementioned variations is Lady Gaga (r.n. Stefani Joanne Angelina Germanota). Luis Miguel and Ricky Martin used their first and middle name for their artistic name. Juanes took his first name Juan and added "es," the first two letters of his middle name, Esteban; and Malú combined the first two letters of her first and middle names, María Luisa. José José (José Sosa) was unique in that he chose to double up on his first name.

Those artists that achieved great heights with a single-word stage name that was not even close to their real names were Chayanne, Apollonia, Zucchero and Maluma. In the case of Liberace and Santana, they used their own last names. Thalia (r.n. Ariadna T. Sodi Miranda) chose to outdo everyone by just using her middle name.

Some Latinos who used their real first name were Madonna, Selena, and Shakira. This is the category René and René fall into.

The following is the story of how René and René came to be as we dig all the way back to the origin of the musical roots that preceded their birth as told by René Ornelas since René Herrera, the other half of this famous music history making duo had passed two decades before this writer was able to further interview him or obtain additional photographs since his gracious widow, Velia, had boxed them up and was unable to access them.

MIKE ORNELAS

Before René was born, his father was already a well-known bandleader as the founder of The Mike Ornelas Orchestra. Furthermore, Cuca, the woman who would bear Mike's children, although not a professional vocalist, possessed a very sweet singing voice. Thus, René Ornelas was born with a double shot of musical talent.

His father was born Miguel Humberto Ornelas on New Year's Day, January 1, 1912, in Camargo, Tamaulipas, Mexico – across from Río Grande City, Texas. It was here that he began playing the drums.

Relating to his father's early years, René said, "As a kid, my father would jam with his brothers, Raúl and Salvador, as they played trumpet and saxophone and Mike kept the rhythm going playing the drums."

Mike was about ten years old when he first ran his fingers across the ivories of a piano, and he was a natural. Not only could he play by ear, but he also read music. And by age 11, he was already playing with different local bands. He became so skilled at playing the piano, that he decided to form a band when he was about 13.

"After creating a repertoire of the hit sounds of Glenn Miller, Pérez Prado, and Agustín Lara, my father became the first Texan to perform in many large cities all over the West Coast, the Southwest, and the Midwest as he conducted one of the first large Mexican American touring orchestras.

"This was during the time when there were signs in restaurants and hotels everywhere that read 'No Negros, No Mexicans, No Dogs Allowed.' My father had a very fair complexion, blond hair, and hazel eyes. So, he looked Anglo and was allowed to enter by the front door anywhere with no problem. However, his dark-skinned band musicians were not welcome, and had to wait in the car while my dad brought them some food. Mike was not only a Tejano music forerunner, but also one of the finest piano players in the state. He was a crooner in the style of Bing Crosby and Rudy Vallee," René said proudly.

"My father Mike was wearing a white suit and a dazzling, flashy white fedora hat when he had some promotional pictures taken at a photo studio in Laredo. He looked so dashing and the pictures had such star-quality that the photographer placed one of them in the window of his shop. As fate would have it, one day, when my mother, María del Refugio Montemayor (nicknamed Cuca), a beauty queen from San Benito, Texas was visiting Laredo, she walked by the studio, took one look at the picture of my dad, then turned to her friend and said, 'What a handsome man! I'm going to marry him.'

"That night, my mother went to the dance where my father was playing piano and singing with his orchestra. To make a long story short, my 18-year-old father flirted with my 17-year-old mother. My father saw how beautiful Cuca was and my mother had already fallen in love with my dad's picture. And since they were both in love with each other, they eloped in 1930.

"Cuca's father, Miguel Montemayor, my grandfather, was furious about the elopement and he went in search of his daughter. Fearing for his life, my dad immediately ran off with his new bride, my mama Cuca, to Ciudad Acuña, Coahuila, Mexico across from Del Rio, Texas. There, he got a job playing the piano at a very popular restaurant-bar called Mrs. Crosby's. Within three years my dad and my mama Cuca became the proud parents of three children: Norma, Raúl and Miguel Jr., aka Mike."

A STAR IS BORN

After their first three children came, the family moved to Laredo, Texas on the north bank of the Río Grande River. There René Víctor Ornelas was born on August 26, 1936. Dr. Lightner came to deliver the baby who was born at home at 502 Grant Street. The doctor spoke very little Spanish and when the birth was very near, Dr. Lightner was sitting on the bed with encouraging words for the groaning Mama Cuca. At the last moment, as she was straining in labor, he told her, 'Mrs. Ornelas, I need *un pújale mas, por favor.*' Cuca was in pain, but she quickly obliged with a grunt and a yell – and swish – René was born.

Shortly before René was born, his aunt Consuelo told the parents-to-be, "It will be a boy and you will be very proud of him. He will be extremely talented and handsome." Sad to say, she died only days before René was born. Next came María Teresa, Rosalinda, and Blanca Estella, Rene's three younger sisters bringing the total of siblings to seven.

RENÉ ORNELAS EXPERIENCES HIS FIRST SCAM

"It was 1940 and World War II was going full blast. Every manufacturer had started making materials for the war. All the companies were now producing bombs, grenades, rifles, bullets, tanks, airplanes, ships and all the components necessary to help the United States win the war. Not a single toy was being made. The stores had no bicycles, no skates, no dolls, no little red wagons. In fact, there were no toys for sale at all. Everything that was being produced was for the war effort.

"We were just kids when my two brothers and I joined The Boy's Club. It had a swimming pool, four basketball courts, ping pong tables and all the fun equipment to keep the kids busy and out of trouble.

"One day, a man came to the club and announced that he needed the members to do a special job for him. The following day we were going to get a very hard freeze and he needed a lot of volunteers to pick tomatoes from fifty acres of land that he owned. For our efforts, we would all get paid. Money – that was the magic word for us because we were always broke. About 100 boys signed up for the job. Very early the next morning, my brother Raúl, my brother Mike and I were the first in line at The Boy's Club. We were ready to go make some money.

"When the truck came by to pick us up, out of the 100 volunteers that had signed up, there were only five of us. All the other boys had chickened out! You see, it was freezing outside and most of the other kids had stayed at home. But not us! The temptation of all the money we were going to make kept us going, no matter what the weather was.

"We arrived at the fields and began picking tomatoes, alongside the regular farm workers. We didn't have any gloves, so it wasn't long before our hands were red, sore, and nearly frozen, but we kept on working. Around 12 noon we were starving. We quickly realized that we had not packed a lunch. We had no food with us, so reluctantly, we began munching on some of the green tomatoes to appease a growling, empty belly.

"The temperature went down to 26 degrees; it was freezing cold, it was very windy, the sand kept blowing into our eyes and we were hungry – we were miserable! After slaving all day, at 6 p.m. they finally loaded us into the truck and took us back to The Boy's Club. From there, we walked all the way home. I stood in front of Mama Cuca's oven for about an hour, trying to get warm. I was tired and nearly frozen, but I was happy.

"We were told to go and meet the man the next day at The Boy's Club, and he would pay us. Baloney! The next day we went and waited, and waited, and waited. Nothing! *Nada*! Zero! Zilch! Diddly! Squat! That's what we got. We never saw the man again. We were duped."

RENÉ ENTERS ELEMENTARY SCHOOL AND JOINS THE BAND

In 1941, the family moved to 1415 Garza Street from where they could walk to attend Sunday Mass at St. Augustine Catholic Church. And right on the church property was a very large Catholic school that taught children from the first to the twelfth grade. A year later, when René was five years old, he was enrolled in the first grade.

"This is when there was a kid in my neighborhood who was about four years older than me. His name was Pepe. He had a hair lip, but he was very popular because, at the back of his house, he had a very large tree. On top, he had a tree house that would accommodate about ten or twelve little kids. There was always something fun going on in Pepe's tree house.

"One day, Pepe had a great idea. He wanted to start a band. He sent us all off to gather some percussion instruments. My brother Raúl got two buckets that he found near a trash can. They were now his congas. My brother Mike found two empty little cans, put uncooked rice in them and wrapped them in tape. Suddenly, he had a pair of maracas. I took Mama Cuca's broom and sawed off two pieces of broom handle that were about six inches long. Presto – I

1940

Cuca & Mike

was playing the claves. For weeks, Mama Cuca wondered who in the world had mutilated her broom. One of the other kids had a ukulele that, to me, sounded like it was always a little bit out of tune. He only knew how to play three chords on the ukulele, so all the songs sounded pretty much the same. But that was okay because we were making music.

"I started singing when I was just a little boy. Therefore, I really wanted to be the singer in the band, but I didn't stand a chance. You see, Pepe owned the tree house where we played and Pepe started the band, so it was his band. He was the leader of the group. It didn't matter that he had a speech impediment. He decided that he was going to be the vocalist in the band. We sounded like *caca,* but we were happy – we had a band, and we played every night. Boy! Did we have fun!"

RENÉ ORNELAS MAKES HIS SINGING DEBUT

A few months later, René was about to undergo an experience that would change his life and determine his future.

"My father was playing the piano at Chulo's Place, a popular restaurant-bar owned by Chulo Flores; and I don't know why he was called Chulo, because he was far from being handsome," René said with a chuckle.

Most important is that it was there that René would sit on top of his father's piano while his dad played for the audience. What he did not expect is that one night his dad invited him to sing a song. René's favorite was a new popular song entitled "Pistol Packin' Mama." But he also knew songs by Frank Sinatra, Jorge Negrete and Pedro Infante.

"You see, I was the only one of the seven children who inherited my father's musical talent, so that's why he took me to Chulo's Place - to get some experience. This was a Saturday night, and the place was packed with World War II soldiers who were stationed at a U.S. military base in Laredo. It was also filled with lots of girls who wanted to dance with them. That's when my father prompted me to sing a song.

"I was really nervous because I saw so many people. But as soon as my dad gave me the microphone, I began singing 'Open the Door, Richard,' a very upbeat popular song. The crowd must have really liked my singing, because so many people were giving me money and asking me to sing more songs. So, I did. You just couldn't stop me then. I was on a roll. I got home with a pocket full of quarters and the applause was still ringing in my ears. I loved everything about it. I was hooked! I may have been only six years old, but it was at that moment that I realized I wanted to be a singer for the rest of my life."

René was just a kid, but he wasn't dumb, as he told Héctor Saldaña about noticing the reactions of the audiences when his father's band would play fox trots and jitterbugs and then follow up with Mexican polkas and cumbias.

(Saldaña, Héctor (1987, March). San Antonio, Texas *Action Magazine*, pp.6,7, 13). "People would go wild over the Latin rhythms and beats."

"Mike, Sr. had played drums in his early years, prior to becoming a piano player. So, he taught Mike, Jr. to play the drums, congas, and percussion. However, this was only because my father needed him to fill in a void because his regular drummer had returned to Mexico," René revealed.

ORNELAS AND RENÉ HERRERA BECOME CLASSMATES

It was at St. Augustine Catholic School that in 1943, Ornelas met René Herrera who was a year older, yet both were in the same 2nd grade class with Sister Cipriani. However, Ornelas never realized it until he found an old school picture and saw they actually sat across from each other in the same classroom with Sister Cipriani.

"I guess we were probably not friends because we lived in different barrios," Ornelas said. "This was the time when our family lived on Moctezuma Street at San Bernardo, which was then called Highway 81, across the railroad tracks and Bruni Plaza. René Herrera lived in El Barrio La X on Cedar and Mier streets. The reason we moved there was to be near Panaderia El Fenix. My dad's brother Marín had left it to him, and it was only one and a half blocks away from our house. My uncles were all bakers and/or musicians, so we always had lots of music and a lot of bread in our house.

As René also recalled, "At the beginning of each school year, we had to buy our books and our school supplies. We could not afford to buy new textbooks for each different class, so our parents would go to the school bookstore and buy less expensive old used books for all of us, but it did not bother me because I covered my books with brand new book covers and presto – they looked good as new. For school supplies, I got some pencils, an eraser, and a Big Red Indian tablet. I was a happy little boy, and I was ready for school where all the Salesian nuns dressed in black habits that covered them from head to toe and the only part that you could see was their face and their hands. There were also three or four priests who took care of the daily Masses."

The school had a cafeteria. However, the Ornelas children always

Courtesy René Ornelas 1944

took their small, brown bag lunch because they could not afford to eat in the cafeteria because there were just too many of them. There was Norma, Raúl, Mike and René. So, Mama Cuca would usually fix something very simple and put it inside a flour tortilla or in a small French bread called a *barrita* from Panadería El Gallo, a family-owned bakery run by Guadalupe and Adela Ornelas.

"It also must have been 1944 when I was around eight years old and Sister Vianney, my favorite teacher, organized a Christmas pageant and taught us to square dance. I had such a crush on that teacher. I never realized she had arms, elbows, and ankles because I had never seen them until she rolled up her sleeves to swing her partner and show us the dance steps. She was quite a dancer. I was clumsy, but she patiently taught me how to move."

See the picture of the square dancers that shows René peering out, from way in the back and in between the two girls in plaid skirts. His brother, Mike, is the third from the left.

"Therefore, I loved the nuns because they were so sweet and loving to me."

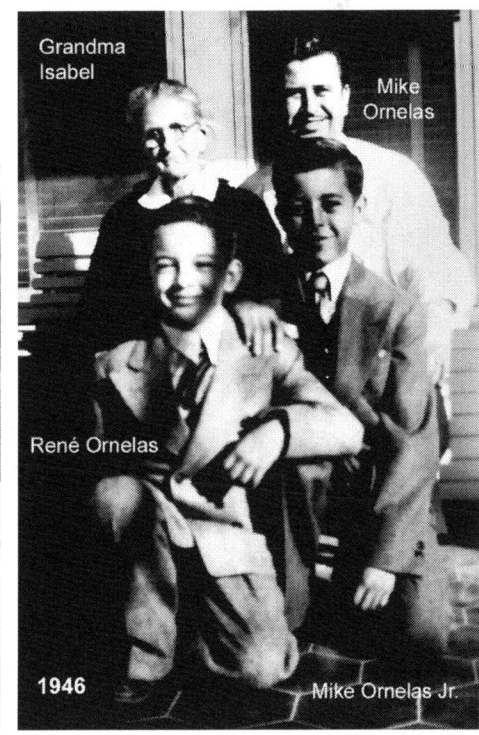

René Ornelas through the years

CHAPTER TWO

RENÉ ORNELAS' MUSICAL HERITAGE - LA CURANDERA

Regarding his interest in music, and giving credit where it is due, René said, "My grandmother, Isabel Garza de La Garza Ornelas, aka Chavelita, is the one who taught me, as a child, to love God, Jesus, the Blessed Virgin Mary and all the saints and to love music.

"Growing up, we lived in many different neighborhoods. For a short period of time, we lived in the Barrio Del Azteca, but the one that sticks out most in my mind is El Barrio De Limón, which was bordered by Garza Avenue and Santa María Street. It was called El Barrio de Limón because Fidel Limón owned and operated the big grocery store on a corner where all the people hung out, especially on the weekend. In addition, that neighborhood teemed with characters.

"Three houses away from us, there was a couple named Mike and Fela Gómez. They had about eight kids and lived in a little house that had dirt floors. Yes, they were very poor, but boy were they always working in order to survive. Mister Gómez was always doing odd jobs all around the neighborhood and he had many skills that all of us needed. His wife, Fela, took in laundry and washed and ironed clothes for some of the families in the barrio. Their oldest son, Mike, Jr., was working in a restaurant as an assistant cook and he would bring home the leftovers to help feed the family.

"Limon's Grocery Store had a meat department and the butcher, Simón, would save some of the pieces of fat from the steaks and cuts of meat that he had trimmed and put aside for Fela, who would then send her kids to pick up the pieces of fat. Of course, I would tag along with them because Mr. Limón would give us some of the fruit that was extremely overripe, and we would eat the delicious fruit on the way home. I always looked forward to this, because to me, it was like having a party and being surrounded by my friends.

"Fela took the fat, put it in an old, black iron cauldron and start a huge fire under the pot by using *leña* (mesquite wood). Then, she would add lye and some strange and unfamiliar powder and liquids, stir it up very well and boil the mixture for hours. It was quite a concoction, and you could smell it all over the neighborhood. After hours of boiling, mixing and adding more ingredients, it would somehow solidify, and Fela would cut it up into medium sized bars. At the end of this procedure, somehow, as if by magic, the bars had turned into soap.

Fela was now ready to do every load of laundry for her neighborhood clients. We, the Ornelas family, were her number one customer.

"And speaking of magic, about two blocks away from our house, there lived a *curandera* (healer) named Doña Petra. There was some gossip going around that she was also a witch, and it was rumored that Doña Petra had magic powers. Therefore, I was terrified at just the mention of her name.

"It was also in the 1940s that in order to get a telephone line that was less expensive, my father decided to get a party line. That meant there were four different customers on the same line. Doña Petra was one of them. All four customers had the same number, but with a different letter at the end. Our number was 1481-W. Doña Petra's number was 1481-J. When our phone rang, it also rang in all four different houses, because it was a party line.

"One day, I picked up our phone to make a call and Doña Petra was on the party line talking to another woman. I didn't want to listen and eavesdrop on her conversation, but what she was saying really grabbed my interest. Some young woman was asking her for advice.

"This was the conversation. Young girl: 'My husband has been cheating on me with a sexy barmaid called Lola. What can I do? Can you help me?'

"Doña Petra responded, 'Of course I can. That's my specialty. All you have to do is use some of this white powder that I'm going to send you. Sprinkle some of it in his underwear and that will be the end of your problem.'

"I immediately hung up the phone because I was too young to understand everything, but I was too scared to keep listening. All I knew was that I should never mess around with Doña Petra."

RENÉ TURNS 13 AND ENTERS THE 7TH GRADE

Although he was just a kid, by the time René became a teenager he was already a 'roadie' in his father's band. He would carry equipment, set up the stage with the music stands and connect all the microphones to the amplifier and all the corresponding wires.

René wanted so badly to be a part of his dad's orchestra that when he entered the 7th grade, he started preparing himself by taking private lessons to read music, how to sight read and to play the trumpet.

Furthermore, this is when he began experimenting with different combinations of English and Spanish music. As an example, he would sing the Top 40 hit parade songs, inserting Spanish lyrics that he wrote, thus alternating the verses bilingually. Right there, the seed was planted for the musical gold vein that René would mine in the 1960s.

By now, the tuition for the Catholic school had increased to $7.50 for each of the four Ornelas children. This came to a monthly total of $30. In addition to their tuition, it also seemed that every year the cost of their schoolbooks kept going up and up. They were a poor family, but their parents had made a commitment to give all of them a Catholic education. Thank God – it made a huge difference in Rene's life.

"However, by the time I had to enter the 7th grade, my father was unable to afford all those expenses. Thus, he reluctantly had to enroll me and my brother Mike in a public school. However, my sister Norma was kept in St. Augustine until she could graduate from the 12th grade."

RAÚL AND MIKE ORNELAS JR. THE ALL-STAR BOYS

"Since my brother Raúl was a problem teenager, my father sent him to a very strict Catholic academy run by the Marist Brothers. It was called St. Joseph's Academy. My father had decided that this was the best solution to straighten out my brother Raúl, and it worked. He joined the football, basketball, and baseball teams. Raúl became a district all-star in all three sports. And that was the end of his behavior problem. He graduated and joined the U.S. Air Force where he made a lifetime career as an air policeman.

"My brother Mike, who was considered one of the best basketball players in Class AAAA schools in Texas became a district all-star. Mike also excelled in baseball at Martin High School where he began playing first base. But he had a fast ball that you couldn't even see, and his coach soon realized that he was a dynamic pitcher. So, he became their star pitcher. The Martin High School team was called the Tigers while Raúl's team at St. Joseph's Academy was call the Antlers. Both brothers had the number 23 and when they played against each other the competition was fierce. Thus, when I sat watching from atop the bleachers, I didn't know which No. 23 I wanted to win."

Raúl and Mike were stars in sports while René was destined to become a star in the music world. The sad thing about the three brothers is that they were separated by different schools.

RENE DISCOVERS GIRLS IN PUBLIC SCHOOL

"When I was in St. Augustine Catholic School, I never noticed the girls since they were all dressed very modestly. They wore a frumpy-looking, dark blue skirt that covered most of their legs. They had on loafers and thick white socks, so all you could see was a part of their ankles.

"But in 1947, when I started 7th grade at a public school called L.J. Christen Junior High School, located on Santa Maria Avenue and Park Street, all of a sudden, I discovered girls. They all looked cute and sexy in their shorter skirts and tight-fitting sweaters, and I had just approached puberty. Wow! What a difference.

"At St. Augustine Catholic School, I sat close to the front of the class and always paid attention to the teacher. I always did my homework and I got A's and Bs on my report card. But when I went to public school, I forgot all about my scholastic responsibilities. I never did any of the schoolwork; I was having too much fun. My desk was at the back of the classroom and the girls were flirting with me and I was flirting back. I was feasting my eyes on all the cute young beauties. I never dated any of them because I was always broke, but I spent a good-for-nothing, unproductive, but flirtatious semester gawking at all the girls.

"At the end of the school semester, I was rudely awakened by a severe and cruel reality. When the teacher passed out the report cards, I received the shock of my young life. I had made two D's – one in math and the other in English.

"At the bottom of my report card, in big red letters, was written: 'Retained in the 7th grade.' I felt a bombshell that hit me like a ton of bricks. I hoped that it was just a clerical mistake. I quickly went to talk to my teacher. She checked her gradebook and all she had to say was, 'There's no mistake. I'm sorry.'

"I staggered out of the classroom and started walking home. I must have taken the long way home, since it took me about an hour to get there, and I only lived two blocks from school. I reluctantly showed my report card to my Mama Cuca and all she said was, 'Just wait 'til your father gets home.' My father finally got home about five hours later. Oh, how I suffered waiting for him. It was the longest and most miserable five hours I had ever spent.

"My father was always very good to us, but just in case, he had a special belt hanging in the closet. I was so scared of that belt, that just the thought of it kept me going straight. He never had to use it on me."

"When Dad got home, my parents talked and discussed my situation. Early the next day, they took me and enrolled me in summer school to make up for the year that I had flunked. I was so miserable and depressed. All summer long, all the other kids in the neighborhood were outside playing ball while I had to sit in the classroom doing all the schoolwork that I had missed. As if it were not enough punishment, when I finished summer school, my father took me to St. Joseph's Academy and registered me for the start of the fall semester in the eighth grade.

My new teachers, the Marist Brothers, were very tough and very strict. After a full day of doing classwork, they loaded us up with homework. The next day, the teacher would pick up the homework first thing in the morning. Any student who failed to bring his homework was put on a list for the beltline on Friday after school. On Friday, all the other students would line up in two parallel lines, the length of the football field. They all had their belt ready in their hand. As the punishment, the guilty student would have to run between the two lines of students who were swinging their belts, aiming to hit his butt). All you could hear was 'whack – whack – ouch – ouch.'

"In the classroom, I was the first one every day to turn in my homework. No beltline for me. I was a fast learner."

On the positive side, attending public school worked for the best because René was able to play the bugle in the Drum and Bugle Corps at Christen Junior High School as part of his preparation to play the trumpet with his dad's orchestra.

CHAPTER THREE

MIKE ORNELAS AND HIS ORCHESTRA:
THE SPRINGBOARD TO THE 1950'S
BEST KNOWN BANDLEADERS AND VOCALISTS

In the early 1930s, Mike Ornelas created the first Hispanic orchestra from Texas and took it all over the United States. His band formed the root of what we now call Tejano music.

In 1948, some of Rene's father's band members included Henry "King" García on vocals and Modesto Compeán, on upright bass. Modesto's sons, José "Pepe" Compeán played the trumpet and Jesús "Chuy" Compeán played tenor saxophone and doubled as Mike's musical arranger, and Rene's private music teacher.

The blind musician, Baldemar Gonzáles, whose expertise was alto saxophone, was also in Mike's band. He too, was a pianist, but Mike was a talented piano player with a prolific repertoire, and the bottom line is that he was the band leader.

Shortly thereafter, Baldemar shortened his name to Balde. Then, following his dream, he went to Corpus Christi, formed his own orchestra, became a successful recording artist, and achieved great popularity. As a vocalist, the new bandleader went on to have a monster hit with "Que Me Puede Ya Importar." Isidro López was another saxophone player who played with Mike for a couple of years before starting his own orchestra.

A little bit of trivia is that Isidro López was uncle to Lisa López, a very talented international recording star whose biggest hit was "Si Quieres Verme Llorar," on Roland and Annie García's Hacienda Records in Corpus Christi.

Later, Isidro decided to join the Balde Gonzales Orchestra. In the meantime, Modesto Compeán and his sons, Pepe and Chuy" Compeán, joined the Beto Villa Orchestra as more and more orchestras began to pop up all over Southwest Texas.

THE MIKE ORNELAS ORCHESTRA'S
FIRST RECORDINGS

It was in 1949 that Mike entered Armando Marroquin's living room in

Mike Ornelas

Alice, Texas to wax his first nostalgic recording. It was "Bonita" b/w "Así Lo Quisiste" (youtube.com/watch?v=qCF7paWQgFw) (Ideal 291) featuring Panchito Rodríguez on vocals, plus "No Te Me Retires" b/w "Blanca Estela" (Ideal 627). Then Mike Ornelas and his orchestra recorded six more 78-rpm singles in the living room of label owner Armando Marroquín in Alice, Texas.

To get an idea of how versatile and great Mike's orchestra was, listen to a sampling of the following tunes:

"La Niña Popoff," youtube.com/watch?v=hIECLofyewE; "Suby A La Mangano," youtube.com/watch?v=8sXf74Xk8u8; "Rag Mop," youtube.com/watch?v=WnKRO2KobnI; and "Quinto Patio," youtube.com/watch?v=dQqvjNM4H94. The latter by Pepe Morales who had replaced Panchito as lead vocalist and had just recorded "Tres Dilemas" b/w "por Pasar El Rato" (Ideal 964).

Next, the entire orchestra trekked to the Rio Grande Valley to wax four more singles for the Falcón label at Arnaldo Ramírez Villarreal's recording studio at 821 North 23rd Street in McAllen, Texas. And it was here that Pepe recorded "Quinto Patio" (Falcón 87A).

When one considers that Balde González, Isidro "El Indio" López, Chris Sandoval, all the Compeans, and later Víctor Garza of the Rondels and Los Peppers had all sharpened their musical talent as members of The Mike Ornelas Orchestra, it can be seen that Mike's orchestra served as the springboard for musicians and vocalists who went on to achieve great success on their own merit. Why Ornelas even did live radio with Lydia Mendoza at Felix Morales's KLVL in Houston.

Mike kept his orchestra until the mid-1960s, but later would hire a guitar, drummer, or horn player as he kept on performing as a trio, quartet, or quintet at venues such as the Holiday Inn and the Castilian Tower at the Hilton Inn, both in Laredo, Texas.

The fact is that seventeen years later, René, at the height of his career as René and René, reunited with his father to write the Spanish lyrics and record "Cuando Llegue a Phoenix" ("By the Time I Get to Phoenix") (youtube.com/watch?v=t4Xcwf0Nun8) and "Amor No Fumes En La Cama" ("My Love, Don't Smoke in Bed") (youtube.com/watch?v=Feaoq2PXoaI) as René/Víctor Ornelas, Su Piano y Ritmos for Falcón Records. Still later, Rene's Torero recording resurfaced on a 1970s El Toro Records compilation album where it listed Rene's artistic name as Víctor René.

ENTERING A NEW DECADE
"In 1950, I was living in Laredo and the population was 59,000. All my family and all my friends were there, so I felt as if everything I needed or would ever want was there in my hometown in Laredo.

"We had an Air Force base, Laredo was the No. 1 port of entry into Mexico, business was booming, and the economy was in full swing and going up every year. Everything was great. I thought that I would live there for the rest of my life. I never dreamed that someday I would be leaving the city that I had always loved. But everything changed when I had an upturn in my career.

"Laredo was a pleasant place to live. There, everybody found a way to have some fun. There was always something to entertain yourself. For the adults, there were frequent short trips to Nuevo Laredo, Mexico. It was only three or four blocks away, right through the international bridge. People would just drive down Convent Street towards Nuevo Laredo, go over the bridge, pay about twenty cents for the crossing fee, then they would just tell the Mexican immigration officer that they were going into Mexico to spend some of their money. He would gladly welcome them and roll out the red carpet. At that time, Mexico badly needed the American dollars to survive.

"Food was one of the attractions for crossing the Rio Grande into Mexico. *Cabrito* was the No. 1 food that brought most hungry tourists across the Mexican border. In those days, most Americans who lived far from the border had no idea what that food was. Now, anybody who eats Mexican food knows what it is. For the few who might not know, *cabrito* is a milk-fed baby goat that is barbecued over an open pit. It is then flame-broiled on a grill. The cook uses mesquite wood to give it that special flavor. For side dishes, you could get some Spanish rice, a dish of guacamole (mashed avocado with diced onion and tomato), and without fail, you would be served a hearty bowl of *frijoles borrachos* (pinto beans cooked with bacon and beer). Brother, you were in for a treat. It was so delicious; you couldn't get enough. It wouldn't be long before you went back to Mexico for more.

"Since Texas did not have a liquor-by-the-drink law, people would also cross the border to have mixed drinks or a favorite highball. Also, the nightclubs in Nuevo Laredo had an orchestra for dancing plus a flamboyant and extravagant floorshow.

"Since the young people were not interested in that type of entertainment, they stayed on the American side and created their own kind of fun. When I was a teenager going to Martin High School, since all of us were always broke, we found a simple and super-inexpensive way to pass the time and to entertain ourselves. Right after school, we would all go downtown and meet at our usual hangout – City Drug Store. It had a food and soda fountain with tables and chairs and about ten booths. Each booth could accommodate four persons, but we would stuff at least eight of us into the crowded booth. Remember, in those days, we were all skinny, and most of us didn't weigh more than 116 pounds. Personally, I didn't weigh even 100 pounds. If more of the gang would show up, they would just put two or three chairs in front of the booth to be able to fit ten or twelve of us around the booth.

"Mrs. Brown, the head waitress, would come to pick up our order and she would complain that we were blocking the aisle and that she couldn't get through, After some shuffling of chairs, the problem somehow would be solved. As I can remember, we always seemed to order the same thing. For ten cents, we would get a half order of French fries, smothered in mushroom gravy. We would also get free glasses of water, an abundance of napkins, a steak knife, and a bunch of forks. The cook knew we were very hungry, so he would pile up the French fries and gravy on a large plate and would throw in some slices of bread. I guess he felt sorry for us. What a nice guy! Then, we would all take turns in wolfing down the messy, but delicious, lip-smacking spread.

"Just for kicks, all of us would at some time, with a lot of flare and style, carve our names somewhere on the table or on the wooden booth itself. We wanted to make our mark and let everybody know that we had been there. Big deal! The trick was not to get caught. We had to be super careful because we had a feeling that Mrs. Brown, the head waitress and manager, had eyes on the back of her head, just like the teachers. After spending more than an hour in the booth, having fun, talking to all our close friends, we got some pennies together, paid our ten-cent bill and went outside to stand on the corner to watch the girls go by. Around 6 p.m., we would all start walking home. We had to walk everywhere because nobody had any money for the bus.

CITY DRUG STORE AND LUIS NORIEGA
"One early Saturday afternoon, I had gotten all cleaned up. I had shined my shoes, had gotten a haircut and had put on some clean, starched clothes. I really looked neat and stylish and dressed to kill. I

was going downtown to stand on the corner in front of City Drug Store and just look and enjoy the girls who would be walking by the store. I had been walking for a while and I was only three blocks away from City Drug.

"I wasn't paying too much attention to the things around me, but all of a sudden, I heard two very loud, coarse and rude voices right behind me. For no reason at all, two men around twenty-five years old started insulting me in a crude and vulgar manner. I could tell that they were on something, either drugs or alcohol, or even maybe on both. They told me, 'You think you're so special and that you're better than us. We're going to teach you the lesson of your life.' They pushed me so hard that I almost fell down. They kept shoving me until they forced me into an alley with walls all around me. I was trapped with no place to go. One of them pulled out a knife. They were very aggressive and determined to kill or cripple me. I was terrified. I've never been a boxer or a fighter, so I had no idea how to defend myself. They kept punching me so hard and so viciously that I was just about ready to give up.

"Unexpectedly, out of the blue, I heard a loud thundering and powerful voice yelling at the two men. It was Luis Noriega, a friend of my brother Mike. Luis was an ex-Marine and one time when he was home on furlough, his mother made a big enchilada dinner and invited all his friends. Mike and I were invited and that's how I got to meet him. We spent a wonderful evening with Luis telling us all about his adventures in the Marines. Luis was in his early 20's and was known as a tough guy and a very good boxer. He was about half a block away when the men attacked me. He ran and quickly arrived at the scene. He grabbed the two savage men by the neck and roughly swung them around. Immediately, they changed their tune and their attitude. They shook their heads and said, 'Luis, we didn't know René was your friend. We don't want to get into trouble with you. We are sorry, sorry, so sorry.' The two nasty men took off and started walking away quickly. I had never seen them before, and I never saw them again.

"Luis Noriega went to California, found a good job, and started living there. Some time later, he returned to Laredo to visit his parents for a couple of weeks. In California, he had bought a brand new flashy, navy-blue Chevrolet Impala which was top-of-the-line and very stylish. He was so proud of his new car, and he took Mike and me for an exciting ride. It was a wonderful treat. Luis had a great visit with his family and all his friends, but he soon returned to California to go back to work.

"We heard from him occasionally about his job, the girls he was dating and his future plans for another visit to Laredo. But before he could visit us again, I was sadly shocked to read in the newspaper that Luis Noriega, the man who literally saved my life, had been killed in an accident in southern California. That was around 1956. That day, I started praying for him and I've been praying every day for him ever since. It scares me to think that if he had not come to my defense, I might have been killed. There never would have been a René René. God bless you, Luis Noriega, my protector, and my friend. May you rest in peace.

THE HIGH SCHOOL YEARS

The first thing René did when he entered his freshman year at Martin High School in September of 1950 was to join the band as an ace trumpet player. All his classmates remember that the 14-year-old adolescent was an ace trumpet player. After school he would go to the gym, sit on the highest bleacher seat and play the very popular 'Cherry Pink and Apple Blossom White' which featured a dynamite trumpet solo.

"I always had my trumpet with me and I would play the tune as loud as I could so everyone could hear me. Just ask my very good friend, Chevo Contreras," René said.

It was a time that René was very shy, and very broke. In fact, he had never had a single date because he had no confidence in himself and was afraid to ask any girl for a date. However, he was not shy about playing his trumpet. But, if one analyzes the situation, shyness was not the real problem.

"I came from a very poor family. So, I had to depend on hand-me-down clothes from my two older brothers. It would have been okay, except that I was a short 5'10" and they were both about 6'3" tall. My pants were too long, my shirts were too large, and I had to stuff newspaper into my shoes so that they would fit me. So, when I was in high school, things were tough. I had no money, and I had no car.

When you are in high school, no car means no girlfriend, no dates, *mas triste* (So sad). No *cuchi-cuchi* for you. There were a lot of cute girls that I wanted to date, Lynn Taylor, Priscilla Dacamara, Mary Offer, Alma Flores and so many others. But I didn't have a car. I couldn't just call up a girl and tell her, 'Let's go out tonight. Wait for me on the corner. I'll pick you up on the bus.' She would have told me, 'Pick me up on the bus? Are you crazy?' So, I had a lot of spare time on my hands, and I started playing the guitar and writing romantic love songs."

RENÉ, THE FUTURE FARMER

One way to take his mind off girls was by becoming a member of the Future Farmers of America (FFA).

"Would you believe that?" he said, "I wanted to be a farmer, but my class project was to buy some *pollitos* (baby chicks), raise them, cut off their heads, pluck their feathers and sell them for a profit. Are you kidding me? After a few weeks, they had become my pets. I had names for all 100 of them, so they became egg-laying hens and roosters and I decided I didn't want to be a farmer after all. I wanted my pet chickens to die of old age. Many of them did, but some of them, without my knowledge, found their way into my Mama Cuca's chicken and rice pot. Yum yum! Mama Cuca was a very good cook."

After his disaster with the chickens, René quit trying to be a farmer and went back to his first love which was music. "As it turned out, I was in the high school band playing the trumpet for two years, but I quit and joined the choir after the band teacher gave me three licks with a paddle because I was late for a band rehearsal. The licks were so bad, that it left three welts and bruises on my you know what," Ornelas said with a laugh.

That is one of his funny experiences in high school. But, above all, René was in the choir because he really loved to sing. Besides that, at age 14, he had joined his father's orchestra as a trumpet player and sometimes sang as the band's vocalist. This was an opportunity that most of his peers didn't get. In those days not just anybody could make a recording. You really had to be somebody special with name recognition or have somebody with lots of money to promote you.

Next was an opportunity to become a recording artist.

CHAPTER FOUR

RENÉ RECORDS HIS FIRST SINGLE

This came about because there was a songwriter, Arturo Vásquez, who had written a song called, "Recuerdo Mi Pasado" and he particularly wanted René to record it.

"I jumped at the chance; I was so excited. That was my big break. I was now a real recording artist. My father, Mike Ornelas, backed me up with his orchestra. The record was released under the name Victor René for the Genaro Tamez label (Torero TO-110). The flipside was a catchy instrumental titled "La Chingüengüenchona," by the Mike Ornelas Orchestra. It was one of the first hot Tejano music polkas!"

"That was when I realized, 'there's gold in them there hills.' Wow, those were the days," René said.

Listen to how good René was as a 14-year-old crooner at youtube.com/watch?v=xWKQSW3_SGg. Next, Chris Sandoval recorded "Amigo" as Mike's orchestra continued to serve as a springboard for future Chicano music legends.

THE MARTINAIRES

"Out of the 100 choir members, the choir director chose some of the best singers and formed a select group called The Martinaires, and I was one of those chosen. We sang popular classic songs like 'Stardust,' 'Chapel in the Moonlight,' and 'Moments to Remember' plus, Top 40 songs of that era, such as 'Sh-Boom,' 'Mr. Sandman,' and 'The Naughty Lady of Shady Lane.'

From Martin High School La Pitahaya yearbook

"It was in the Martinaires that I reconnected with the other René (Herrera) plus two guys named Juan. In order of age, Juan Garza-Góngora was born December 20, 1934. Juan Orfila was born John Eugene Orfila on July 18, 1935, and René Herrera was born on October 2, 1935. And I, the youngest in the group, was born on August 26, 1936.

"Eucebio 'Chevo' Contreras had nothing to do with our group, I wanted to caption and mention his name because he was my best friend, whom I just learned passed. May he rest in peace," said the Grammy award winning green-eyed vocalist.

What did transpire is that the two Renés and the two Juans clicked musically, and they went from fellow choir members to close friends. As can be expected, almost overnight, they got together after school to jam as a vocal group.

An added bonus was that all except Garza-Góngora played acoustical guitar. Therefore, they were able to musically accompany themselves."

In fact, Orfila was already performing with Adrian Mireles and Edmundo Gutiérrez as Los Tres Ranchos at school assemblies and private parties. In describing their rapport, a caption in the high school yearbook read: "At the P.A.S.F. Sport Dance, guests ... thrilled to the voices of Los Tres Ranchos."

"My goal from then on was to become popular by singing on stage in front of all the girls," Ornelas quipped.

Youth gave them the energy to juggle full-time classes, participate in choir events and rehearse as a quartet. Perhaps the live wire dynamos got their stamina from the exercise they got in school from also participating in one sport or another.

Herrera was on the high school's Tigers football team, Garza-Góngora participated in football, basketball, track and baseball; and Ornelas excelled in track.

"I also wanted to play basketball, but at 5-feet-10-inches tall, I was too short for the team," Ornelas revealed. "But I was skinny, and I jumped like a *chapulín* (grasshopper). So, I was a good runner and high jumper.

"We stayed so busy that at times, we would not do our homework because we were practicing, singing for five hours a day, but we still managed to make fairly good grades."

THE CASA BLANCA QUINTET

Victor Garza, who grew up in *El Barrio de la X*, across the street from René Herrera's house, says that being exposed to the music of his talented neighbor inspired him and his brothers – Guillermo and Santiago Flores - to later form the group called The Dots.

Yes, the 1950s was a time when the drive-in theaters and the burger joints with car hops attracted all the kids. It was also a time when you would see guys sitting on their car hoods playing their guitar and singing. Some guys would take their girlfriends, or their *movidas* (pickup date), to go make out at Lake Casa Blanca.

The famous recreational area, Lake Casa Blanca, also boasted a country club for Laredo's elite. Soon, the four choir members became the house band at the ritzy club. Each night they performed at the club and since the audience consisted of an older crowd, they would call the still-unnamed four young men, the Casa Blanca Boys.

So much for singing in front of an audience of girls. But that didn't bother the teenage foursome because they were paid $6, given a meal,

1952 THE CASA BLANCA QUINTET
Juan Garza-Góngora, René Herrera, Joe Quesada, Juan Orfila & René Ornelas

plus whatever they made in tips. What bothered Ornelas was that the combination of three nylon-stringed acoustic guitars sounded terrible.

"All I could hear was click, click, click and I felt we needed a smoother, deeper sound. So, it was my idea to add a bass player because I wanted to hear a bottom; and I knew just the guy who could solve the problem. He was a classmate who played upright bass. I spoke to him, and he said, "Yes, I'd love to join your group.' He was our age and a real nice guy named Joe Quesada.

"Once we added a fifth musician, the club manager began calling us The Casa Blanca Quintet. Five to six months after performing with us, Joe Quesada quit the group and this left the group with four members.

THE QUARTER NOTES

After Quesada left the group, they were no longer a quintet. Therefore, the remaining foursome agreed to change the name of the group. Ornelas recalled that he wanted the group to be named, "Los Intocables" (The Untouchables), but Orfila wanted to call the group "The Masters."

"I thought the name was too 'uppity' so we discussed having another name entirely," Ornelas stated.

Patterning themselves after The Four Aces, The Four Freshmen, The Hilltoppers, and The Ink Spots, the Laredo Martin High School students settled on the name, "The Quarter Notes." In Mexico, the people could not pronounce Quarter Notes, so they called them "Los Cuernos'" (The Horns) and that sounded very funny!

Juan Garza-Góngora was the emcee; Herrera was a guitarist, Juan Orfila played the *requinto (*a small guitar that played the melody) and Ornelas played guitar and sang the lead solos. In addition, since Ornelas was the only one who could read music, he always arranged the group's four-part-harmony vocals.

"It was an era when *serenatas* (serenades) were common, so people would hire us to serenade their sweethearts for birthdays, anniversaries or just to say, 'I love you.' And at the end, the girl had to fall in love with the guy, because the *serenata* showed how much he loved her," Ornelas explained.

This is perhaps something Ornelas learned from his father who would rent a truck and a PA system to drive from house to house with a small group of musicians to perform prepaid serenades for the clients' wives or sweethearts on Valentine's Day and other occasions.

1953 — Juan Garza-Góngora, René Ornelas, René Herrera, Juan Orfila

The Quarter Notes

DOO WOP VS CONTEMPORARY POP

Doo wop was very popular at that time. However, The Quarter Notes stuck to their contemporary pop repertoire and garnered more media attention than other vocal groups, as the following magazine article describes:

"The guitars and voices blended in the cool breeze of the early morning hours. It was the early 50s and another young girl was serenaded by Laredo's most popular singing quartet, The Quarter Notes.

Even to this day, there are many who still cherish that very special moment - to recall the thrill of rushing to school the next day and breaking the news to her friends. The boyfriend bragged to his friends about having the Quarter Notes serenade his girl." (Sullivan, Tom (Fall 1990) *Si'Laredo Magazine*, p. 5)

As icing on the cake, Ornelas was in for another highlight when they pooled their resources and recorded the catchy, bouncy doo-wopish "Pretty Pretty Eyes" which he wrote, and they recorded for Guyden Records. This is one tune you absolutely have to check out at youtube.

com/watch?v=MHEKNjIi2OM to get an idea of what teenagers were listening to before rock'n'roll and before the era of 'Grease.'

But most important, be prepared to listen to some fantastic four-part harmonizing. I mean, these guys were good. Unfortunately, the flipside to this single, "I Don't Want to Go Home," is not on YouTube. However, it is available to purchase as a download on Amazon Music Unlimited.

From their first single on, Ornelas would sing lead vocals on both 'Side 1' and 'Side 2' of each single.

"This was also a time when there were ten boys hoping to be voted 'Most Handsome' in the senior class of Martin High School." René said, "I was unaware that I was even in the running. Without my knowledge, there were two very popular girls who had submitted my name. Thus, I was totally surprised when the Student Council president announced my name at school over the PA system that I was the winner. I had been voted the 'Most Handsome' boy in the senior class of 1954!"

On the musical side, the demand for local professional dates had increased to the point that the four teenagers realized they were in business, but not big business. Thus, they set their sights much higher. They aimed to become full-time national entertainers. However, life threw a monkey wrench into their plan.

THE SUMMER OF 1954

After René graduated in May, his father Mike decided to move the family to Denver, Colorado because orchestra bookings were in a slump and financially, he had fallen on hard times. Reluctantly, René obeyed his father and went with the family.

Mama Cuca had just given birth to her last baby, Blanca Estela. Mike, Cuca and their five kids, Mike Jr., René, Maria Teresa, Rosalinda and newly born Blanca Estela, were all packed like sardines on hard bench seats in a black Ford panel truck that had no windows and no air conditioner. Therefore, it was a very long, hot, unbearable, and uncomfortable ride to Colorado's capitol.

"My dad had been promised a job there by Paco Sánchez, a rich man who owned a radio station and other businesses. However, we found out that he was dishonest when he did not come through on his commitment to hire all of us as he had promised. So, there we were, stranded and broke.

"Fortunately, Beto Villa, who was one of the top traveling bands of the era, was on tour in the Denver area.

"My dad contacted Beto and as Lady Luck would have it, Beto had just lost his piano player plus one of his trumpet players. *Que suerte* (What luck) for us. Beto hired my dad to play piano and my brother Mike to play congas. And I was extremely good so Beto hired me to play trumpet in his band."

"My brother and I were also paid extra to drive Beto Villa's two station wagons," René added. "We were saved. God was on our side."

Looking back, one wonders if René realizes that regardless of the brevity of his gig with Beto Villa, "The Father of Orquesta Tejana" he can honestly say he was once a member of this historical orchestra.

In the meantime, back in Laredo, hungry to achieve their goal at all costs, Herrera, Garza-Góngora and Orfila borrowed $100 from the Kiwanis Club of Laredo and went knocking on Jack O'Toole's door in Galveston. However, O'Toole who was one of the best-known promoters in the Houston area, told them to come back when their fourth member returned so that he could hear all four of them.

In the interim, Mike, Mike Jr. and René Ornelas were on the road doing what they did best, making music.

"We did ten engagements in the Denver area, then traveled to California where we did twelve more. After that, and before summer ended, our family went back home with money in our pockets," Ornelas said. "Above all, I was happy to rejoin The Quarter Notes who had been performing as a trio in my absence."

In September, Ornelas entered Laredo Junior College on a voice scholarship and Garza-Góngora enrolled at Southwest Texas State University (now Texas State University in San Marcos, Texas).

JACK O'TOOLE

Garza-Góngora only attended one semester since this is when the foursome called him to set up an audition at O'Toole's night club. After listening to them, O'Toole was undoubtably impressed with the group's unquestionably talented quartet as he told them, "Boys, you have what it takes – talent – but I need to polish you up before you experience the bright lights of the stage."

Recalling his first impression of O'Toole, Ornelas said, "Although a little on the plump side, the ruddy-faced, impeccably dressed, distinguished-looking, blue-eyed musical talent scout seemed to be the perfect example of a successful businessman."

So, when Fat Jack – as the group nicknamed him - promised to take them under his wing and groom them for stardom, they agreed to sign on the dotted line, and he became their manager.

True to his word, the slick Irish night club owner not only took them on, but early in 1955 he drove to Laredo to personally pick them up in his brand-new Cadillac. Happily, they packed and loaded their bags in the trunk of O'Toole's new baby blue and white Caddy.

"His club, Ciro's, which was right across from the beach, was the most popular place in Galveston because it had music, gambling, mixed drinks, and a floorshow. And this was to become our boot camp, our training ground. This is where O'Toole promptly began to whip the act into shape," Ornelas said.

"I remember Jack would sit all alone in the dark, near the center of Ciro's club, while we worked on our vocals and on choreography that looked professional. It was uncanny how Jack had a sharp eye for what looked good and for what looked bad; for what worked, or for what didn't work."

During six months of rigorous training, O'Toole toughened, tightened, and polished up their act as he got them to learn choreography, introductions, jokes, attitude and, in short, how to work Ciro's audience into the palm of their hands.

Next, O'Toole put The Quarter Notes in the Balinese Room, a famous night club built on a pier stretching 600 feet from the Galveston Seawall. That was where strippers and famous vaudeville acts were sometimes on the same bill. It was without a doubt, one of the more prestigious venues where the group performed.

THE QUARTER NOTES
BECOME A TOP-NOTCH NIGHTCLUB ACT

Having proven themselves to be a class act, O'Toole soon began booking The Quarter Notes throughout the United States.

Consequently, the quartet left Galveston and began working in New Orleans, Chicago, New York, Miami, and other big cities. While in these places, they worked with Sofie Tucker, Jimmy Durante, The McGuire Sisters, Spike Jones and actor-comedian Paul Gilbert, the father of actress Melissa Gilbert who starred in the hit TV show, "Little House on the Prairie."

"This was before rock'n'roll, when, if you used electric guitars, you needed amplifiers and electricity to power them," Ornelas said with a laugh.

San Antonio Express-News writer Héctor Saldaña noted that The Quarter Notes had been right there when rock 'n' roll was being invented.

"They were there during the changing of the guard. Therefore, The Quarter Notes can be considered one of the true transitional groups of the 1950s," Saldaña stated.

"Later, when rock 'n' roll became popular, we included tunes by Bill Haley and the Comets, Elvis Presley, and Chuck Berry in our repertoire," Ornelas said.

Gimmicks are good, and The Quarter Notes had a good one.

"We took the hit song, 'Rock Around the Clock,' kept the same beat and changed the words to, 'Here's Juan. Here's René. Here's Juan. Here's René. Here's the rock 'n' roll done the Latin way.'

"Then, we would join our voices to sing '*Ay te watcho cucaracho, al ratón chicharrón ...*' to the tune of 'See You Later, Alligator.'

"The people went wild when we sang it at the Blue Room of the famous Roosevelt Hotel in New Orleans during the 1967 Mardi Gras," Ornelas boasted.

"Orfila hated to be called Juan, but the name 'John' didn't fit in with their opening introductory theme song. "So, I had to put up with being called 'Juan' for the duration of the Quarter Notes," Orfila said with an irritated tone in his voice.

Orfila described their manager by saying, "Jack O'Toole was like a snake charmer; he was a con man, but darn if he didn't get us the greatest gigs."

32   THE QUARTER NOTES BECOME A TOP-NOTCH NIGHTCLUB ACT

Orfila was referring to getting The Quarter Notes booked at The Copa Cabana in New York, the Black Orchid in Chicago, the Chez Paree in Chicago, Bassell's in Niagara Falls, New York, and other prestigious venues where they shared the stage with Mel Torme, Bobby Darin, Andy Williams, Burl Ives, Percy Faith, Joan Blondell, plus countless other big-name stars.

"Imagine, four little Mexican Americans from Laredo, Texas rubbing elbows with some of the greatest super star entertainers of that day, thanks to Jack O'Toole!" René said with wonderment.

That publicity helped spark a national tour of The Quarter Notes performing their musical magic at other prestigious venues, theaters, and clubs.

THE QUARTER NOTES
L-R: Here's René Herrera, René Ornelas,
Juan Garza-Góngora (behind Ornelas) and Juan Orifa

Photo courtesy René Ornelas

CHAPTER FIVE

THE QUARTER NOTES BECOME NATIONAL RECORDING ARTISTS

The Quarter Notes' popularity had reached a height to where the next step was to record some songs. Calypso music was the rage at that time. So, in 1956, when Harry Belafonte made Trinidad's calypso music a worldwide craze, they recorded "Come De Night" (youtube.com/watch?v=4LzsLUY4mTE) as the flipside to "Loneliness" (youtube.com/watch?v=Z0amAgdM4qA), in which they took turns on lead vocals on this ballad for DeLuxe Records, a subsidiary of King Records in Chicago.

Their follow up single was the vocally delightful "My Fantasy" (youtube.com/watch?v=Sil7eZsnICA) in which Ornelas croons the lead. "Ten Minutes to Midnight" is the flipside to this 45-rpm single on which Ornelas also sings the lead. That national release came out at about the same time as Mando and the Chili Peppers' album which was released on Golden Crest Records. However, the two popular groups had never met.

Next, they recorded "Who Am I," written by Herrera (youtube.com/watch?v=5qOy8VvWjj8) and "Teen Age Blues" (youtube.com/watch?v=05fDBD8IV9Y) for Fox Records.

"As was the norm, Herrera and Orfila sang tenor, Garza-Gongora sang in the middle; and because of my range I sang lead on all recordings. So yes, that's me doing the bass on 'Who Am I,'" Ornelas said as he sang some bass notes to make his point.

The Quarter Notes' two singles came out in the golden era of the 1950s doo-wop music scene. Their awesome recordings made the Top 10 survey at KONO Radio in San Antonio, Texas, and they were on their way up.

This was during an era when their recordings, just as those of Dion and the Belmonts, Chip and the Quarter Tones, the Royal Lancers, Julito and the Latin Lads, plus later the Royal Jesters, Johnny Maestro and the Crests and other Latin American street corner vocal groups were referred to as "white doo-wop music."

The Quarter Notes' first three singles made enough waves and sold enough records to grab the

Randy Wood

attention of Randolph Clay "Randy" Wood, the tall, lanky, handsome 39-year-old president of DOT Records.

He was intrigued by the mastery of their unique sound, one that stressed harmony and vocal counterpoint. Thanks to Chuy Compeán, who wrote their musical arrangements in Houston, The Quarter Notes always carried with them their musical charts for their original compositions, a rarity among new groups.

Much to The Quarter Notes' credit, their professional night club experience set them apart from dozens of unpolished acts who wanted to record for the Dot label. The fact that the Laredo quartet's musical accompaniment was simply a piano, an upright bass, plus a couple of acoustic guitars was also a great testament to their tremendous singing talent and to the developing skill of René Ornelas' vocal arrangements.

Recalling their audition for Dot, Ornelas said, "For the audition, I sang the verse in the style of Nat King Cole. On the bridge part, we sang in the style of The Four Freshmen. We sounded great and Randy Wood ate it up."

In layman terms, Ornelas said that he did not think he had a unique voice and he basically imitated Nat King Cole's smooth, mellow voice. Then, they went into a Four Freshmen's

BIG FIVE PLATTER PULSE
Week of June 17, 1957

SAN ANTONIO'S TOP "20"

1.	Love Letters In The Sand	Pat Boone	Dot
2.	Young Blood	Coasters	Atco
3.	Teenage Romance	Rickie Nelson	Verve
4.	Dark Moon	Gale Storm	Dot
5.	A White Sport Coat	Marty Robbins	Columbia
6.	Come Go With Me	Del Vikings	Dot
7.	Talkin' To The Blues	Jim Lowe	Dot
8.	So Rare	Jimmy Dorsey	Fraternity
9.	It's You I Love	Fats Domino	Imperial
10.	Little Darlin'	Diamonds	Mercury
11.	Gone	Ferlin Husky	Capitol
12.	I Like Your Kind of Love	Andy Williams	Cadence
13.	My Fantasy	Quarternotes	Deluxe
14.	My Dream	Platters	Mercury
15.	Old Cape Cod	Patti Page	Mercury
16.	Four Walls	Jim Reeves	Victor
17.	School Day	Chuck Berry	Chess
18.	Let There Be You	Five Keys	Capitol
19.	Empty Arms	Theresa Brewer	Coral
20.	Souvenir D'Italie	Leroy Holmes	M-G-M

jazzy, four-part harmony on the bridge. Randy Wood was floored. The Quarter Notes passed the audition. They were in like Flynn.

On the day of their recording session in Hollywood, Randy Wood brought in three future Grammy Award winners - Joe South (Joseph Alfred Souter) to play electric guitar, and pianist Ray Stevens (Harold Ray Ragsdale) to record as studio musicians to back up The Quarter Notes. The third was a bushy-haired, long bearded, wild-looking, very talented electric bass player named Charlie Daniels. All three of those talented musicians would soon become super-stars in their own right.

Just like RCA and Columbia, the Dot label was one of the 'it' labels from 1950 to 1979. Their impressive list of artists under contract at that time also included two more of The Quarter Notes' idols, The Four Lads and The Mills Brothers. Also on Dot Records were Eddie Fisher, Tony Martin, Ivory Joe Hunter, Tab Hunter, Pat Boone, Gale Storm, Jimmie Rodgers and countless other internationally known artists. Therefore, it was quite an accomplishment for The Quarter Notes to be in Dot's catalogue of famous artists.

Thanks to that Dot Records single from where their Side 2 "Please Come Home (to Daddy)" (youtube.com/watch?v=ybCKGFj13oQ) written by Ornelas became a huge hit, the Quarter Notes' career took off and they received their next big break, when they were seen by millions of television viewers, and heard by millions of radio listeners, when they appeared on the "Arthur Godfrey's Talent Scouts" national television broadcast alongside Julius La Rosa, Carmel Quinn and the

36

Monsignor George Gloeckner

Herrera — Ornelas — Garza-Góngora — Orfila

René and René

Juan and Juan

1957

Laredo U.S. Congressman — Jack O'Toole

Juan Orfila
René Herrera
René Ornelas
Juan Garza-Góngora

Enjoying a cold beer

Juan Garza-Góngora
René Ornelas
René Herrera
Juan Orfila

1958

Photos courtesy René Ornelas

McGuire Sisters, on November 27, 1957, in Miami, Florida.

The program was a talent show competition and The Quarter Notes sang their version of the song "¿Quién Será?" ("Who Could It Be?") which is better known as "Sway With Me" in the American market. They won the competition with 1st place honors and the grand prize of $2,000 dollars, which they never saw.

"Our manager, Jack O'Toole, got away with all the money again! He was always driving a brand-new luxury car. And, sometimes, he even let us ride in it! Our compensation was that we got to appear on Arthur Godfrey's morning TV show for a whole week in Miami, Florida," Ornelas said with a laugh.

Their five-day appearance on the "Arthur Godfrey Show" led them to more headline performances at leading supper clubs and hotels. Despite their success, their personal manager was only paying them ten dollars a night and you can guess the rest.

"We weren't making that much money, but we were happy because we were on stage, and people were listening to us. And this was way before *la onda chicana*, or *la onda tejana* (Chicano music or the Tex-Mex music wave)," Ornelas said.

In the interim, one of their 45-rpm records was on the charts and it was selling. Night clubs were offering them more money, and more recordings with Dot Records seemed to be on the horizon. Although they never released an album on Dot Records, The Quarter Notes' fan clubs sprang up in Pittsburg, Pennsylvania, also in Joliet and Chicago, Illinois, in Houston and many other cities.

The Quarter Notes had high hopes because it was Randy Wood who was directly responsible for Pat Boone's stardom. They knew they were in good hands. Then all hell broke loose. Jack O'Toole was furious because he had not been included in the recording deal. He threatened legal action against Dot Records and Randy Wood.

As Ornelas remembers, "Jack was a nightclub guy, and he was blind to the fact that he was burning the bridge with Dot Records. Randy decided it wasn't worth the hassle and he literally dropped us like a hot potato."

Their star was rising to new heights when almost overnight, the airplay stopped, and all their records were pulled from store shelves. Immediately, The Quarter Notes severed their ties with Jack O'Toole.

The fun, the girls, the adulation, the traveling, the money stopped, and the group floundered. What were they to do now? Uncle Sam had the answer.

THE QUARTER NOTES JOIN THE U.S. ARMY

Once more fate stepped in to lend a hand. The four buddies, no longer teenagers, remained such a tightknit group that when Juan Garza-Góngora was drafted in 1958, the entire group joined the army under the "buddy system plan" in what seemed to be a loyal attempt to stay together.

After raising their right hand in a joint swearing-in ceremony and signing the paperwork at Fort Sam Houston in San Antonio, they were sent to Fort Carson, Colorado for basic training.

There, they kept on singing in the showers, on guard duty or in the mess hall. It was like being in the middle of a musical movie when they broke into a song at any given place and at any given moment.

René shaves off peach fuzz

Pvt René Ornelas at U.S. Army Garrison Stuttgart in Germany

Photos courtesy René Ornelas

Lucky for them, two weeks into basic training, Sergeant Honky Harvel, their new friend, found a way to get them off-base to perform.

Ornelas recalled, "I'm sure he pulled a heck of a lot of strings and bribed other soldiers to pull it off, because no one is able to get a weekend pass when they're in boot camp (basic training).

Somehow Sgt. Harvel would sneak us out in his car so we could go sing for free beer off-base at a night club in Denver, also to sing at the Caravan Club in Colorado Springs, and at other venues in the Pike's Peak area."

As a side note, Ornelas remembers this: "As soon as we finished basic training, we all got a two-week furlough and went home to Laredo. While we were there, I heard on the radio that the careers of three American singing legends were unfortunately cut short as a plane carrying the three stars crashed in Clear Lake, Iowa after doing a concert show. Killed were Ritchie Valens, J.P. Richardson (The Big Bopper) and Buddy Holly.

I'll always remember the date because it happened on my mother's *cumpleaño* (birthday). It was February 3, 1959, and it is remembered as 'the day the music died.' After all these years, I am still saddened by this tragedy."

When the foursome got back to Fort Carson, the army kept them at the base hospital as medics for another six months. Then, they were transferred to Fort Dix in New Jersey to await further orders. But, when the orders arrived, the army had them all going in different directions, one to the Pacific, one to Alaska and two to Germany.

The guys panicked. That same day they called their friend in Laredo, Monsignor George Gloeckner, who in turn called their congressman. The politician called a high-ranking general and within 24 hours, thanks to their intervention, The Quarter Notes were able to stay together on the buddy system plan, as they were initially promised.

They were all shipped to U.S. Army Garrison Stuttgart, a few miles south of Ludwigsburg, Germany.

In Ludwigsburg, they were assigned to the Southern Command and 128th Evacuation Hospital as medics in a tent setup that resembled the one seen in the TV hit show "M*A*S*H." The acronym stands for Mobile Army Surgical Hospital.

DIVINE INTERVENTION PLACES
THE QUARTER NOTES ON A NEW PATH

After that, they entered the U.S. army entertainment contest where they won first place in all of Germany. Next, they won 1st Place in the Finals of the All-Europe Army Entertainment Contest.

Then, as fate would have it, on August 30, 1959, the four home-grown Texas Army boys won 1st Place in the All-Army Entertainment Grand Finalists Contest, hosted by Ed Sullivan with their song, "Who Am I." Now they were considered the "Best Vocal Group in the Army." Many of their songs were included in 'Side Four' of the Army Entertainment Program Album produced by the Special Services Division.

Blessed by their God-given talent, in 1960, the winners were sent to Washington, D.C. to start, what was to be, a Department of Defense world-touring show known as "Rolling Along 1960" and named after "The Army Goes Rolling Along," the official U.S. Army song. The result is that the "Rolling Along" All-Army Entertainment contest album features the Quarter Notes on its 10-record-set cover and 'Side 6' contains "Mobile," "The End" and "Lazy River" by the Laredo foursome.

Consequently, for an entire year, they entertained U.S. military personnel, Department of State civilians and their family members at military bases in France, Germany, Italy, Panama, Spain, Japan, Okinawa, Hawaii, Alaska and many other states and countries.

After performing at countless USO shows all over the world, on April 4, 1961, at the end of their three-year military stint, they received their honorary discharges and the four Tejanos returned in triumph to Laredo, Texas, where they were greeted by a parade of proud hometown

U.S. Army National Contest winners

Department of Defense world-touring "Rolling Along Show"

Garza-Góngora, Herrera, Orfila, Ornelas

Photo courtesy René Herrera

1960

supporters and their biggest supporter, Monsignor George Gloeckner. That same day, the Quarter Notes were also met by Mayor Guajardo and received the key to the city.

"With the encouragement of Msgr. Gloeckner and the Catholic Youth Organization, the four boys had but one way to go – to the top," (Ramírez, Verónica (1985, Thursday, July 18). Flash – High Profile. *Laredo Morning Times*, pp 7E, 8E)

RENÉ ORNELAS BECOMES A CIVILIAN AGAIN

René Ornelas loves to tell the following little story: "When I finished my stint in the US Army and went back home to Laredo, I found out that my father and my mother were not living in the same house anymore. My mother had moved to live with my sisters in Austin, and my father now had his own small apartment in Laredo. I had no place to call home, so I asked René Herrera if I could stay with him in his house until I could find a place of my own. He said it would be okay for a while. His parents had a large house and Herrera had his own spacious bedroom with a big and roomy bed. Despite this fact, he told me that I could sleep on the floor. Good grief! I sure wasn't expecting that!

"However, one good thing that I really enjoyed was the delicious meals that Herrera's mother, Paula, prepared for us every day. What a good Mexican mother! I stayed there for about a month, until I found employment and I could now afford my own apartment.

THE QUARTER NOTES REGROUP

As a flashback to life after the army, The Quarter Notes were not quitters and attempted to pick up where they left off, but it wasn't the same as before.

Garza-Góngora married his high school sweetheart, Alma Mora and moved to San Antonio. His spot had to be filled. Thus Lizandro L. Héctor "Chando" Guerra was then groomed to replace Garza-Góngora, but it never really worked out.

According to Herrera, "Garza-Góngora was a natural emcee and entertained audiences with his charming manner and playful humor on stage." Now it was up to Ornelas to pinch hit on the microphone.

Ornelas added, "So, I had to start being the emcee. But I wasn't too comfortable with it because I only wanted to do the shoo-be-doo-be-dos and just forget about talking to the audience. I wanted to watch the girls. I was the shy one and Juan (Garza-Góngora) had an extraordinary gift of gab."

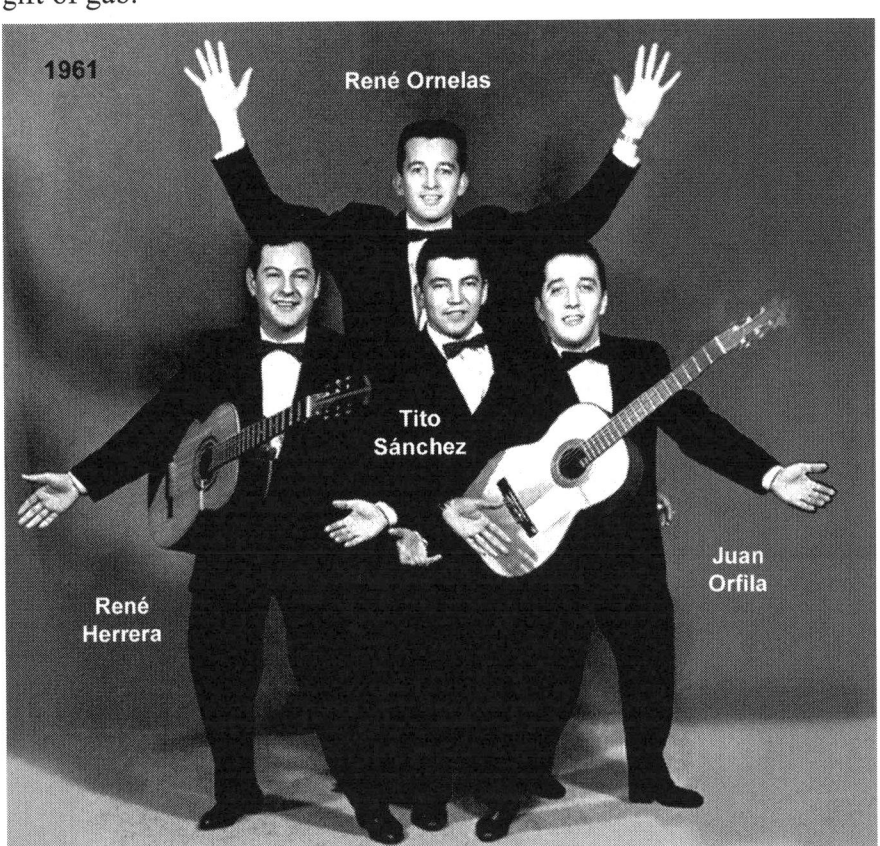

As it turned out, Orfila's good friend, Jorge "Tito" Sánchez, had attended all of the Chando Guerra practice sessions and he knew just about all of the songs. However, Tito, according to Ornelas and Herrera, was not a trained and ready entertainer. He was not yet prepared to be on the stage.

"But we chose him and trained him because he was able to sing, was single, and was able to travel," Herrera said.

"And he was a good-looking young man. Besides, he was a friend and a nice, easy-to-get-along-with guy," Ornelas added.

After Tito was ready, The Quarter Notes purchased a brand new 1962, baby blue Mercury car and by sheer luck, famous Mexican composer, musical arranger and orchestra leader, Luis Arcaraz came into town to audition new acts. The quartet went for a tryout and Luis loved their polished look. He was very impressed with the way they sang, so he took The Quarter Notes to Mexico City where he would be their representative/manager for Mexico.

True to his word, Arcaraz booked them in Acapulco, Guadalajara and at one of the most important venues in Mexico City, El Teatro

Blanquita. This was the showplace for "who's who" in the history of Mexican bands, vocalists, comedians, and other acts. If you didn't perform at the El Teatro Blanquita, you really hadn't made it yet in show business in Mexico. "And we made it!" said René Ornelas.

It was at that famous venue that these four young Laredoans shared the stage with such distinguished stars as Pedro Vargas, Trio Los Panchos, Trio Los Aces, Los Tecolines, Toña La Negra and the comedy team of Los Polivoces. They had now arrived. Unfortunately, on June 1, 1963, the 58-year-old Luis Arcaraz was killed in a car accident in San Luis Potosí,

René Herrera, Tito Sánchez, Juan Orfila and René Ornelas marked the end of their era with a last appearances on a Mexico City televison program in 1962.

Photo courtesy:
René Herrera

close to Matehuala. This left the Quarter Notes stranded in the Mexican Capitol with no contacts, no booking agent or manager; and nobody to open the right doors for them. They felt lost. They didn't know where to turn.

After getting stranded in Mexico City, they had some bad experiences and when they finally got back to Laredo, each one went their separate way.

"The Quarter Notes disbanded for more reasons than that," Herrera said. "Quartets primarily went out of fashion because other singing styles became more popular," Ornelas added. "Some of those quartets that faded were The Ink Spots, The Mills Brothers, The Four Aces, the Four Coins, The Four Esquires, The Four Freshmen, The Four Lads, The Bobby Peterson Quartet, The Hi-Lo's and many others.

"That was the end of the era for quartets," Herrera stated.

THE MOST HORRIFYING MOMENT

"After we got back from Mexico, I started working for the Vumore Cable Company in Laredo. There, we were trained to climb utility poles, how to lay cable lines all over town and how to install residential connections for TV cable service. It was summer and it was blazing hot. We were all sweating so much that we started calling Laredo "The Armpit of Texas." We worked in the scorching sun all day long. I was miserable, but in a way, I was happy because I had a job, and I was getting paid $1.25 an hour. That was the new minimum wage, up from 50 cents an hour, and it was a lot of money in those days. Wow! What would I do with all that money!

"On Friday, November 22, 1963, at 1:00 o'clock in the afternoon, I had just climbed up a pole and started to lay some TV cable when suddenly, I heard a news flash broadcast on my small portable radio which I always carried. The announcer said in a loud and shocked voice, 'President Kennedy has just been shot.' I was so startled, that I almost fell off the pole. Soon after that report, another announcement was made, saying that President John F. Kennedy was dead! I will always remember that devasting and horrifying moment in my life."

CHAPTER SIX

"ANGELITO" IS BORN

"Quartets might have gone out of style," Ornelas said, "but duos such as Jan and Dean, the Everly Brothers and others were now in style."

All the teenagers in Laredo started to listen to KTSA and KONO radio stations from San Antonio where they listened to the Royal Jesters plus Sunny and the Sunliners. So, before going their separate ways, René Ornelas and René Herrera, decided to go to the Alamo City to record "Angelito," a song that they wrote when the quartet was in Mexico.

As a matter of trivia, Ornelas revealed that he got the idea for this song to attract the attention of Rosalinda Ramos, a beautiful, young Mexican *vedette* (dancer) at Teatro Blanquita.

"But she never even looked at me. I was only a lowly Quarter Note, always broke and not yet a successful René René. Little did she know how badly she missed out."

As for life after The Quarter Notes, Ornelas' plans were to move to California to explore the possibilities of working and singing as a soloist, while Herrera's goal was to obtain a college degree in business and to work in Laredo.

ABRAHAM "ABE" EPSTEIN'S RECORDING STUDIO

Despite their separate plans, before they parted, they decided to record "Angelito." In late 1963, they went to Abraham "Abe" Epstein's recording studio. It was actually a real estate office/part-time recording studio at 735 North General McMullen Drive in San Antonio.

Ornelas stated, "Before I left for California, we recorded 'Angelito' (Jox JO#17) with a group of musicians that had shown up for the recording session."

One may hear this original version with a basic drum beat that was typical of a 1960s combo at youtube.com/watch?v=hqOvBrw3Mj. And the flipside, "Write Me Soon" (youtube.com/watch?v=CsIexAveF_k) written by Herrera, featured a nice saxophone accompaniment.

"I gave one half of the songwriters' credit to René Herrera because he had written some of the English lyrics and we were friends. In return, he was supposed to give me half of a song that he had written."

Ornelas and Herrera signed a contract with Epstein, which virtually guaranteed Abe Epstein everything and René and René nothing; and that was it, period."

The studio had a very simple Magnacord Recorder and two microphones – one for the singers and one for the band. Some of the musicians on this recording were Ramiro Cervera on vibes, Fred Salas on piano and bass, Ornelas' hairstylist Blas Bustamante (Mr. B) on acoustic guitar and three other musicians on trumpet and drums – all awesome musicians.

Ramiro Cervera said, "I know that we recorded on a Monday because Epstein called me on a Sunday and asked if I could play vibes for René and René the next day."

Afterwards, as they walked out of the studio, Ornelas, who felt that the results were less than encouraging, sarcastically said, "Not even my grandmother is going to buy that record." But Epstein eventually released it anyway and after it was leased to CBS Columbia Records, it sold over a million copies and became their first gold record.

SUNNY OZUNA AND OTHER RECORDING ARTISTS

Ildefonso "Sunny" Ozuna was already enjoying the success of "Talk to Me" and celebrating with pride regarding his November 2nd appearance on Dick Clark's "American Bandstand." Yet, René and René were not even aware of Sunny's success.

According to Ornelas, "Laredo and San Antonio may be only 150 miles apart, but to us, San Antonio was like another world, and our cultures and our preferences in music were very different.

"In Laredo, even the Anglos spoke Spanish while Mexican Americans in San Antonio spoke more English, and the musicians there were into a local San Antonio thing (the Westside sound).

San Antonio was already in the musical stage that, decades later, was referred to as the "Westside Sound." The only rockin' teenage bands in Laredo emulating this sound were the Valencianos – Jesús, Tony, Reymundo "Ray," Javier and Eddie – who recorded "Sincerely" and "Time Was," a translation of "Duerme," a Mexican tune.

The other bands were The Uniques, the Viscounts, the Dial Tones, the Royal T's, and the Tune Ups. There were also Chuck (Fidencio Vargas) and The Dots, and The Latin Gents featuring Albert Esquivel on lead vocals, Víctor Garza, bass; Ray Valenciano, guitar; Tony Valenciano, alto saxophone; Rich Casso, tenor saxophone, César Prudo Casso on drums and J.J. Barrera's Dismal Swamp.

Before that, Albert Esquivel had formed the group called The Endings in 1959, a trio featuring Charlie Mata on guitar and Mike Treviño on bass.

Esquivel later moved to the Alamo City and became a prominent promoter, formed the original Texas Talent booking agency, and owned two record labels – Chicano Records of America and Texas Best. In 1962, Esquivel recorded "In the Still of the Night" and "That's My Desire" with Luciano Duarte while stationed at Warner Robins AFB, near Macon, Georgia.

The Uniques were a doo-wop group consisting of Jorge Ramírez, vocals and guitar; his brother, Manuel, Danny Castle (r.n. Daniel Castillo), guitar, and Sergio Cavazos.

Ramirez said, "Prior to them, only orchestras – such as those of Mike Ornelas, Eleazar (Eli) Treviño, Luis Ramos and the Valdez Brothers – played at the high school dances. That's not what we wanted, but that's what we got."

That was the extent of Laredo's rock music scene up to 1963. Bt inspired by Sunny and the Sunlines, Noé Esparza, Carlos Landin and the The Rondel; Víctor Garza and the Peppers featuring Ely DeHoyos, Joe Argaiz and Sergio Ruiz soon followed.

RENÉ ORNELAS MOVES TO CALIFORNIA

As can be seen, Texas is so large and the people's taste in music is so different, their influences are so unlike, that it is almost like living in another country. So, unhappy with his most recent experiences, René Ornelas decided to leave the state and start a new life elsewhere.

Ornelas recalled, "After we recorded 'Angelito,' I went to Santa María, California where I washed dishes and worked as a waiter at 'Chico's Casita,' my brother Mike's restaurant. While there, I borrowed a guitar and an amplifier. After waiting on tables, I would change my clothes, get on the stage, play my guitar and sing for the customers.

"Later on, I formed a group that I named the Vic René Four. We played at a popular place called Las Flores Night Club. The gig lasted for a month.

"After that job finished, I went back to work for my brother at Chico's Casita. One day, while I was washing dishes and listening to a small radio that I had in the kitchen, I got the surprise of my life. The DJ was playing my song, 'Angelito' and he announced that it was #2 on the Top 40 list in California and it was one of the most requested songs. I dropped all the pots and pans that I had been washing and I immediately called René Herrera in Laredo. He told me that we had a hit record that was being played all over the United States. The bookings were lining up and I needed to get home quickly to go on tour.

"I was low on funds and didn't have the airfare to go to Laredo. But the next day, I was talking to a customer at the restaurant and he turned out to be a booking agent in California. When he discovered that I was half of the René and René duo, he offered me a booking in northern California. He was putting on a show that included The Beach Boys, Diana Ross and the Supremes and some other super stars. He asked if I wanted to be a part of it. Naturally, I agreed and said yes. I had to quickly find another René to complete the duo. I chose a musician friend who had worked with me at Las Flores Night Club. I taught him the harmony parts in 'Angelito' and some other René and René songs. Would you believe he was an Irishman with red hair and freckles? But who knew? Nobody really noticed because we were both wearing hats. Everybody wanted to hear René and René and we were a great success. They loved us. After the concert, I was paid $5,000 and I was on my way to Laredo to start the René and René tour."

"ANGELITO" REUNITES THE ORIGINAL RENÉ AND RENÉ

In the meantime, Herrera was working at Hachar's clothing store as a credit clerk and Ornelas was in California when "Angelito" was released in early 1964. Ironically, not one of San Antonio's Top 40 radio stations would play the record until Bruce Hathaway broke it on KONO radio. The tune caught the attention of radio listeners and it quickly sold 50,000 units in Texas.

One of the first to hear "Angelito" was Sunny Ozuna, who said, "This is cool. These guys are on a spin of their own; and I thought they were local because they recorded for Abe Epstein.

"And yes, every one of us was in a different world. Alfonso Ramos was doing his thing in Austin, and Little Joe was making strides in Central Texas; so, we were all too busy making a mark for ourselves to keep up with other bands.

"I remember names like Mando and the Chili Peppers would catch my ear in the late '50s just because of the name, but that was it."

Capitalizing on the regional hit, Epstein leased the recording to national record companies with worldwide distribution.

On April 28, 1964, the radio station copy was released on red vinyl with "Angelito" on both sides as Columbia 4-43045 / JZSP 77617.

Recalling how he got the news about "Angelito", Herrera said, "One day Abe called me and said, 'René, the record is taking off here in San Antonio, but we've got to go to radio stations and promote it.' I said, 'Are you going to pay me?' 'Yes,' he answered.

"In the meantime, I was trying to find Ornelas and couldn't locate him. People wanted to see René and René, so I took Willie Flores and dressed him up like me and passed him off as René Ornelas hoping to get away with playing the record and miming it," Herrera recalled.

Little did Herrera realize Ornelas was about 1,800 miles away.

"I was going to stay in California, and I was never going back to Texas – that is, until the day that I discovered we had a hit record," Ornelas said.

Herrera was going crazy trying to locate Ornelas so they could reunite as René and René. Finally, René Ornelas called Herrera to find out what was going on.

"Where have you been," Herrera asked. *"Pues lavando platos"*

("Washing dishes"), Ornelas answered.

"We've been looking for you, so come back home as soon as possible because we've already lined up some tours," Herrera said.

It was hilarious to picture Herrera using someone in Texas and Ornelas using someone else in California as the other René, but that's what they had to do to pacify promoters in both states.

"If it weren't for Epstein, we would not have made it," Ornelas said of the label owner who leased the first master to Columbia Records.

"The only boo-boo on several releases of this tune is that the labels read (Herrera & Ornellas). So, for years, my royalty checks misspelled my name as Ornellas, but the bank still cashed the royalty checks. The single went on to sell millions and to become an international hit.

That's amazing for a record that 'never made' Billboard magazine's Top 40 pop singles charts. (Whitburn, Joel (1996) *The Billboard Book of Top 40 Hits from 1955 to 1996*. New York: Billboard.

Years later, when asked how he felt after the recording of "Angelito," Ornelas changed his tune when he responded, "Well, I knew it was something special ... it was such a simple, romantic song and it had a hook that would make even Neil Sedaka proud."

The hook was that it was in English and Spanish which was a first. Nobody had ever recorded an English and Spanish bilingual song in the Top 40 market. It made a big hit! It went on to sell over a million copies.

What was amazing, or unexpected, is that even though René & René were native sons of the southern Texas-Mexico border region where the most popular genre was regional Mexican, they went against the grain and their mainstream musical contribution was essential to the genesis of rock & rock at this period in time.

It's also amazing how one telephone call can change a person's life.

"Epstein's main guy at Jox Records was Milton "Milt" Lance, a Jewish New York native who worked as a publisher," Ornelas said. "After some negotiation, Milt began to handle all our bookings. Promoters, such as Memo De Anda in California wanted to work with us, but we were loyal to Epstein. Lance was also the one who answered the phone when Dick Clark's representative contacted Epstein's office to book our appearances."

CHAPTER SEVEN

RENÉ AND RENÉ
ON DICK CLARK'S "AMERICAN BANDSTAND"

On August 8, 1964, René and René not only performed "Angelito" on Dick Clark's nationally televised "American Bandstand," but they were also interviewed by him. Clark introduced the song as "one of the most delightful, most interesting records to come along and become popular in many, many a moon."

During the interview, Clark asked Ornelas, "Who is the telephone lineman? I heard one of you was, no?

"I used to be," Ornelas responded. "I used to be climbing poles"

"You mean up on the top ... playing with the electricity? What turned you on to this? Did you get a shock one day?" Clark continued to grill him.

"No, I got tired of climbing poles. That's all," Ornelas answered.

"Fair enough," Clark said, then he turned to Herrera and asked, "What made you decide to change format to this?"

"I don't know," he responded. "Maybe it was a hit record."

"So, what does the future hold for you?" Clark continued.

"Well, I have to get a manager first," Herrera said as the YouTube video came to an end.

Ornelas' comment on the Dick Clark show caused many people to wonder about that part of his life, and he was gracious enough to answer that question.

"After I was discharged from the army, a cable company came to Laredo, and they needed to hire about 20 people to work for them. Although I had never climbed a pole, or even a tree, I applied for the job. I got the job and after a week of training, I started to work climbing poles and installing lines and cables.

Incidentally, the entire performance plus the Dick Clark interview can be seen at youtube.com/watch?v=bXDb5ktGQ_8.

Joking about "Bandstand," Ornelas said, "Before us, the only Mexicans allowed on the TV studio set were the guys who brought in the tacos through the back door for the staff; but we walked right in the front door. Yes! We broke the barrier. From then on, it was cool to sing in Spanish."

As a result of their appearance, the show's host took them on two Dick Clark Caravan of Stars tours with the Beach Boys, Jan and Dean, Three Dog Night plus Diana Ross and the Supremes.

The icing on the cake came when Lance told them that Johnny Carson wanted them to appear on "The Tonight Show." Up until 1957, all guests, no matter how famous they were, were paid a union scale of $265.50. Scale was up to around $400 when René and René were invited. Therefore, they would have had to pay their own way to Burbank, California. So, they turned down Carson's offer. What a loss because that appearance would have resulted in still more record sales.

"ANGELITO" OPENS THE DOOR FOR ALL HISPANICS

Yes, René and René hit the big time and they could have been bigger yet, if they had capitalized on this once in a lifetime opportunity. However, Laredo provided the world with one of the most popular singing artists of its time.

In the process, they also went down in musical history as the first Hispanic artists to record an international bilingual song – long before Johnny Rodríguez or Freddy Fender did it.

The publicist for Epic Records, in his liner notes in the "Mucho René and René" album, wrote: "During the summer of 1964, when the usual musical tournament was under way on the radio, one song was exceptional. ... Teenagers, commuters, housewives – record buyers – made "Angelito" popular.

"It was perhaps significant to consider the remarks of a fringe member of the music business, commenting on what he assumed was the cleverness of 'that guy René. First, he records the melody,' our friend observed, 'then it is played back while he records the harmony part. It's a cute gimmick ...

"Theirs is a romantic, intimate musical approach that provides quite a change from the omnipresent 'English Sound.' Furthermore, it seems to bridge the gap between rock 'n' roll and bossa nova, appealing to fans of both. As this album shows, René and René can be extremely diverse within the framework they have chosen ... they achieve a pleasantly uncomplicated blend of vocals ... and they display the same 'feel' that made 'Angelito' a success.

"Throughout the album, they refute what one misinformed soul characterized as 'a cute gimmick.' René and René present themselves as one of the most pleasant vocal groups heard from in years." End of album liner notes.

"We were recording in Spanish when it wasn't cool to speak Spanish," Herrera commented.

"The romantic music that I was writing at that time shows that I was on a bilingual kick, Ornelas added, "During that period, we were so hot that we even did an opening show for a television station in Venezuela for $15,000 and, that was a gazillion dollars at that time. 'Angelito' was so big that Epstein made deals to re-release the song with major labels and of course, Epstein made tons of money."

In Mexico, their hit earned them three of the most prestigious awards: La Estrella de Plata, a Disco de Oro, and El Globo de Oro.

IRENE RAMÍREZ AND DENISE

During his travels performing in concerts from city to city, René would sometimes call and speak to one hometown girl long distance from his hotel or a pay phone.

"Our recording of 'Angelito' had just been released and it was a monster hit when I met a young girl in Laredo. Her name was Irene Ramírez. It was at a time when I was swamped with offers from agents for bookings and performances all over the United States and Mexico.

"All of a sudden, somehow, I found myself engaged to her. I came back to Laredo, and we got married. Nine months later, in May 1965, we had a cute baby girl, and we named her Denise. I really wanted to name her Palmyra, but Irene refused and said, 'No!' Denise is still very grateful to her mother for that.

"Then, I got back on the road again, having fun and performing mostly one-nighters. It was party time again! Our marriage didn't stand a chance. Soon, we were divorced. But the good part about that relationship is my daughter Denise. Although I did not have a big part in raising Denise, I did teach her Spanish. She turned out to be a good woman, and because she is bilingual, she has a great job. She grew up, married a wonderful man, Louis Villarreal, who now is the owner of his own trucking business. They have two great kids, Nicholas and Mandy. I love them all and thank God for them."

"CHANTILLY LACE" (JOX JO-032)

Their follow-up to "Angelito" was "Chantilly Lace." This one featured Jox/Cobra recording artists, The Dreamliners, an all-female vocal group that was made up of Sylvia "Sol" Wilburn, Cecilia Sílva and Claire Peralta, who later married Sunny and the Sunliners' tenor saxophone player Johnny García.

The flipside, "I'm Not the Only One" ("No Soy El Unico"), was a tune penned by Lance.

"I was the Dreamliners' lead singer when the girls and I went to a studio in Houston to record the Big Bopper's cover; plus, I later did all the harmony on different dubs," Sylvia revealed. "I remember that one. That was really a kicker. I really loved to do that one.

"The engineer, a Cajun guy from Louisana, had the girls and me do it. Then he had me stack my part twice. I guess we had to do that to anchor it. I remember doing that one because it was so much fun."

Their version of "Chantilly Lace" was so good that ABC Paramount (catalog number 45-10699) picked it up for national distribution. Next, it was leased by H.M.V. Records (His Master's Voice) for release in the United Kingdom; and CBS released it in the Netherlands.

Two more singles on Epstein's JOX label followed (see discography). One of those was the super catchy, happy-go-lucky, Ornelas written "Loving You Could Hurt Me So" (youtube.com/watch?v=sM_xHaT5PE).

This Fred Salas-produced ditty featuring the musical backing of The Dell Tones is of special importance because it rivals any of the then popular British tunes.

THE BEATLES EXPLOSION

"All this was happening as the British Invasion hit the United States. This is when we found ourselves in the middle of an eruption called The Beatles, who made everything happening in music in 1964 look and sound old-fashioned and out-of-date," Ornelas recalled.

Many of the era's top rock 'n' roll bands got wiped out by The Beatles, the Rolling Stones and other mop-top-haired groups, yet the short-haired, clean-cut duo René and René kept on trucking.

"Thank God our fans were still marching to our drumbeat," Ornelas said with a laugh. "Our gigs were still solid and steady. What hurt us is that the record company was taking in all the money and keeping all the sales royalties for 'Angelito' and we never saw one penny from that.

"However, Milton Lance was nice enough to look out for us and did ensure that we were able to collect our songwriter's royalties by having us sign up with BMI. Thanks to him, we were eventually able to afford a car, a house and some of the other finer things in life."

The bottom line is that they were cheated out of so much money that Ornelas and Herrera sued the label owner. He counter sued them and neither side won. The only ones who won were the lawyers.

Ornelas said, "The best thing to come out of it is that he finally released us. We were so happy because, at last, we were free from Abe Epstein."

After they removed that noose from around their necks, Ornelas and Herrera spent the next few years touring and basking in the adoration of their fans all over the United States. But most admirably, they did not forsake their Chicano fans in Texas.

GILBERT SEDEÑO

They left no stone unturned as they performed at the large coliseums in Austin, Corpus Christi, Lubbock, Midland and San Angelo, Texas where Gilbert "El Coyote" De Anda's Tejano Brass band opened for them. And as drummer Gilbert Sedeño recalled, "Shortly before they went on stage, they panicked because their drummer did not show. So, I volunteered to fill in and that's my René and René story, "said Gilbert Sedeño, who later switched to saxophone plus organ and went on to become the piano player and music arranger for Little Joe and the Latinaires.

Perhaps some people remember him as Oblio, the nickname Little Joe gave him before this nationally known award-winning pianist, composer, arranger and producer went on to become a part of Antonio "Ham" Guerrero's Tortilla Factory, Sol, and the musical director for the Pura Vida Awards.Next, he embarked on a musical trip with some of the best nationally known country western and jazz artists. Artists such as Willie Nelson, Ray Price, Merle Haggard, Freddy Fender, Steve Tyrell, Bubbha Tomas, Resolution, Spring High and others.

A few other venues where René and René performed in Texas were at the Carousel in Corpus Christi, the Pan American and the Stardust Ballroom in Houston, the Civic Center in Laredo, Charro Days in Brownsville, and La Villa Real in McAllen.

RENÉ AND RENÉ
RECORD FOR ARV INTERNATIONAL/FALCÓN

In 1967, they realized they needed to produce another hit to keep the momentum going. So, Lance, who lived in Northwest San Antonio and the two Renes drove down to the Rio Grande Valley, to 821 North 23rd Street in McAllen, Texas to be exact. We went to talk to Arnaldo Ramírez Villarreal, Sr. who owned both Falcón and ARV International record labels, with distribution to the international market."

As can be seen, ARV stood for his full name. He was also the founder and host of "Fanfarria Falcón TV," a television program that was originally created to spotlight his artists on Weslaco KRGV-TV, Channel 5, from 1966 to 1982.

"Carlos Guzmán, a very popular, well-known international singer who recorded for Falcón, later became Arnaldo's TV co-host. But at this time, Carlos was working as the administrator of RAMMS Music publishing company, and we became life-long friends," said Ornelas.

As Arnaldo "Nano" Ramirez Villarreal Jr. recalled, "My father was into recording orchestras, *conjuntos* and *norteño* groups. And the Renes were doing bilingual pop, so he really wasn't interested in them."

However, Nano Sr. was a fair man, and he took a chance on them. The United States was smack dab in the middle of the Vietnam War and the first single they recorded was "Enchilada José." It was a tune they had written about a friend who lost his life in Vietnam.

"His name was actually Eddie García, but we use Enchilada José as a novelty," Ornelas revealed.

The flipside was "Hiding in the Shadows," another of their original compositions.

"We recorded those two songs at Falcón' recording studio where Nano Sr.'s brother, Rafael Ramírez was the sound engineer. As you know, Rafael had his own orchestra and was also a songwriter. So later, he had us record 'Llorarás' and 'Creí.' But that came after they built a larger studio in Mission, Texas at which time, Nano Jr.'s brother Marco became the new sound engineer," Ornelas explained.

Photo courtesy of Arnaldo Ramírez Villarreal

Well, the single was released as ARV International 5007. However, the problem was that both tunes were in English. They weren't even bilingual, which is what René and René were known for.

"My father put out the first single and it didn't do well," Nano Jr. said. "They only sold about 500 or 600 records. So, they told Ornelas and Herrera, 'Sorry, we made a mistake. The songs did not sell.'"

The real problem is that the record company didn't know how to promote their music genre.

"MORNIN'"

The mid-sixties were a time when Jorge Ramírez – then performing as Spain and Jason with Roberto "Beto" Peña - would hang out at René Herrera's house in barrio X where Ornelas would often be present.

"One evening, Beto and I sang a few of my compositions before them in hopes they would record my material. The song they liked was 'Mornin.' But that was it," Ramírez said.

"Two years later, I ran into René and René at a recording studio in Houston, where I was then living. I was in the same studio because Milton Lance, who managed them, arranged for me to record some English pop tunes as Spain and Jason. They were nice enough to let us sing a few of my compositions. And once again, the one they really liked was 'Mornin,' so much so, that they decided to record it. In turn, Herrera, showed us 'Far Away' and said, 'Here, why don't you record this one.'

True to their word, Ornelas and Herrera recorded "Mornin', but the label songwriter credit read "George Ramírez" instead of Jorge. It was so good they decided it would be the "A side" to their next single. The snag was, that it was another all-English language tune.

In the meantime, what were René and René to do? They had a monster hit with "Angelito" and now ARV wanted another huge bilingual hit so they would not be just a one-hit wonder.

"Looking back, that was a most fortunate musical break because that tune is what later got me into René y René," Jorge revealed of things to come.

CHAPTER EIGHT

"LO MUCHO QUE TE QUIERO"

Flashing back to 1963, before blue-eyed guitarist Samuel "Sammy" Ibarra Jr. graduated from Laredo Martin High School that year, he and Noé Esparza recorded "Lo Mucho Que Te Quiero" (youtube.com/watch?v=M_ucFCTvACU) with the musical backing of their own band, the original Rondels featuring Humberto "Humbe" Donovan on rhythm guitar; Robert "Chore" Alonzo on bass; and Joe Lee Vera on drums.

The 45-rpm single was recorded for Luciano Duarte's Frontera Records (DC-107), a label based at 1817 Garfield Street. Duarte was not only a disc jockey at KVOZ Radio but also the first to spin tunes by Mexican American *conjuntos* and orchestras on his "Serenata Nocturna" radio show beginning in the 1950s.

The duet by the two childhood friends from a barrio known as "El Catorce" went nowhere. The sales of their version of "Lo Mucho Que Te Quiero" were almost nonexistent. No other radio station would play the record, so the song fizzled out.

Recalling their impression of this now four-year old bilingual tune, Ornelas said, "When Herrera and I heard this record, we thought it had some potential, but boy, it really needed a lot of work."

Ornelas and Herrera enhanced the melody and the chords, strengthened the lyrics so the words would rhyme, and so that the tune would flow better in an effort to make it another international hit. Finally, after months of hard work and exhausting editing, the song had been reworked into the simple sweetness of a romantic bilingual million-selling top-40 hit song. But since Ibarra had written the original raw lyrics, the three agreed to share songwriting credits.

Therefore, foremost on the René and René list of recordings for Falcón would be "Lo Mucho Que Te Quiero." However, they did not want to record it in a local studio.

THE RECORDING SESSION

"Angelito" had been recorded in a very simple, uncomplicated 2-track studio. Ornelas had heard that there were some recording studios that had more than two tracks, but he didn't know where they were. So, he searched for and found one in Houston.

"We were thrilled and excited because Doyle Jones' recording studio had an eight-track recorder and that was the latest thing at that time," Ornelas said. "I was sure we had hit the big time!"

"As soon as a slot was available, Ornelas and Herrera drove there with Milton, their promoter. Freddy (Salas) and I went on our own," said Sylvia "Sol" Wilburn of The Dreamliners.

Fred Salas, who had just married Sylvia on July 26, 1967, brought his wife along because she did not want to be alone in their Lackland AFB apartment and that turned out to be a blessing because she vividly recalled all the details of that historical day.

"I believe Frank Peña and Tony Esquivel, the two trumpet players, went together, but I don't know if Little Johnny Rodríguez, the bass player; or Nick Adams, the drummer went together or alone.

"I recall Ornelas really didn't want to record 'Lo Mucho' because he thought it was an old crappy arrangement. *'No hombre --- se oye muy feo.'* Worse yet, they had not even rehearsed the song with the band."

"Don't worry," Freddy said. "Because when I get through with it, it's not going to sound like that. It's going to be so catchy that when people hear the intro, they're going to know what song it is; and that's what makes a hit,"

By the end of the recording, Herrera really loved it. And Ornelas, who was at first reluctant, got used to it and ended up loving it saying, "Wow Freddy, that was a great sound!"

"And he was right," Sylvia added. "Freddy branded that song. People hear the first few notes, and they know it's 'Lo Mucho Que Te Quiero.' And it became one of the most-played songs on jukeboxes, whether it was a cantina, a diner or anywhere else.

"He wrote the whole musical arrangement, but of course he kept some of the melody, which is right.

Then, Freddy walked to the studio's old C-3 Hammond organ, sat down, started adjusting the setting and began picking on the keys as

62   THE RECORDING SESSION

he wrote the music to the instrumental intro and the solo because he wanted everything to go the right way as everyone waited.

"However, Tony had this thing where he would get nervous when nothing was happening. So, he went across the street to a little bar to get a beer. Then, Frank said, 'No, no, no, if you're going, I better go so I can bring you back on time.' So, both disappeared, but made it back to record their part.

"But as the session went on, the horn's vibrato got wider and wider. It was like *la banda está borracha* (the band is drunk)," Sylvia recalled. "So tired of the numerous retakes, Freddy said, '*Sabes que* (You know what) Tony, I think all your parts are great.' Then he had Frank do both parts and Tony never noticed. And later, Freddy also re-recorded the bass part."

August 8, 1967

The Renés go over the lyrics

Fred Salas rearranging the intro to "Lo Mucho Que Te Quiero"

Making history at the Doyle Jones studio in Houston

Fred Salas

Bert Frilot

Our most sincere thanks to Sylvia "Sol" Wilburn of The Dreamliners for taking these priceless photos and sharing her memories.

Coincidently, one month before this book went to press, Sylvia casually said, "In the meantime, I sat in a corner having a wonderful time just watching. But I had my camera with me, and I started taking pictures during the recording session."

"What? Do you realize those never-before-seen photographs are priceless?" I told her. What an unexpected, pleasant surprise and a treat for you, the reader.

In the meantime, Herrera waited by the microphone while Ornelas drank a 12-ounce A&W root beer out of an embossed brown bottle.

Once Fred wrote the new musical arrangement, he also played keyboards on the entire production. So together, they worked their magic and put new breath in an old song.

Now, with all the changes, enhancements, and new Fred Salas arrangement, "Lo Mucho Que Te Quiero" had all the makings of a national hit.

"LO MUCHO QUE TE QUIERO" IS PUT ON HOLD

As previously mentioned, the two tunes that made up the first single on Discos Falcón were sung in English and released on a label that had made a name for itself due to their roster of orchestras, *conjuntos*, and *norteño* groups. Hence, it did not do well.

Ornelas and Herrera were so happy and proud of their new recording after they turned over the two-inch analog tape reel to Arnaldo "Nano" Ramírez Sr., they sang all the way back to Laredo. Little did they realize Nano Sr. had placed their recording on a storeroom shelf because the A side, "Mornin'" was completely in English.

This was also about the time when René and René had virtually disappeared from the local scene.

ARNALDO GÓMEZ "NANO" RAMÍREZ JR'S SIDE OF THE STORY

Nano was a high school student when he joined the U.S. Navy Reserves in 1963. And a year later, he met his (now) wife, Lucy González. She played piano and he would accompany her on guitar as a duet with no name. Next, Nano and two of his cousins Kelly Ramirez on keyboards and Antonio "Tony" Gómez (cousin) doing second voice; plus, Eddie Pérez, lead vocals and alto/tenor saxophone; Luis

"La Wicha" Anzaldúa on bass; Juan Farías, alto saxophone; Sunny González, tenor saxophone; Albert Theis, trumpet; and Julio De La Garza on drums, formed The Unknowns.

"The fact is, that we were the first Chicano group in the Rio Grande Valley to include a trumpet in a band," the Chapala Beach Boys bandleader stated.

According to Manuel Mario Gómez Sáenz of The Cruisers, who was instrumental in giving this writer most of the band members names, Nando, Kelly, and Tony were cousins.

"The reason I know is because my mom and Nando's mom were sisters," Mario said with a chuckle.

As the band's name implied, they originally gave themselves that name because they were unknown. But shortly after a change in the lineup that now included Floyd Hanna on keyboards and Fidel Ballie on drums, they changed their name to the Chapala Beach Boys (The Unknowns) and recorded four 45-rpm singles, an extended play album (Falcón FEP-115) followed by a long-play album (Falcón FLP-2033) containing the "Chapala Theme" (youtube.com/watch?v=8ukEoChfR7o).

While 95 percent of their music was instrumental, when they entered the studio to record the album, they only had eleven instrument tunes. One of them was "Twine Time" (youtube.com/watch?v=vW4fWPhNrT0). Needing one more tune, Óscar Villarreal wrote, sang and played guitar on the twelfth tune – "No Te Perdono" – and that's a piece of unknown trivia about this album; and about the track that stood out because it did not fit their instrumental style.

Then, after their popularity reached Central and South America, Nando did the unexpected.

"In 1966, I went on active duty and got stationed aboard a Navy tanker. A year later, when the two Renes and Milton Lance came to see my dad about recording for Falcón, I had already made YN2 (Yeoman Second Class Petty Officer).

"This is when my father mailed me some newspaper articles. He told me he had signed René and René who were all excited to have Milton Lance included. He also told me they had been in

Arnaldo "Nano" Villarreal Jr.

the studio recording with my uncle, Rafael, who was the engineer.

"And my father used to tell us that they had recorded five selections, but they needed six tunes to make up one side of an album. But they were all in English. So, he told them to go back home and write a sixth selection then come back so they could finish the album.

"After I got my honorable discharge from the Navy, I went to work for my dad. My office was in the control room," Nano continued. "One day I was doing inventory when I saw a tape of 'Lo Mucho Que Te Quiero' that had been sitting on a storeroom shelf, no telling how long.

So, I took it out and started listening to the song. I thought it had so much national potential that I said to myself, 'You know what? I'm going to put it out. So, I took it upon myself to put out the single (ARV International A-5011) against my father's wishes.' On top of that, everybody in the office didn't think it was a good idea. But I disregarded everyone's opinion and had it pressed.

"Now I had to get the ball rolling, break it, and generate radio airplay. Suddenly, I remembered that when I had the Chapala Beach Boys in high school, we used to do a form of payola by giving two DJs at KRIO, a then popular Top 40 radio station, a gift or other freebies and they would announce all my gigs for a month.

"As it turns out, these two DJs were at my wedding to Lucy on June 6. By now I had started producing some English music – *unos poco loco* (a few crazy) country bands and I played 'Lo Mucho Que Te Quiero' for them. Of course, the first thing they said was, 'Nah, it's bilingual man, nobody's going to play it.' Why not I argued. 'Angelito' was bilingual, and it was a hit.

"They refused to hear me out, but as it turned out, Pro Call Records had a weekly Top 40 chart. So, guess what? Here in the valley, it was the 'number one' song for almost three months while The Beatles tunes would only last three or four weeks.

Next, Lo Mucho Que Te Quiero" was re-released, again as a vinyl single, but now as Falcón 1774 in Mexico.

All together it sold 2,000 45-rpm singles the first month. Then, it started picking up in other cities until it sold over 50,000 copies in Texas alone."

Once the airplay extended to overseas, "Lo Mucho" was leased out for release on numerous foreign record labels.

NANO JR. HITS A HOME RUN WITH "LO MUCHO QUE TE QUIERO"

Defying naysayers and all odds, Nano Jr. went against the grain. Remember that persistence overcomes resistance.

"Before you knew it, it snowballed all over the nation and in Mexico. Suddenly, René and René were getting awards in Monterrey and all over. At the same time, we began getting calls from major record labels – A&M Records with Herb Alpert, Capitol Records, CBS and others trying to lease the single. In the end, I decided to lease it out to White Whale, a worldwide known company that had a hit record with The Turtles. They gave us a $25,000 advance, released it and before you knew it, it had reached No. 14 on *Billboard* magazine's Top 40 Hits on December 14, 1968, where it stayed on the charts nine weeks. It never got to 'number one,' but it was huge.

"Next, Ornelas and Herrera recorded another six songs for the album. That's the outcome of the forgotten tape I dusted off and gave a life because I liked the song. I also recall jokingly telling both Renes, 'If it weren't for me, you would still be teachers in Laredo,'

On White Whale, "Lo Mucho Que Te Quiero" became René and René's second international hit, quickly selling over one million copies. A little trivia is that Falcón Records was owned by two brothers in

ARV INTERNATIONAL Records publicity photographs

NANO JR. HITS A HOME RUN WITH "LO MUCHO QUE TE QUIERO"

McAllen, <u>A</u>rnaldo and <u>R</u>afael <u>V</u>illarreal, thus the ARV label.

If you're too young to remember this tune, listen to it at youtube.com/watch?v=F6p1XIdM6Ks.

It turned out, this tune was covered by around thirty different artists and everyone copied it, even Al Hirt. That was such a trip to hear that version (youtube.com/watch?v=JVdFkYilJy4).

"I believe that at the last count, Falcón had sold a total of four million records. Later, Falcón became part of a corporation called Certron Records. They took over the label and we had other recordings under that label. Nothing happened, we sued them, we got the Falcón label back and continued as Discos Falcón until the late '70s.

As Sylvia Wilburn-Salas recalls, "When it became a hit, I was so proud of everyone. As for my humble husband, he said, "It was great. Now let's go on to something else – that was Freddy. As he would say, *"No me gusta darme paquete"* ("I don't like to brag."). That's because Freddy was not that interested in those things, the main thing was that it came out to be a hit for René and René.

Forging ahead, "Lo Mucho Que Te Quiero" took René and René out of the 'One Hit Wonder' category because they now had two hits --- and they were million-sellers. That fueled their popularity even further. But what Ornelas and Herrera quickly learned is that a hit record is just a calling card.

As Herrera said, "the artists make the money with the concerts that keep you on the road."

"The record company makes money off the sales. The songwriter makes money off the airplay. That's the way it goes, but yes, a hit opens doors," Ornelas said.

Unbeknownst to Ornelas and Herrera, their music publisher was about to make more money. You see, at some point in time, Ibarra fell on hard times and had decided to sell his share of the songwriters' rights of "Lo Mucho Que Te Quiero;" and Milton Lance, who was their music publisher, seized the opportunity by making Ibarra an offer for his share of the song.

In need of immediate capital, Ibarra sold and transferred his entire rights including (but not restricted to) his share of any, and all royalties due him from Pecos Music or any other source for "Lo Mucho Que Te Quiero." This included performance royalties from BMI. So, as of May 1, 1969, Milton owned a full one-third interest in the writer's royalties by contract with Pecos Music.

Meanwhile, Ornelas and Herrera were completely unaware of that transaction and didn't find out about it until much later.

"Milton Lance was about five-feet-five-inches tall, a little pudgy and bald. So, he always wore a golf cap. And remember, he was Jewish, so he was a shrewd businessman," Ornelas said.

"LO MUCHO QUE TE QUIERO" GOES INTERNATIONAL

Up to the time of this writing, Ornelas was so busy touring during all those years that he was not aware that besides his records

René and René broke into the American market with "Angelito." However, a second million seller elevated their already rising star and suddenly everyone wanted to know who this guy René was because people assumed it was one singer. Even seasoned pros in the music industry would remark, "First he records the melody. Then it is played back while he records the harmony part. It's a cute gimmick, except that he records as two vocalists." They had no clue about René and Rene's individuality until they saw them on tour or television. This time they hit so hard that their ARV/Falcón records were released all over this planet.
Furthermore, record labels that they recorded for as far back as their Quarter Notes days re-released new 45 rpm singles with a picture sleeve to cash in on a piece of the pie. The proof is in the above photos.

being released in the United States, and in Mexico, Arnaldo Ramírez Sr. had also leased, or licensed, "Lo Mucho Que Te Quiero" to the following record companies: Mafer in Spain, Major Minor in the United Kingdom, Island Records in the UK, President Records in the Netherlands, Frankie in Belgium, Polar in Norway and Sweden, Stateside in Australia, and other companies around the world. But it was all good. They couldn't complain because the worldwide airplay meant more songwriter royalties.

CBS also released follow-up René and René singles in Italy and the Netherlands. That's some hefty leasing with some heavy-duty sales checks for Discos Falcón.

What was very impressive, if one stops to think about it, is that the red hot "Angelito" appealed to all age groups at a time when Elvis, the Beatles, the Rolling Stones, and other popular singers and groups dominated the Top Ten charts.

"Yeah, we were in competition with some heavy hitters," Ornelas said with a smug look of satisfaction.

"What created their hits was the combination of Ornelas' and Herrera's voices, and a lot of luck," a friend, Jorge Ramírez said.

As Javier Villanueva, then director of Tejano R.O.O.T.S. Hall of Fame in Alice, Texas, told Ramiro Burr, "Those guys set the mark and also influenced a lot of other groups," (Burr, Ramiro (2001, July 11). Duo earns hall of fame honor for role in Tejano music history. *San Antonio Express-News*. S.A. Life pp 1G.)

On October 23, 2022 *San Antonio Express-News* columnist Paula Allen wrote, "Both Renés were talented songwriters and that helped the pair take off ... although they had hits with some covers, the songs that boosted René and René to national fame were original compositions."

So, it's no doubt that those two mega-hits plus countless albums and national tours by René and René made them a household name in The United States and all over Mexico, Central America, South America and the Caribbean. This resulted in tours to Panama, Puerto Rico, Venezuela and other Latin Hemisphere countries.

In Europe, Laredo's most famous duo performed in France and Italy. On the Pacific Ocean side, it was Japan, Okinawa plus Korea. This doesn't include touring just about all over the United States, including Alaska and Hawaii, plus Canada.

In 1969, BMI (Broadcast Music Inc.) gave them the Radio Airplay Achievement Award for "Lo Mucho Que Te Quiero." That award was given for a song that reached over a million in airplay. That song continues to receive airplay on oldies-but-goodies radio stations and is a song that continues to provide both René and René with royalties.

When you add to that their touring income, you can say René and René were rolling in it, so they really didn't "knead" the dough. However, fans are fickle and if you don't hit the road, you will soon be forgotten. Besides, Ornelas also had the Tijuana Jail to fall back on.

ARV INTERNATIONAL & FALCÓN RECORDS' FOLLOW-UP TO "LO MUCHO QUE TE QUIERO"

As you learned earlier in this chapter, "Lo Mucho Que Te Quiero" was originally Side B to Jorge Ramírez's "Mornin" (ARV International

RUDY & THE RENO BOPS MEET RENÉ & RENÉ
Center: Rudy Tee Gonzales
L-R: Ray Martínez, Manuel "Red" Gonzales, Chano Elizondo, René Ornelas, René Herrera, Rubén Arispe, Phil Quiroz and Johnny Wing
Photo courtesy Chano Elizondo

5011 / Falcón 1774) but once it hit, "Lo Mucho" was released as Side A and Side B was changed to "Las Cosas" under the same Falcón 1774 number. "Las Cosas," which featured Fred Salas' unique organ style sounded very much like "Lo Mucho," so much so, that the next single was "Las Cosas" b/w "Relampago" (Falcón 1801).

Long story short, the sister labels, ARV and Falcón released 16 vinyl singles in 1968; and that's not counting the leasing of "Lo Mucho Que Te Quiero" to labels in 14 other countries.

The reason is that having found that there was an international market for Spanish-English bilingual songs, they began taking popular hits by Mexican trios, translated their lyrics to English, and recorded bilingual versions of those songs. And *voila*, another set of hits. A classic example is "Creí" (youtube.com/watch?v=1qvDHNvAdeU), written by Jesús "Chucho" Monge Ramírez (Falcón 1843) backed with a new recording of "Angelito" on the flipside.

Little did anyone know the can of worms this re-recorded new version of "Angelito" would produce.

ABE EPSTEIN TAKES RENE AND RENE TO COURT

In an attempt to get a piece of the pie, real estate agent and music producer Abe Epstein hired attorney Robert Arthur "Bobby" Allen, who graduated from Baylor Law School in May 1968, to sue René and René for breach of contract.

"Epstein's basis for the lawsuit was that they had a money-making record out, and he claimed he wasn't being paid his agent commission," Allen told *San Antonio Express-News* columnist Paul Allen. Read the article at expressnews.com/news/local/article/Rene-and-Rene-Tejano-music-mainstream-17526008.php.

"The Renés were represented by a very fine gentleman, attorney Albert McNeel. Along the way, there was a dispute with one of the Rene's over whether he had to take off his sunglasses during his oral deposition," Allen continued.

Furthermore, Epstein told an interviewer that he had something to do with their success because he helped the pair take off on his Jox label. The record producer also said he suggested they add some English lyrics to "Angelito" and that he also recalled René Herrera wanted to sell the song to him for $100, but he talked Herrera out of it and the record went on to sell 30,000 copies in less than a month.

As for the lawsuit between Epstein and the Renés, a *San Antonio Light* story from January 16, 1969, states Epstein filed it against the singers and their manager, Milton Lance, a former employee of Epstein Enterprises. He was asking for $75,000 in punitive damages --- $25,000 from Lance, $50,000 from Falcón Records and a percentage of the income earned by Herrera and Ornelas because the plaintiff contended that the recording artists signed a contract with him on January 18, 1964. It included a provision that they would not record songs with other firms for a five-year period, and they recorded a new version of "Angelito" for Falcón Records, an alleged breach of contract.

When asked about the outcome of this lawsuit, Ornelas said, "I have no explicit recollection of who refused to take off his sunglasses during the deposition, nor that lawsuit, other than it was settled out of court with no damages paid.

RENÉ HERRERA ATTEMPTS TO QUIT THE DUO

All of this did nothing to soothe Herrera's troubled spirit, because he realized that getting slapped with a lawsuit and being on the road was not for him.

As Herrera said, "Every time I came home, I looked beyond the glamour, fame and adulation. I knew this was not going to last forever. My wife Velia (née Castillo) and I wanted more stability."

Aside from the road, the duo also had to continue churning out more hits. So, in early 1970, they went into the studio to record "El Mexicano," (youtube.com/watch?v=WLQXt2yPy2A) a song that they wrote together.

It was their third single on Milton Lance's East Bend

René Herrera, a fan, and René Ornelas
Photo courtesy René Herrera

label, and it was produced by Doug Sahm of Sir Douglas Quintet fame. On the flipside was "You're Really Hurtin' This Guy" (youtube.com/watch?v=5UnfOsAl4xU), a song written by Ornelas and arranged by Fred Salas.

Other songs that Ornelas wrote for this production, which was released in 1971, were "Dices Que Me Dejas" and the bilingual version of "Mienteme" (youtube.com/watch?v=JR6tJWdxaVU). The album also included a song written by Sunny Ozuna called "Put Me in Jail," which René and René made into the bilingual version called "Castígame Ya" (youtube.com/watch?v=c-PaSevTiaY).

Sometimes this writer wonders if Herrera was aware of the influence of René and René in Mexico since all the hits by Mexican artists were usually written by their top songwriters, while these two Texans achieved success with their own songwriting skills. The songs that René and René wrote were so popular that they were also recorded by the top artists of the Latin Hemisphere.

After graduating from Texas A&I University, Herrera went to work for Union National Bank until it closed. Then he joined the Laredo Model Cities and Community Development. His last job was with the Laredo Independent School District from which he retired.

As Herrera said about retiring from René and René, "I enjoyed the ride. It was a great experience, but I don't regret quitting the road at age 35."

Although he said he was quitting, Herrera never completely got rid of the desire to sing and play the guitar and to be in the spotlight, he often sang at private parties for his friends in Laredo and he also enjoyed singing in church.

René Herrera and Ramón Hernández following an interview at Herrera's home in Laredo, Texas

Photo by Martha Hernández

CHAPTER NINE

TOMMY PHARR & FERMÍN DOS SANTOS

Interjecting two unknown facts for trivia seekers, Milton Lance had connections all over, one of whom was songwriter Aubrey Mayhew in New York City. Mayhew is the man who discovered Donald Lytle, changed his name to Johnny Paycheck and convinced his boss at Pickwick Records to record him. They did and Paycheck charted. Seeing he had a winner, he quit his job and along with Paycheck, steel guitarist Lloyd Green, and Mayhew started Little Darlin' Records.

Despite a few hits, the label ran out of money and closed in late 1969. But Mayhew was shrewd and quickly struck a deal with Certron Corporation to start a music division in Nashville and they set up an office at 1226 16th Avenue South.

Now in search of new talent, in mid-1970 Aubrey called Milton and he brought up René and René. However, Milton knew it wouldn't be long before Herrera quit and looking out for Ornelas, he suggested him to Mayhew.

"This is when Milton sent me to Nashville," Ornelas said. "The problem was that I didn't know how to sing country; and I didn't want to sing it either. But in those days, you didn't argue with record producers. So, I just went along with it."

Thus, Ornelas recorded two country and western songs with the musical backing of three famous recording artists - Ray Stevens, Joe South and Charlie Daniels. The end result was "Touch My Heart" b/w "Apartment #9" (Certron C-1007), two tunes written by Johnny Paycheck and one of them co-written with Mayhew.

"And to top it off they changed my name to Tommy Pharr," Ornelas said with a laugh.

Other artists on this label were Bobby Helms, future country star Don Williams and Pozo Seco in the beginning of their careers. After a couple of dozen singles, and little in the way of cash coming in from record sales, Certron pulled the plug in early

1971. Paycheck took this "outlaw" music style to Epic and went on to become a big star with "Take This Job and Shove It."

"I took the 45-rpm single and put it in our jukebox at Tijuana Jail. However, when they took the jukebox, that record was still in there and that was my only copy," Ornelas wistfully said about his loss.

Next, Ornelas recorded "He Sabido Que Te Amaba" and "Háblame" (EB-105) as Fermín Dos Santos in what was his first record for East Bend Records, a label owned by Milton Lance. The first was re-released as East Bend EB-505 (youtube.com/watch?v=pwhiBGTZTHw). The two latter tunes were later re-released as East Bend EB-503 (youtube.com/watch?v=73J1kuN3Ah4) –as René & René.

RENÉ ORNELAS DIVERSIFIES

Herrera had entered the business world and not wanting to stay behind, Ornelas invested his money wisely. He invited his brother, Mike, to come from Santa María, California to join him in opening René and Mike's 'Tijuana Jail,' the most crowd-pleasing night club in Laredo, Texas.

"Our night club was extremely popular since I was 'the first' to get a liquor-by-the-drink license for a private club in Laredo. Prior to that, people could only buy beer at the night clubs. I was able to sell mixed drinks and as an added attraction, I had live music, strobe lights and gorgeous go-go dancers; and my sister, María Teresa, best known as Terry, was the prettiest dancer we had. Wow!! The place was packed every night."

"When I owned 'Tijuana Jail' in 1970, it was always party time. I was having so much fun; I was making a lot of money and I was a recently divorced single man."

René and René were at their all-time high. This meant Ornelas still had to fulfill his performance contracts. But without skipping a beat, he managed to balance touring and running a club.

"In my absence, my brother Mike would take care of the business as I would fly out of San Antonio to perform some shows. And when I returned, it was party time again. To keep the customers and my fans happy, I would sometimes perform at my club.

"Some radio disc jockeys from San Antonio came to check out the Tijuana Jail; and when they saw all the crowd and how packed it

René Ornelas' sister and go-go girl María Teresa "Terry"

was, one of them said, 'René, you have perfected the art of extracting money from another man's pocket without resorting to violence.' It was a compliment I never forgot.

"I also owned a popular Mexican restaurant, called La Bonita, in downtown Laredo. It was another one of my moneymakers. I was hardly ever there, so my dad, Mike Ornelas, Sr. would run the restaurant business for me. Life was great and it couldn't get any better."

BACK TO THE DRAWING BOARD

Yes, life could not get any better, until Herrera decided to quit the duo in 1972. However, Ornelas was still determined to continue his life-long dream. He gave the club, Tijuana Jail, to his brother Mike and moved to San Antonio.

Ornelas knew he needed stability and continuity because fans were going to catch on when they didn't see the same second face that was on album covers, posters and in concerts. So, Ornelas decided to move to San Antonio with the determination to continue his life-long dream of entertaining.

He remembered Jorge Ramírez and lost no time in selecting this fellow Laredoan as the second René. To carry out his plan, René Ornelas had Milton Lance ask Ramirez to become the new half of René and René. Ramírez accepted and moved from Houston to San Antonio because that's where Ornelas decided would be their home base.

Now, women would have two handsome hunks to ogle. Here's a quick condensed bio on Ramírez ...

JORGE RAMÍREZ – THE NEW 2ND RENÉ

Jorge Alberto Ramírez was born on November 1, 1944, in Laredo, Texas. He graduated from Martin High School in 1962, and Laredo Jr. College in 1964. However, his musical story started in 1958, when he formed The Uniques, a doo wop group, that at one time or the other included his brother Manuel plus classmates Richard Applewhite, Danny Castle (r.n. Daniel Castillo) and Sergio Cavazos.

Jorge said, "Later, I took two Laredo Junior College choir members, César González and Irene Treviño, formed The Folk Three, and we patterned ourselves after a very popular folk-singing trio called Peter, Paul and Mary. Prior to that, I had put together a group similar to the Quarter Notes with three guys in the choir to record a station break jingle for KVOZ."

After junior college, Ramírez moved to Denton, Texas where the 5-foot-11-inch-tall North Texas State University student teamed up with Carol Beyer. Together, they sang folk songs on campus, at parties, and at pizza parlors. It was then that Ramírez also became a songwriter.

In 1967, after he graduated with a degree in journalism, the singer-songwriter went back to Laredo, teamed up with Roberto "Beto" Peña, a green-eyed, sandy blonde-haired *güero* and formed the singing duo called Spain & Jason. I was Jason, Roberto became Spain. When I entered school, no one could pronounce Jorge Alberto, so I became J.A. That's why I went with Jason and in college we had a guy from España with a similar name problem. Thus, everyone called him Spain. And musically, we patterned ourselves after Pete and Gordon plus Chad and Jeremy, but unfortunately our act didn't last very long.

"A year later, I moved to Houston where I was employed by KTRK-TV and worked as a solo act at Steak and Ale during my free time. It was also during the late-1960s that J.C. (John Charles) Crowley and I formed a musical group called Just Friends. Who was to know that 17 years later, Crowley would become the co-founder of the extremely popular Top 40 group called Player and landed a number one smash hit with 'Baby Come Back' (youtube.com/watch?v=1qNVMaYWuwY)."

That's it in a nutshell. Now we resume where we left off and that's Ornelas' decision to leave his beloved hometown, move to the Alamo City and find a replacement for Herrera.

RENÉ ARRIVES IN SAN ANTONIO

"Parties are a lot of fun, but you can't party forever. There comes a time when you have to go home. That's exactly how I felt, but I didn't have a real home anymore. I was renting a luxurious apartment, but somebody was always dropping in at all hours and starting another bash. So, at my apartment in Laredo, there was always a non-stop shindig going on in full swing. Besides, I had some serious personal problems in my life. I just had to get away. I gave my night club to my brother Mike and my restaurant to my father Mike Ornelas, Sr.

"I packed my things, filled up my yellow 1965 Oldsmobile with gas and I took off for San Antonio. I didn't know anybody there, but I just took a chance because it sounded interesting."

What Ornelas did not realize when he signed a one-year lease is that the Alamo City apartment with a fantastic looking swimming pool turned out to be a senior citizen's apartment complex. So much for ogling a bevy of young women in bikinis.

"After a few months, I realized that most of the people in those apartments were older married people and the ambience was very dull and humdrum."

"MIRA" EAST BEND RECORDS EBSLP 1015

In the meantime, Ornelas lost no time in sitting down with Ramírez to co-write new songs.

"I must say I learned a lot about songwriting from Rene Ornelas and I can't say enough good things about his writing talent," Ramírez said with great fondness.

"As a songwriter, it's so easy when you have a vehicle, and my vehicle was Ornelas because I would write very personal autobiographical tunes' and he was a musical craftsman who would rewrite the lyrics to commercialize a lot of what I wrote."

Then, they lost no time in bringing those new songs to fruition by going to Houston and recording the "Mira" album. This production features six of their joint compositions. Those songs were "Mira" (youtube.com/watch?v=ju3nOE4e8N0), "Como Has Cambiado Mujer" (youtube.com/watch?v=_cGRldoSG9U), "Al Amanecer" (youtube.com/watch?v=6fK3jy_s2n0), "La Noche Es Fría" (youtube.com/watch?v=1_zGBhTfpuI), "Para Que Me Enseñaste" (youtube.com/watch?v=xuq5BUuXPww), plus "Poquito A Poquito" (youtube.com/watch?v=tpn47vEqAAk) and they belonged to Pecos Music BMI.

"As is the norm, we recorded three 45-rpm singles for radio airplay."

Commenting on the album, Fred Salas, who did all the musical arrangements and instrumental solos, said, "Adding Ramírez's modern style injected a youthfulness into the duo's recordings which resulted in a more contemporary feel to their music."

"Yes, the '¡Mira!' album was powerful, but some of the songs lost energy in our live performances because all we had was two guitars and a bass player. Thus, we lacked the synthesizer, brass, flute, drums, and percussion heard in the recording. So, that was a challenging time," Ramírez said with a hint of frustration.

One of their gigs together was at Arturo's Ballroom at 3310 South Zarzamora Street where among the crowd was Lee Comasco Woods, a US Air Force Senior Airmen stationed at Laughlin AFB in Del Rio, who worked as disc jockey at KDLK (FM 94.1) during his off-duty hours spinning what are today's oldies. This was at a time when Wolfman Jack (r.n. Robert Weston Smith), based across the border in Ciudad Acuña, Coahuila, Mexico ruled the airwaves because the signal emanating from the console on his show on XERF (AM 1570) was blasted out on-the-air with up to 500,000 watts of power. However, that didn't faze Woods as he spun any recording by René and René.

"I knew Arturo Villarreal, the owner of the popular club. Therefore, I had the opportunity to meet them. I don't know where the second René was, but I got to meet a clean-cut Ornelas. Then, at a closer look, I noticed his wardrobe was meticulous, his shoes were spit shined, his shirt was perfectly ironed, his jacket was perfectly tailored, and every hair was in place. Women wanted to touch him. I witnessed them swoon over him and I could understand why. He was a class act.

"Unlike other famous singers who are full of backstage demands, he never puts on airs. I've worked with him many times over the years and all I can say is that as a person he is just the nicest gentleman, always a cordial human being. And musically, onstage he's always just spot on," the former KITY/KONO disc jockey recalled.

This is a classic example of Ornelas' charm and he, along with a charismatic Jorge, could have landed loads of national television interviews if they had based themselves in Los Angeles, New York, or Miami.

"That's why I kept trying to get René (Ornelas to move to California because that was a good market for us, but at that time, he didn't want to move. We were also offered a Las Vegas audition, but we couldn't do it because we didn't have our own band. We could have been a great Las Vegas act because René and René were so popular."

That same year, singer-songwriter Marvin Palacios, who knew Jorge's cousin, Sunglow recording artist Tony Rey (r.n. Antonio "Tony" Reynaga), gave him a tape to pitch some of his songs to Jorge. He in turn played it to Ornelas who loved Marvin's material so much they recorded "Te Vi Por Primera Vez" with the English version, "The First Time I Saw You Girl" (Orfeon 15084), on the flipside of their single. Both were Marvin's songs. Moreover, from that point on, Marvin would sometimes join René and Jorge as a guitar player.

CUPID'S ARROW HITS RENE'S HEART

With the "Mira" album out of the way, as soon as his lease was up in 1973, Ornelas was more than ready to relocate to another apartment.

"This is when I met a guy named Henry Garcia and we became very good friends. He knew everything about San Antonio. In fact, he knew everything about everything. He had an apartment in a very active, youthful, and fun complex called La Plaza Apartments. At his insistence, I went to check it out and I saw their swimming pools, their tennis courts and all the good-looking young girls."

"There was a vacancy right across from the tennis courts and very close to one of the swimming pools. I immediately signed a lease and moved into my new apartment. Wow! What a difference. That apartment complex was alive.

I soon learned how to play tennis and I was playing every day. So, when I was not traveling and doing concerts everywhere, you could catch me on the courts playing tennis, either singles or doubles. I had never before played tennis in my life, but now that I had learned, I was very good, and I was hooked. My friend, Henry, and I were a pretty good team, always looking for another twosome to challenge on the tennis court.

"One day, I was waiting to start a game, when out of the blue I saw a very good looking and slender girl wearing shorts and holding onto a leash with a cute little dog on the end of it. I was attracted to her, but she kept on walking and disappeared from my sight. I wanted to know who the girl was, so I asked my friends.

One of them said, 'Oh, it's Phyllis and Saundra. She lives in the apartment next to the office.' I planted that information in my computer brain as I didn't want to forget about the beautiful girl I had just seen.

"Later on, I was talking to Macario, another new friend, and I asked him if he knew Phyllis, the fascinating girl who lived in the apartment next to the office.

"He said, 'I know the girl who lives in that apartment and her name is Saundra Sessions. But Phyllis is the name of her dog.' I felt like a fool, but I had to laugh." René continued.

"I know you like her and want to date her, but don't even bother. She will quickly turn you down. She knows you are a wild entertainer who can have all the girls he wants. But Saundra is different. She's the marrying kind. She's a good Catholic who takes her grandmother to church every Sunday," Macario said.

So, who was this young statuesque five-foot-eight-inch tall, blue-eyed cutie that caught René's eye?

SAUNDRA SESSIONS

Saundra's parents were married in 1935. In 1936, her brother Billy was born and in 1940, she was born in San Antonio. She was two years old when her parents got divorced and went to live with her grandmother, Ellie Beaumont, whom she called Mama. Saundra's mother Stella went to work at Kelly Air Force Base where she met and married an airman, and of course,

Saundra Sessions

the couple was moved frequently from base to base across the United States. For more stability, she stayed with her grandmother, who took the place of her mother. Mama (Ellie) made all her clothes, fed her good meals, did everything a mother should do, including making sure that the now teenager had a good Catholic education at St. Teresa's Academy for Girls. The Teresian nuns were awesome. They were a godsend and always made her feel special.

Through thick and thin, Saundra made enough money working at Sears to attend Our Lady of the Lake College where she received her B.A. degree in English and earned her secondary teaching certificate. When she was 21, she got her own apartment and began teaching.

In short, she was a good girl, a great catch.

THE MAGIC OF WHITE LEATHER

René continued, "A few days later, I had to catch a flight to Los Angeles because we were booked to do some concerts in southern California. One of those was at the famous Hollywood Palladium in California; then we went on tour, headlining as the stars in an all-star show that included the group Malo and other very popular bands.

"Before I came back, I went shopping at an exclusive men's clothing store in Hollywood. I saw the most beautiful and captivating white leather sports jacket that I had ever seen. It was made of the softest, finest leather. I tried it on, and it was a perfect fit. It was extremely expensive, but I had just made a good chunk of money, and I really had to have that jacket – so I bought it.

"The day that I returned to San Antonio from my trip to the west coast, my friend Macario was throwing a party for me. To my surprise, he said he had invited Saundra, the girl who had attracted me with her good looks. He told me that at first, she had said that she was not going to the party. Her reason, as she said, was "I don't smoke or drink alcohol, and that's the main thing that people do at a party, and they get drunk and irrational."

After Macario insisted that she had to come to the party, even if it were only for fifteen minutes, she reluctantly agreed to go.

As Ornelas recalls, "When I arrived at the party, Saundra was already there sitting on the sofa. I grabbed a highball, took a sip, and casually walked over toward her. I put my foot decisively on the coffee table in front of her, and leaning in close to her face, I told her, 'I'm never getting married again!' I think I must have scared her because she stood up and went home.

"Minutes later, I went to her apartment and knocked on the door. She would not answer. A couple of days later, I went back and knocked on her door again. She still would not answer the door. But luckily, I later saw her at the swimming pool, and I got my courage up, went over and talked to her. She had a very funny sense of humor, and we had a good time talking together."

After they returned from that tour, they went to do a television interview at San Antonio's Univision KWEX-TV, Channel 41 where former Quarter Note, Juan Garza-Góngora, was now a TV producer.

Ramírez said, "That's where I formally met Garza-Góngora. We exchanged phone numbers and stayed in touch after that meeting throughout the 1970s and '80s."

While all this was going on, René Ornelas, the romantic lyricist was falling in love.

RENE AND SAUNDRA'S COURTSHIP

"We began dating, but I was also going out with other girls. I finally realized that Saundra was the one for me. She was a sexy, blue-eyed, very intelligent brunette who taught English at Tafolla Middle School and I was in love. At the time, I was on the west coast doing some concerts and I had been writing letters to her. One evening, I told myself, 'This is it.' So, I picked up the phone and dialed her number. We talked for a while and then I said to her, 'I was just sitting in the park here in Los Angeles and suddenly, I got very lonely and I don't want to be alone anymore. So, let's get married,'" René proposed.

RENÉ AND SAUNDRA GET MARRIED

"After completing my singing commitments in California, I took a flight home and a week later on May 11, 1974, we were married in Saundra's home at La Plaza Apartments on Loop 410 and Isom Road."

Judge Mike Hernández officiated in the civil ceremony in which Rene's brother Mike, Jr. was best man and Saundra's sister, Pamela Morse was her maid of honor.

May 11, 1974 Mr. & Mrs. Ornelas

Mike Ornelas sang at his son's wedding

On honeymoon in Chicago

"The wedding reception was held at the La Plaza Party Room and all their friends and relatives attended. Ornelas said proudly, "My dad Mike and my good friend Fred Salas played music on the piano for dancing." Fred's wife, Sylvia Sol, a very beautiful and talented singer, was also at the reception. Saundra's mother Stella Beaumont and her good friend Rose Humphreys made all the arrangements for the food and flowers. Very beautifully done, Ladies!

A convalidation rite and blessing of the marriage later took place in a Catholic ceremony at St. Henry Catholic Church on South Flores Street. The Very Reverend (Monsignor) Emil Weselsky, a good friend of René and Saundra, performed the ceremony and said the Holy Mass. Their friends, Rob Malloy and his wife Laurel, were their witnesses. They are still very happily married, 50 years later.

"Thank you, Jesus!"

THE HONEYMOON

René and René had a three-week concert tour in Chicago and the Tri-State area and Saundra was still teaching. But as soon as the school year ended, she joined him for their honeymoon in the Windy City.

The couple saw many interesting sites in the city, but because René was so interested in life and after death and the supernatural, he wanted to see the new movie, "The Exorcist."

At the hotel, René went to freshen up in the bathroom. But after half an hour, he had yet to come out. So, imagine Saundra's surprise when she opened the door and saw him lying on the floor unable to get up. His bad back condition had returned with a vengeance. She called an ambulance and the attendants quickly came to the 27th floor with a stretcher to take him to the hospital.

The doctor prescribed a week in traction; but René refused and went back to the hotel with a prescription for Tylenol 3 (with codeine) for the pain. However, René is very allergic to codeine. Thus he got a very negative reaction to the drug and he flipped out! He just wasn't making any sense at all.

That same evening, Saundra received a call that her beloved grandmother had just died. Jorge Ramírez promised that he would take care of René, so she reluctantly returned to San Antonio for the funeral. René needed medical attention. But would you believe that Jorge brought a *curandera* (Mexican quack witch doctor) to heal him? Her treatment lasted a whole week, but it didn't help. René called Saundra every day, but all he could say to her was a very garbled "Hi." He still wasn't making any sense at all.

The concerts were cancelled so René had to go back home. Saundra had to buy four first-class tickets to accommodate René lying on a stretcher in the airplane. When René was being carried out of the plane in San Antonio, he gave Saundra the "peace sign" along with a very slurred "Hi." He was still out of it. An ambulance took him to the hospital where he stayed in traction for three days.

He went home and stayed in bed for a month. He couldn't even walk. Saundra took complete care of him and all his needs. She finally took him to a Swedish chiropractor who miraculously healed him and had him back on his feet in less than one hour. René had crawled into the doctor's office but he came out dancing and ready to play tennis again. What a honeymoon!

CHAPTER TEN

THE BROWN ALBUM

Their next album release was "René Y René" (Orfeón 12-38020) However, everyone calls this 1974 release the "Brown Album" due to the sepia-toned cover.

Side A, which was arranged and produced by Fred Salas, was recorded at Amen Studios with Manual "Manny" Guerra serving as technical advisor. Side B was recorded at Jones Studios in Houston, and it was arranged and produced by Esteban "Steve" Jordán, who also played accordion on half of the cuts. What is also unique is that this album contains only eleven tunes instead of the standard 12-song format used during the 1970s. Unfortunately, not one of the eleven tracks is available on youtube.com.

Also on two of the recording sessions was the very awesome René Sandoval on alto saxophone. He was a gifted, genius musician who

Just married and about to enter a new musical union with Jorge Ramírez and later with Marvin Palacios

The new René and René

The 3rd René — Jorge Ramírez, René

The 4th René — David Villanueva, Marvin Palacios, René Ornelas, Juan Zertuche

Photos courtesy Jorge Ramírez and Marvin Palacios

made the songs sound even better and more modern. People might still remember Sandoval when he was playing with the Eugenio Gutierrez Orchestra back in the 1950s. Sandoval's wife, Minerva, was also a very talented singer in that band from the Rio Grande Valley.

"The brown album was a classic. However, the people at Orfeón Records thought the six tunes making up 'Side B' were too modern and too progressive," Ramírez said.

However, before the year was over, Orfeón released an extended-play album (EP-1204) with four of the Steve Jordan-produced tunes.

After the album was released, the dynamic duo recorded "Where Is The Love" and the Bob Gallarza-arranged "Yo Soy Chicano" (Orfeón 45-15080) (youtube.com/watch?v=X3MVvWsV3cY), was a Royal Jesters cover b/w "Di Que Pasó." (youtube.com/watch?v=-UFgz9bD1rI). If the latter sounds familiar, it's because it is the Spanish translation of "Where Is The Love."

CAPITALIZING ON TWO INTERNATIONAL HITS

The international popularity of "Angelito" and "Lo Mucho Que Te Quiero" kept René and René's momentum high as they traveled from city to city and state to state to perform when one pleasant early summer day, Ornelas and Jorge boarded an airplane in Houston and settled down for a three-hour flight to Los Angeles where they were scheduled to do a concert in East L.A.

Upon their arrival at LAX, the booking agent and some of his crew picked them up, then took them to one of the top radio stations to do an interview and invite the audience to see the show. Afterwards, the booking agent took them to do a soundcheck at the venue where a crowd had already begun to arrive for the concert that was scheduled to start at 5 p.m.

"The concert was being held at a huge open-air park in East L.A. By 4:30 p.m., the place was jam-packed. The concert had a lineup of twelve recording artists, but René and René and the group called Malo were the top headliners. The weather was perfect, just as the weatherman had predicted. It was sunny with the temperature around 95 degrees and it seemed to be getting hotter by the minute. At five o'clock on the nose, just as it was scheduled, the loud downbeat signaled to the enthusiastic crowd that the show was on and it would run until ten o'clock that night."

Ornelas said, "The booking agent came backstage to let us know that we had attracted a record crowd. There were more than 15,000 people in attendance. I had never seen so many people in any of our performances – ever! Yes, 'Angelito' and 'Lo Mucho Que Te Quiero' were two of the most popular songs and two of the most requested songs on the Top 40 charts; and there was nothing better than seeing this duo perform their hit songs live.

"When it was our turn to go on and we got onstage, the charged-up and electrified crowd went wild. The mass of wall-to-wall, standing-room-only crowd of people started to move forward in order to be closer to the stage where we were. But, between the crowd of people and the stage, there was an area filled with water. It was a trench-like moat meant to keep the performers safe and away from the multitude. Many of the girls were wearing shorts and other summer clothing, so they started jumping into the water and swimming or dog paddling trying to get to us on the stage.

"A group of girls made it and they swarmed all over us. They all wanted a hug and a kiss from René and René. We were all wet and saturated with water, but the girls wanted more. They started pulling on my clothes. They snatched the handkerchief from my coat pocket, grabbed some of the sheet music from the music stand and helped themselves to anything they could get their hands on as a souvenir. One of the girls even ran off with my hat. I was all wet; my outfit was a disaster. My hair was all messed up and I had lipstick all over my face. But I was happy. The fans loved René and René."

After the concert, when Ornelas got back to the entertainers' green room, after his wife, Saundra, saw him all wet, half dressed, full of lipstick and bedraggled, she broke into laughter as she asked him, "Well, do you still have your *calzones*? (underwear)?"

RENÉ ORNELAS, JORGE RAMÍREZ, MARVIN PALACIOS

Later that same year, The Quarter Notes were asked to perform for a high school reunion in Laredo and since René Herrera was no longer singing professionally, Jorge Ramírez filled in as the fourth Quarter Note.

"This is when I met Juan Orfila," Ramírez said. "I already knew

Juan Garza-Góngora, so this was the start of a relationship with another Quarter Note."

"In May 1975, I no longer wanted to be part of René and René. I quit singing as the second René just to do something else," Ramírez said.

That something else turned out to be the formation of the original Río Rami Band with Marvin Palacios plus Cenobio Javier "Bubba" Hernandez on bass.

"Rami is a shorter version of my last name and 'Río' is special to me because it could stand for the Río Grande, close to where I grew up; or it could also stand for *El Río de San Antonio*. Both rivers are very special to me, but we tell people *río* means we play a river of music," Ramírez explained.

Within a year, Río Rami evolved into a large group, which included Víctor Montez, guitar; Ricky Guerra, drums; Stanley David Solís, keyboards; plus, later Ray Zuly, guitar; and Joe "Jama" Perales - formerly with the Royal Jesters and leader of his own La Fuerza band - played bass and sometimes alternated with Jorge on vocals.

RENÉ RECORDS AS 'RENÉ ORNELAS' AND AS 'RENÉ RENÉ'

Away from their adoring fans, Ornelas sensed Ramírez's imminent departure. So, he went to Bob Grever, owner of LADO A and CARA Records, to test the waters as a solo artist. The result of their meeting is that he recorded under his birth name.

All the Lado A recordings were done with Fred Salas and Bob Bruce's United Audio Recording (UAR) Studios on Mossrock Drive on the north side of Northwest Loop 410 in San Antonio. An inside story on UAR is that Bruce never liked the abbreviation because he was concerned that someone would think it stood for "United Arab Republic."

It was there that Ornelas was accompanied by Salas, the musical director who wrote the piano arrangements, plus played flute and tenor saxophone. Add to him George Finney on guitar, and Joe Sílva on percussion.

The first song they recorded was Rene's translation of Paul Anka's "She's Having my Baby" to "Esperando A Mi Hijo" (youtube.com/watch?v=hHHNiOHglAE) b/w "Ya Volví" (youtube.com/

watch?v=vTQMD5JREDo) (Lado A 5016) featuring Salas playing the then very popular pulsating San Antonio organ sound.

As a matter of trivia, the female voice you hear in this recording is that of Sylvia "Sol" née Wilburn Salas, Fred's wife.

"I remember that gig because before the recording started René asked if I would sing. And I responded, 'Of course, I'm always ready to sing.' It was a song I quickly learned because it had a very logical chord progression, so it was very easy for me.

"But then, Freddy started it out in a different key. So, I argued that it was not the right key and he said, 'What's the matter with it?' I answered, 'It's not the right key.'

"He looks at me and I look at René and I said, 'Oh no, it's not like the record' and nobody said anything because they didn't want to contradict Freddy. Still, I said, 'This is the key.' So, I started singing it acapella. René finds it on his guitar, he looks up, and he says, 'Wow, Freddy, she has perfect pitch.'

"After Freddy heard me prove him wrong, he gave me this wide-eyed look and said, 'okay, okay.' Then he quickly rewrote it and then we sang it in one take.

"It was kind of fun, but I never had enough confidence in myself, and I don't think I gave it the right feel. I was never too comfortable with the way it turned out. I didn't like the way my voice sounded because I heard it one way in my mind, but when it came out of my mouth, what I heard in my head was not there, not what I wanted. But René loved it and everybody else loved it. So, we went with that. It sure was fun doing that song. That's what I remember."

"Later, I went on to do background vocals on a few more of his recordings," Sylvia added.

"As I recall my days with The Dreamliners, I would sing lead and do the harmony on different dubs. I also sang background on a Jimmy Edward Christian song. I would also stack my voice two times to anchor it. And now I found out that René was good at stacking and it's important not to mess up when you're stacking."

Under his own name, Rene's next recordings were "Un Momento" (youtube.com/watch?v=P_fTr8EQNQQ) and "Una Carta De Cuba" (actually "Guantanamera") (youtube.com/watch?v=teN0dQNFNPU) (Lado A 5021) for Bob Grever's label.

The latter features Sylvia doing backup vocals throughout the entire song. However, when I played the song for her, she said, "That can't be me because I don't have that vibrato."

A year later, now determined to prove that people will listen to him as a solo act, Ornelas recorded a Spanish version of "Hey Baby" (youtube.com/watch?v=WLEUbVi9VUI) b/w "Bajo Un Cielo Azul" (youtube.com/watch?v=ebCeN6zx_40) (Lado A 5038), which he co-wrote with Marvin Palacios. This is another tune that features Sylvia Sol on backup vocals.

The follow up single was "La Llevo En La Mente" (www.youtube.com/watch?v=yn32q9lFdag) b/w "No Vivo Un Dia Sin Ti" (youtube.com/watch?v=_T4LZb8pwYQ) (Cara CA-120).

This came at a time when Grever was making the transition from LADO A to CARA Records.

A year later and now resolved to prove that people would accept him using José Jose's formula of doubling his first name, in 1976, he recorded "I'm Sorry Sir," a song he co-wrote with Marvin Palacios and released on Lado A (5038)(youtube.com/watch?v=BE-TZ6eNIvw) b/w "Try Me Again Tomorrow" (youtube.com/watch?v=MDqjzuuM7IQ) (Lado 5038) as René/René.

Next, Grever had him re-record "Lo Mucho Que Te Quiero" b/w

"I'm Sorry Sir" (Lado A 5042). This single was also released on Lado A Records in 1976 – again as René/René - as Jorge plus other vocalists who were performing as 'the second René' fluctuated back and forth during this period of time.

ENTER MARVIN PALACIOS – THE 3RD RENÉ

This is when Marvin Palacios, whose songs René and René had recorded two years earlier, stepped up to the plate as a pinch hitter as the other René, but only for weekend commitments since Marvin was on active military duty in the U.S. Army and stationed in nearby Killeen, TX at Fort Hood.

From this point on, René Ornelas' musical biography gets more confusing since Palacios was in the Army and when he was unable to get away to perform with Ornelas, Jorge Ramírez unofficially continued to fill in as the other René until 1982.

Marvin Roy Alaniz Canales Palacios was born on August 9, 1954, in San Diego, Texas.

Palacio's story is that of a small-town boy who does well, yet the singer-musician-songwriter has managed to remain humble and down-to-earth.

This hazel-eyed singer-songwriter was reared in Benavides, Texas until 1967, when his father, Leandro Palacios, Jr., moved the family to Kingsville, Texas.

There, his father played guitar and saxophone with Los Rancheros, his own group. Noticing that Marvin enjoyed strumming on a broom, his father started teaching him to play guitar at age four. By eight years of age, Marvin was already singing and playing guitar at various public functions.

When Marvin signed up for speech and joined the Henrietta H. King High School choir, Laura Canales aka "*La Reina (de la música chicana)*," was his classmate in both classes.

As a matter of trivia, three of Marvin's cousins and/or distant cousins are bandleader-radio-television personality Johnny Canales, Laura Canales aka "La Reina de La Onda Chicana," and tenor saxophone player Florencio "Lencho" Palacios III of The Lemans, Pura Vida, Libertad, Llamarada, GTO, plus Ricky G and the Dreamglows.

Palacios was still in high school when he joined One More Time, a top-40 cover group. Five months later, they changed their name to The Young Society. Finally, in May of 1972, he and Laura Canales graduated from high school.

By Fall, 1973, Palacios and Elio Ramírez had formed Society Sounds, a group that included Luis Bernal – brother of Eloy and Paulino Bernal. In between gigs, Palacios would freelance with the Beto Leal Orchestra.

A patriotic American at heart, Palacios joined the U.S. Army in January of 1974. He went to boot camp at Fort Polk, Louisiana. Then, he was sent to a military training school in Fort Ord, California. After completing specialized training, he was transferred to Fort Hood outside Killeen, Texas.

This is when Marvin would sometimes sing and play the guitar with the René and René team of Ornelas and Ramírez when they were still fulfilling contracts as René and René.

However, based on a gut feeling about the other René, Ornelas was also recording as a soloist. He was right. In May of 1975, Jorge Ramírez called it a day with René and René.

When Ramírez stepped down, Palacios, who had often joined them as a guitar player, was on active military duty. Nevertheless, he was ready to step in as the other René.

The week that Ramírez quit, Palacios found himself on his way to the Windy City on a long weekend pass. In Chicago, René and René were booked for two shows backed up by Los Hermanos Ríos, a very talented music group originally from San Antonio.

The next day, they performed in Bowling Green, Ohio, and René Ornelas' brother, Mike Ornelas, who was a professor there at Bowling Green State University, showed up to see his younger brother perform.

From that point on, Ornelas and Palacios began to perform as René and René.

"I was able to get four-day weekend passes; and if I had a duty weekend, I would swap weekends with someone, buy them a bottle of booze or pay them to take my duty," Palacios said.

In 1976, they did enough gigs as René and René to warrant several publicity pictures. Then his fellow servicemen found out about the celebrity among them, and the *Fort Hood Sentinel* did an article on Palacios, an article that was later published worldwide in *Army Times*.

Palacios said, "That's when we actually had a band made up of me and Ornelas on guitar, Juan Zertuche on a big Hammond organ on which he played bass with his left foot, plus David 'Takatá' Villanueva and Kido Álva alternating on drums and percussion. The band was still called "René and René.

"We would wear white pants with different colorful jackets or black pants with colorful shirts, or sometimes suits. If we wore a tuxedo at a fancy restaurant, we joked around that people might mistake us for waiters," Palacios recalled with a laugh.

Since Palacios was a soldier on active military duty, and was only a part-time René number two, Ornelas continued to record as a solo artist. However, recording under the name 'René Ornelas' was not effective enough. So, in mid-1976, he went back to ARV International Records in the Rio Grande Valley and began recording simply under the name "René."

That year, he recorded three singles and a Spanish cover of Lou Rawls' "You'll Never Find Another Love Like Mine," as "No Te Encontrarás Otro Amor."

Before the year was over, there were wedding bells when Palacios married the former Petra "Pat" Camarillo on December 18, 1976.

Marvin Wedding Day — Pat
December 18, 1976

CHAPTER ELEVEN

JORGE RAMÍREZ COMES BACK IN AND THEN OUT AGAIN

Dissatisfied with the lack of promotion by Bob Grever, Ornelas decided to change record labels. In the meantime, Ramírez and Palacios were flip flopping back and forth. So, by fall 1977, when they decided to disband Río Rami, Ramírez went back to singing as the other half of the duo of René and René; and they recorded two albums for ARV.

That worked out perfectly for Palacios, the newlywed, who wanted to stay home with his wife and write songs for other artists.

True to his word, by 1978, Palacios had written "Tengo Ganas de Tu Amor," "Que Pasaría," and "Promesas Sin Cumplir."

All personal problems aside, the label compiled ten tunes previously recorded by Ornelas and Herrera and released it as "Creí" with a misleading drawing of Ramírez and Ornelas on the cover.

In the interim, Ornelas and Ramírez recorded two albums for ARV as René and René. Those albums were "Cuando Vuelva A México (ARVLP-1045) and "Quisiera Ser" (ARVLP-1050). They were all released in 1978 and included Marvin's compositions.

"Now let me tell you the story behind 'Alli En Laredo,'" Eleazar "Ely" DeHoyos of Los Peppers said. "David Curiel gave it to me, when I was the lead vocalist for Conjunto Nozotros in 1976 and its original title was 'Mi Laredo.' So, we – Félix Lozano, bandleader, and lead guitarist; Óscar "Chompón" García, accordion, bajo sexto and backup vocals; Roberto Macías, bass and second voice; and Alfredo "Fred" Medina on drums – came up with a great musical arrangement. Then, we spent the next year performing it to audiences from Laredo on up Interstate 35 to Dallas. When Marcelo Tafoya heard it, he wanted us to record it on his record label, but that never happened. But tired of waiting, Curiel gave it to René and René."

"When we got the song, the title sounded like a love song to Laredo and we worked on the musical arrangement with Los Fabulosos Cuatro and a trumpet player," Ramírez said.

"In addition, we changed some of the words and the title to 'Alli En Laredo' to make it rhyme and more commercial," Ornelas revealed. "That's why the songwriter credits read: Curiel/Ramírez."

Curiel also wrote "Quisiera Ser" and if the name sounds familiar it's because he also wrote "Eres Casada y Te Regaña Tu Señora," a monster hit that was recorded by a slew of artists, but erroneously

1976 to 1979

The Jorge & Marvin Era

Raúl Velásco

March 25, 1979 - Accepting EL GLOBO DE ORO in Los Angeles

René Ornelas, Carlos Guzmán, Jorge Ramírez and Arnaldo "Nano" Ramírez at the Mike Chávez Chicano Music Awards in 1978

Photos courtesy Jorge and Marvin

credited to Carlos Landín when he headed Los Rondels.

Getting back to the two ARV vinyl albums, Ramírez and Marvin Palacios played acoustic guitar; Encarnación Fuentes played keyboards; Eddie Fuentes and Léo J. Léo were on brass; René Sandoval on saxophone; René Ornelas and Juan Sánchez, on percussion; and David Garza on drums on those two albums that were recorded at Falcón Studios and engineered by Nano's son, Marco A. Ramírez. As icing on the cake, Lucio G. Cárdenas came up with a good concept for a powerful album cover and Corky Naulte, who was known for his creativity in the record business, did all the photography.

RENÉ ORNELAS GETS HIS DEGREE AT UTSA

Before leaving his hometown and moving to San Antonio in 1973, Ornelas had transferred his Laredo Junior College credits to San Antonio College where he excelled in algebra, music theory, guitar, and piano.

Despite his busy schedule as an entertainer, Ornelas obtained his Associate in Arts degree at San Antonio College. Then, he attended the University of Texas at San Antonio where in May 1977, he graduated from UTSA with a Bachelor of Arts (BA) degree and received his teaching certificate in Spanish and bilingual/bi-cultural education. He also studied music theory, guitar, and keyboards to strengthen his musical compositions.

That summer, Ornelas and Ramírez appeared on the Raúl Velasco "Siempre En Domingo" TV show. Other guests who appeared on that show, which was taped in Corpus Christi, were Isidro López, Freddy Fender, Gilbert Rodríguez of the Blue Notes, Carlos "El Minero" Miranda and Chelo Sílva.

Steve Jordan, the number one accordion player in Texas, was supposed to perform, but he didn't play due to differences of opinion concerning his part in the production of the show. After the taping, Freddy Fender invited Ornelas and Ramírez to his house for a jam session, some food and a lot of fun.

By late 1979, the honeymoon was over; Ramírez had tired of being a harmony voice for René and René and he quit again – one more time. That was a shame, because Jorge's voice blended so well with René's. However, before they went their separate ways, Ornelas and Ramírez

98 MAZZ OPENS FOR RENÉ

recorded a fourth album, but it was not released until 1980.

Those four albums were released as René and René. Therefore, the demand to see René and René continued, but with Ramírez and Palacios no longer in the picture, Ornelas was back to being the Lone Ranger in search of Tonto.

MAZZ OPENS FOR RENÉ

Jorge Ramírez's departure created a new void and René Ornelas found himself faced with searching for a new partner again. However, René was persistent and as the lead vocalist of the famous duo, his voice was instantly identifiable. Moreover, he had a knack for persevering over the greatest odds as he forged ahead on his own.

As Lorenzo López said, "I remember I was the PR man and roadie for my brother Joe López who was the lead singer in the then up-and-

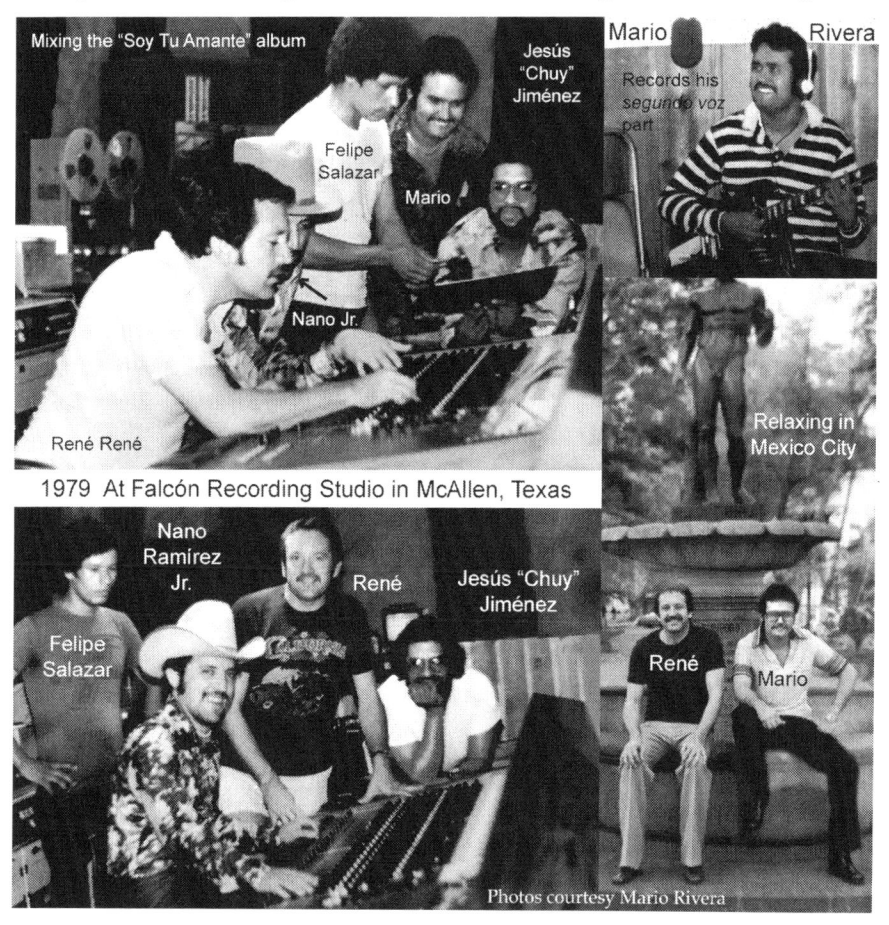

Mixing the "Soy Tu Amante" album
Jesús "Chuy" Jiménez
Felipe Salazar
Mario
Nano Jr.
René René
Mario Rivera
Records his *segunda voz* part
Relaxing in Mexico City
1979 At Falcón Recording Studio in McAllen, Texas
Nano Ramírez Jr.
Felipe Salazar
René
Jesús "Chuy" Jiménez
René
Mario

Photos courtesy Mario Rivera

coming new band called MAZZ when René Ornelas was very much in demand. Hence, René was the headline act and Mazz opened for him at the Corpus Christi Coliseum.

"I remember the musicians began to play, and Rene could be heard singing. However, he was not anywhere to be seen. Slowly the lights came on when I saw his trademark hat moving down from the highest balcony. Bands were just starting to use wireless microphones and René used one to pull off his grand entrance. No need to say, the crowd went wild as he walked down the stairs and up to the stage without missing a note. Even the promoter, Genaro Tamez, who thought he had seen it all, was blown away by Rene's showmanship."

He pulled off such an impressive stunt that no one bothered to ask for the other René.

MARIO RIVERA – THE 4TH RENÉ

Still, the fact that Ornelas was now recording as René René did not stop promoters from wanting two Renés so they could advertise that René and René would be performing at their function. Having a show with both Renés would be a greater attraction and a bigger draw than having only one René.

In the meantime, Ornelas was now left with the task of hiring a substitute for Jorge, the other René, who had quit the duo. Once more, he had to fulfill commitments that were already under contract as René and René.

Ornelas initially picked up substitute vocalists here and there to sing harmony with him in order to fulfill contracts that required the presence of René and René.

"As long as there were two of us and the sound was there, the people didn't notice and they were happy," Ornelas said. "However, it was very frustrating to teach each new substitute exactly what to do. I needed stability, and this time I found Mario Rivera, who already knew all my songs.

"And I didn't have to go too far to find him, because he had been in my musical group for some time. He was a seasoned guitarist and vocalist in the band that I had started, which at the time consisted of Mario on guitar; Felipe Salazar on keyboards; Ezequiel "Zeke" Escobedo, bass; and and former Royal Jesters' drummer Jesús "Chuy"

Jiménez. Those are the musicians who played on my 'Soy Tu Amante' album."

However, it is David "Takatá" Villanueva, another drummer, whose picture appears on the "Soy Tu Amante" album. The reason is that he replaced Jiménez, after the album had been recorded in late 1979. This happened before the back-cover photo was taken.

As Mario Rivera explained during an interview in Salt Lake City, Utah, "At live performances, I sang the harmony part along with Ornelas singing the lead. I played guitar on the album, 'Soy Tu Amante,' but on all the recordings, René always sang both voices, lead and harmonies, by going back and singing all the parts on different tracks. Therefore, René sang all the vocals on the recordings."

Raúl Velasco was so impressed with René and René's performance on the TV special he taped in Corpus Christi, that he wanted them to go to Mexico City to appear on his weekly Sunday night TV show, "Siempre En Domingo."

"I had just quit," Ramirez recalled, "So, that meant that Mario Rivera lucked out when René Ornelas took him along as the other René to appear on the television program that was seen by millions of people all over the Latin hemisphere,"

"When René took me into the band," Rivera said, "I already knew all his songs because I had been in his band for some time, so it was easy to get started as the other René. We did a lot of gigs at the NCO clubs. We went to Lubbock and as far north as Chicago for a show with the number one

Clockwise from bottom left: Felipe Salazar, David "Takata" Villanueva, René Ornelas, Ezequiel "Zeke" Escobedo and Mario Rivera.

promoter in the area, the Zuñiga Brothers: Joe, Richard and Frank; but the highlight of my eight years with René is when we did 'Siempre En Domingo' with Raúl Velasco. I was very proud to be the other René; and it felt good to be signing autographs as René and René.

"In Mexico we also did shows in the Capitol, Mexico City, DF; in Guanajuato, in La Feria de San Marcos, in Aguas Calientes and in Villahermosa, Tabasco. In short, we enjoyed ourselves big time. Everybody treated us like the stars that we were. And we also did 'Fanfarria Falcón' and 'The Johnny Canales Show' in Texas."

Ornelas was also still recording as a solo artist under his own name; but there were promoters, festival coordinators and special events bookers who still wanted René and René. So, Rivera spent eight years touring with Ornelas from 1977 to 1985.

HERE WE GO AGAIN

Nonetheless, Mario was not immune to love, so when Cupid's arrow pierced his heart, he wed his Filipino sweetheart in 1984. A year later, when the couple moved to Salt Lake City, Ornelas' first reaction was, "Here we go again! I've got to start looking for another René to sing harmony with me."

"However, the bug was still in me and shortly thereafter I joined Brown Brandee," Rivera admitted.

In the interim, what helped René was that Marvin Palacios and Jorge Ramírez were always there to take turns and substitute as the other René whenever the need arose. Unlike other groups that break up, go their separate ways and sever their ties, it was marvelous to see this trio stay friends and there were even times when the three guitar playing vocalists – Ornelas, Ramírez and Palacios – worked together as a group and could easily have been billed as René & René & René.

In January of 1977, a 23-year-old Palacios finished his three-year stint with the U.S. Army. Shortly thereafter, he recorded "Gracias Mi Amor Y Perdona," which he co-wrote with Ramírez, and which they recorded as Jorge Alberto y Marvin. It was later released as "Perdóname" by Joe López and Mazz. And on the flipside, they recorded "No Quiero, No Puedo."

They also co-wrote "Promesas Sin Cumplir" for their second single; and Side 2 was "Cual Fué La Razón," written by Palacios.

102

Late in 1978, Marvin replaced Rudy Palacios in the Rudy Tee Show, a music revue where Rudy Palacios sang harmony.

The renewed Ornelas-Ramírez-Palacios on-and-off again union only lasted until mid-1979 at which time Ornelas had begun to record as a solo artist as he continued to record some of Ramírez's songs.

THE RESURRECTION OF RIÓ RAMI

That same year, Jorge Ramírez, Marvin Palacios, Cenobio Javier "Bubba" Hernández, and a skinny, Afro-haired Joe Revélez re-grouped as a stronger Río Rami with the addition of Jorge Alejandro on congas and Steve Solís on drums.

Río Rami grew so popular that they landed a recording contract with Melody Records in Mexico. Their album, considered to be one of the best all-time Tejano records, was released in 1980. However, the label changed their name to Banda Río Bravo, and they didn't know it until the album hit the stores.

"Pushing and promoting us as urban cowboys, they released 'Buscando Amor' (youtube.com/watch?v=YM6jkcmflCM). It was a Spanish version of 'Looking for Love' which they had José Rosario translate. And the flipside was 'Creo En Ti,'" Ramírez said. "This one was Graciela Carballo's Spanish translation of 'I Believe in Love.'"

While all this was going on, in 1980, Bob Grever released an album by René Ornelas (Lado A LP-113), which contained songs that were recorded back in 1974. Furthermore, Ornelas continued to promote himself with guest appearances on television shows such as the Albuquerque-based "Val De La O Show." That 1980 program, on which he sang "El Amor De Los Dos," can be seen at youtube.com/watch?v=yX1d_dWxoro.

In 1982, all the René # 2 substitutes began to follow their own path.

SEPARATE WAYS

Despite the musical chairs, in the interim René and Jorge were racking up awards as El Globo De Oro and La Estrella De Oro. As a solo artist, René served as a presenter in the 1981 Tejano Music Awards. And in the Rió Grande Valley he was runner-up for three KIWW awards such as– "Male Vocalist," "Songwriter," and "Album of the Year" - but Ornelas was dissatisfied with the lack of promotion and airplay of his singles as a solo artist. So, he decided to change record companies and what transpired is covered in the next chapter.

Rió Rami had since disbanded. However, Ramírez had recorded his own 'Niña Preciosa' (youtube.com/watch?v=t0c2uf3c2AA) b/w 'Vuelve, Vuelve Corazón' (Cara CA-252) under the name of Rio Rami.

"Trùth be told it was just me with my guitar; and I did both tracks with a click track. That's just a beat (steady pulse) with a metronome. Then, Manny Guerra started dubbing in instruments in layers with studio musicians."

"Niña Preciosa," a catchy spirited rhythmic tune with a hook, is probably one of the best recordings in Jorge's career. Nonetheless, by 1985 Ramírez had done a gig as a radio announcer and had entered the field of public relations.

Marvin Palacios had gone on to record much of his own material with TH-Mex Records as Cañabrava. Two years later, he received his first recognition as a songwriter when "Me Sigues Rogando" was recorded by Grupo Mazz and was nominated for "Song of the Year."

CHAPTER TWELVE

RENÉ RENÉ ORNELAS AT HACIENDA RECORDS

Next, René Ornelas began what turned out to be a long-term relationship with Hacienda Records. Based at 1236 South Staples Street at the corner of Morgan Avenue in Corpus Christi, Texas. The label, which was owned by Roland García, had an impressive roster of artists under contract that included Freddy Fender, Isidro López, Isidro's niece, Lisa López, Rubén and Alfonso Ramos, Roland's own daughter, Michelle, plus most of the best-known bands and *conjuntos* in South Texas.

Among those in the label's roster of conjunto musicians was Valerio Longoria, Tony De La Rosa, Steve Jordan plus many others.

This is the record company that had quickly made a name for itself with Lisa López's now internationally famous recording of "Si Quieres Verme Llorar" (youtube.com/watch?v=A6FEzJotGas). Roland's brother, Rick García, was the chief recording engineer with his younger brother, Arnold García, sometimes working the boards. Roland's wife, Annie M., did all the graphics; and his green-eyed, blonde sister-in-law, Alicia Rodríguez, doubled as receptionist and secretary.

To make a long story short, in 1982, Hacienda released "Hoy Amanecí Pensando En Ti" (youtube.com/watch?v=LC1FDDy80po) and "Dímelo" (youtube.com/watch?v=54lrRfF8_o4).

"Hoy Amanecí Pensando En Ti" went on to win "Song of the Year" at the KFLZ 4th Annual Music Awards and it also garnered René the Texas Association of Spanish Announcer's (TASA) El Zenzontli Award for "Most Requested/Most Popular Song."

Now in view of the fact that he made his first recording in 1952, what seemed weird, or out of place is when he received the El Zenzontli Award for "Most Promising Artist" on October 14, 1983. Most promising artist? After 30 years in the business!

The album (Hacienda LP #7002), which was released in 1983, also included the beautiful "Voy A Descubrir Un Paraíso" (youtube.com/watch?v=qdEv501VZ8I), which was written by René Ornelas and produced and arranged by Fred Salas was recorded at Salasound Studios in San Antonio. Furthermore, Patricia and Rick García also did the lush, beautiful background vocals on the Spanish and English versions of this song.

Other songs on this album are "Hay Cariño En Este Amor"

(youtube.com/watch?v=nEseOtRCzDw) "Quiero Dormir" (youtube.com/watch?v=2eu3V7Sx-QM) and "Yo Quiero Que Vivas Conmigo" (youtube.com/watch?v=Q5N9jcpdH7E) all written by Ornelas. Listen to all the contents in this production and you may agree that this could easily be the best album Ornelas ever recorded.

Trivia wise, Patricia and Rick García recorded the backup vocals on "Hoy Amanecí," and David and Héctor Saldaña of The Krayolas sang the harmonies on "Dímelo," "Mafioso," and "Se Fue Mi Vida."

"A little fact is that we, my brother David and I started writing and recording with René at the end of 1979 and early 1980," said Saldaña, now the music curator at the Wittliff Collections and longtime contributing writer to the *San Antonio Express-News*.

"I wrote the music, melody and the English lyrics and a respectable chunk of the Spanish lyrics to "Dimelo," "Mafioso" and "Se Fue Mi Vida."

Sure enough, the credits on the album read: Ornelas-Saldaña-Saldaña. In fact, Héctor Saldaña also co-wrote "Chica Chica," "Donde Nací" and "Hey Sayonara," which were included in the "Vamonos A Cozumel" cassette.

"That's because I always thought the instrumental arrangements and production were too tame and smooth on the six tracks I listed (I personally like a more raw, simple rock and roll approach). I wanted them like Buddy Holly-ish

"So, if you listen to those songs, they are different melodically, harmonically and structurally than any of the other René stuff. You can hear the Beatles and '60s Brit pop influence in it.

"I'm proud of them. And I loved working and hanging out with René. I've got lots of memories of that period with him and his manager at the time, Milton Lance. Those were some of my happiest times. He's a musical genius and he knows vocal harmonies like Brian Wilson. He's also hilarious. That's why I love him and his music.

This was not René's first collaboration with The Krayolas since he in turn helped arrange the vocal harmonies to their song "Sunny Day." Furthermore, Héctor also played rhythm guitar on the sessions René did at ZAZ Studios with the West Side Horns.

"HOY AMANECÍ PENSANDO EN TI"

The album was released under the name "René René Ornelas." But the change of name did not matter, for it was the romantic voice, the dreamy lyrics and the rich musical arrangement coupled with massive airplay that turned "Hoy Amanecí Pensando En Ti" into a monster hit.

Almost overnight, Onda Chicana artists, Tejano artists, *conjuntos, música grupera* groups, *norteño* groups and many other bands picked it up and recorded the René Ornelas composition in their own style. Also, Little Joe and Melinda Hernández recorded it as a duet with a brassy, big band interpretation. See video at youtube.com/watch?v=TtgYOgFpcpg.

In the Rio Grande Valley, it was covered by several *conjuntos* with accordion and *bajo sexto*, natch. As the hit trickled down into Mexico, it was covered by *norteño* bands. For credibility, for your listening pleasure, and for a study in musical genres since the original love ballad was later recorded as a cumbia, a polka and other musical styles, the following list is provided for research purposes:

Mr. Chivo: youtube.com/watch?v=KbQMtmb4SEk
Los Hermanos Ortíz: youtube.com/watch?v=YgYATjaYpzg
Grupo Detalle: youtube.com/watch?v=Ca4dtCRm0bk
Los Unicos de Mel Villarreal: youtube.com/watch?v=0-ul22XoS-M
Conjunto Sereno: youtube.com/watch?v=BfiepCGKx8k
Joe Lara y Grupo Xprezzión youtube.com/watch?v=wgaiNCZmq4o
Joey Lopez: youtube.com/watch?v=ppVTm_ucjHc
Brillo De Luna youtube.com/watch?v=7bGFmQa46w4
Conjunto Oro: youtube.com/watch?v=r2A4Sp-VGpU
Grupo Super Jet: youtube.com/watch?v=1qLIiXDXsEI

The original album with the hit song by René René Ornelas, "Hoy Amanecí Pensando En Ti," was released in 1983. In the meantime, René Ornelas suffered a great loss when his father and former bandleader, Mike Ornelas, died on September 7, 1983. Thus, it was a bittersweet year.

A year later, René Ornelas' father was posthumously inducted into the Tejano Music Hall of Fame on February 26, 1984. That same year, René Ornelas followed "Hoy Amanecí Pensando En Ti," with another of his compositions, "Voy A Descubrir Un Paraiso" (Hacienda HAC 306)(youtube.com/watch?v=qdEv501VZ8I), a song he co-wrote with E.J. Ledesma and it did very well when it was released as simply René.

108

Freddy Fender

Roland García
Hacienda Records owner

STANDING OVATION

Mike Cosley
Richard Noriega
Teddy Mulet
Charlie
Eddie Fernández
Freddie Montilla

Courtesy Richard Noriega

Richard Noriega and René reunite years later

Trini López, Saundra & René Ornelas
© Ramón Hernández

René is interviewed by Elsa García who, according to Sam Almanza, was the the first Tejano artist to work at KYST Y92 in Houston. She was later followed by Sunny Ozuna and Laura Canales. KYST was also the first Tejano formatted radio station in Houston.

© Ramón Hernández

"Hay Cariño En Este Amor" (youtube.com/watch?v=-nIG8L5z2ao), which Ornelas co-wrote with Marvin Palacios, was the B side to this single.

In 1985, René Ornelas translated his song, "Hoy Amanecí Pensando En Ti," and scored a huge Hacienda hit called "Let's Turn Out the Lights" and he put the original Spanish version on the flipside. Furthermore, in what was a brilliant move, when RCA took over Hacienda's distribution, the English-version was also released as the Side B to "Love Is the Answer" ("Un Paraiso").

Best of all, the RCA album listed the artist's name as René René.

RICHARD SÁENZ NORIEGA, JR. - THE 5TH SECOND RENÉ

Although now recording as René René Ornelas, or simply as René René, he still had performance contracts to honor and fulfill as René and René. So, it was time to find another René #2.

This time, Ornelas turned to a musician who had been the vocalist for the Ramiro Cervera Orchestra. The name of this handsome, young, talented vocalist and guitarist with that well-known orchestra was Richard Noriega. After having played in that band, in 1975, Noriega joined a Puerto Rican group called Standing Ovation with whom he performed at the Flamingo Hilton in Las Vegas.

Noriega said about his 1978 music credits, "Next, I recorded several disco albums as Amant for Paris Productions in Miami with Ray Martínez, an American dance music icon and producer with T.K. Disco Records."

According to bsnpubs.com, "No other record label .... epitomized the sound of mid-1970s disco as TK Records, aka "the Miami Sound" or "the Sound of Sunshine." Thus, Noriega was among the Miami elite.

As Amant, Noriega and Martha Roque can be heard singing "If There's Love" (Columbia KS -40,024), a song that had a disco quality, at youtube.com/watch?v=MwLlmzpyywo. Also check out "Hazy Shades of Love" (T.K. Disco 115) at youtube.com/watch?v=jN7InRxlGk8.

"This tune gave us the opportunity to appear on 'American Bandstand,' but we would have had to pay our own way plus hotel and meals, so we passed on the offer since we couldn't afford the trip," Noriega said with a hint of regret.

Going back to his musical roots, Noriega, the San Antonio native

110

March 1, 1981

L-R: Frank Rodarte, Ben Tavera King, René Ornelas at podium, onstage behind René are Gilbert Velásquez, andRubén Cubillos. Seated at the table are Rick "Güero Polkas" Dávila, Jimmy Edward and Joe "Pepe" Sánchez.

Photo courtesy Joe "Pepe" Sánchez

1981
Steve Solis Lisa López
René
Little Joe and Johnny Hernández
René
Gibby Escobedo

Photo courtesy Joe Pepe Sánchez

Mike Ornelas
Happy days with his dad & brother
Jr.
Sr.

HACIENDA RECORDS
1984
SIDE B
HOY AMANECI PENSANDO EN TI
(René Ornelas)
René

and 1968 Luther Burbank High School graduate, started singing and playing guitar at age 16. And when he joined René Ornelas in 1979 at the young age of 29, the former studio group singer slowed down his Miami Sound musical beat.

Noriega stated, "Together, we toured the country as René and René for a couple of years. Everything was great. One of the highlights of being with René Ornelas was appearing on a popular TV program, the "Val De La O Show" in Albuquerque and performing at a national LULAC convention during our stay in New Mexico in the early 1980s.

"I remember Abe Epstein was at that convention and approached us about recording an album for his label as René and Riche," Noriega said with a laugh.

"After what happened to them in the '60s, Ornelas wouldn't have anything to do with Epstein ever again.

"Following that episode, René and I went on a multi-city tour with Sunny and the Sunliners and other popular Tejano artists of the time."

In 1983, Richard Noriega began juggling four jobs at the same time when the college student started working at WOAI Radio 1200 and at KSAT 12 as a television reporter and anchor from Monday through Friday, while still performing on weekends with René and René.

But in 1988, when Richard was offered the position of news director and anchorman at KGNS, the #1 television station in Laredo, Texas, he couldn't say no to the opportunity. And René said, "What! Again?"

This is when René Ornelas finally decided that he had had enough. He didn't really need another *compadre* (good friend) to sing with him. So why not go solo with a name that sounded like the world-famous duet?

RENÉ RENÉ – THE TURNING POINT

In 1985, he decided to stop flip flopping from using Rene Rene Ornelas, Rene Ornelas and Rene/Rene – as the Lado A record labels listed him in two 1976 45-rpm singles.

René stated, "In the world of music, many people did not realize who René Ornelas was, but everyone did know the name René and René. So, I capitalized on the name."

René Ornelas figured it never hurt José José or later, Lisa Lisa, so why not double the name René? And it worked! In September 1985, the name René and René officially became just René René. No more going back to René Ornelas. From then on, he would use the name René René for recordings, performances, promotions, and everything pertaining to his musical career.

"That way they'll expect only one of us, right?" Ornelas said in his characteristic sense of humor. People accepted the change without question. They just loved René.

"To be successful again, Ornelas didn't stray too far from the name René and René. All he did was to take out the word 'and' from René and René," Jorge Ramírez added jokingly.

The first sign of a major revival came when Ornelas was selected to perform as René René in a Fats Domino oldies concert, which also featured Sunny of the Sunliners, Rudy Tee of the Reno Bops, Sonny Ace and Latin Breed. This sold-out concert took place on Friday, August 1, 1985 at Fiesta Plaza, aka the Pink Elephant, in San Antonio.

RAMÓN HERNÁNDEZ – PERSONAL MANAGER / PUBLICIST

Ramón Hernández said, "This writer, Ramón Hernández, became his publicist and personal manager. I, in turn, also brought in *Billboard* magazine executive Marv Fisher as co-manager.

I wrote out scripts for radio station drops and promos, compiled a complete list of Spanish-language radio stations, radio and television programs, record shops and distributors and we hit the road.

After doing radio interviews, we would go to record shops where René René would do an autograph signing. Before leaving, he would autograph a poster or publicity picture. Then, he would help the owner, or clerk, put the poster up on the wall. Henceforth, the poster served as an advertisement and a subconscious reminder or suggestion to buy Rene's new single and/or album.

In addition, we would give the owner or manager a 45-rpm record for 'in-store play.' This means that whenever the store had a few customers, they would play the new single. The angle is that when they heard Rene's unmistakable voice, it would catch their attention and prompt them to react with, "Hey, I love that tune." Or "What's the name of that tune?" Therefore, this ploy also instigates a sale.

At clubs, we would give the in-house DJ an album because we knew that they were also mobile DJs that were hired for weddings, *quinceañeras* (a girl's 15th birthday), other birthday parties and private functions. They did not have to invest their hard-earned money to buy Rene's album. Then, there was no excuse not to play one of René's many songs during those gigs.

Again, this was to reach more and more listeners and for a younger crowd that was not familiar with René, to introduce them to his music, make them new fans plus turn them into a new generation of buyers.

HITTING THE ROAD ON A PROMOTIONAL TOUR

We left no stone unturned. We stopped at many tiny out-of-the-way radio stations in remote locations. Disc jockeys were pleasantly shocked to see an internationally-known singer walk into their humble surroundings. However, we knew their high-powered 50,000W and 100,000W antennas would reach thousands of listeners in their area.

We would depart the Alamo City, stop at the *Floresville Chronicle* for an interview with Lucinda González followed by a visit to KWCB 94.3. Then, we'd head south to KAML 99, a radio station that services Kenedy/Karnes City, Texas. Some station owners, program directors, and disc jockeys were so flattered that René René went out of his way to drive to their small town and visit their humble studios that they immediately put his latest release on their playlist and KAML was a perfect example. Here, the disc jockey was so much in disbelief that after René gave him a copy of the 45-rpm single and as he invited René into the booth for an impromptu interview he turned to René and said, "I still haven't heard this record, but the fact that you personally came to my show, I feel honored and I'm going to play the hell out of your record."

When we left each radio station, we stopped at the *Karnes Countrywide* newspaper office where I filled in the names of the radio DJ personalities and cited the visit by René René. Next, we stopped to see Rodolfo René Rodríguez at KIBL 1490 in Beeville followed by the radio station and newspaper in Odem. Then, we drove to Corpus Christi where we finally called it a day.

The next day, after stopping at KCCT 1150, KKHQ 98.3, KUNO 1400 and KMIQ 105.1, it was on to KFLZ Que Feliz in Bishop, then head for the Rio Grande Valley. We were just like Johnny Appleseed planting the seeds for airplay and stopping to give the editor or publisher in each town a standard press release. The prepared opening paragraph of the press release said, "RCA International recording artist, René René, paid a surprise visit to K___ radio where he personally hand delivered a copy of his most recent recording and autographed pictures for everybody at the radio station.

Even though we didn't set up scheduled appointments, radio station DJs and PDs never hesitated to give René a live on-the-air interview; and, if it was an automated station, the owner would call someone in to interview René, which was normally the case at KBIC 102 in Alice, Texas.

Next was KDSI Que Dice, also in Alice and *vamonos*. René and I would get into my car to continue our record promotional tour. Of utmost importance is that the reader of this book is aware that all of the aforementioned actions were not an act because René genuinely loves people. And he's a ham when it comes to posing with fans. He enjoys what he is doing from the core of his being. And that is why he is the star he is.

As can be seen, we went beyond visiting the big city mega stations. We didn't overlook anybody. We also went to barter-stations where DJs had one-hour or 30-minute shows and they appreciated the personal touch and attention bestowed on them."

In addition, we would visit some of Rene's friends, such as Raúl Hernández and his wife Aurora in McAllen. And also songwriter E.J. Ledesma in Houston. Add to that Alberto "Beto" Villa's wife in Falfurrias, Texas, whom most everyone simply knew as *la señora* Villa.

That's why Rene's recording got on playlist charts, got airplay and were placed on heavy rotation. As a result, he was nominated for four KIWW Music Awards, two KFLZ awards, two El Zenzontli awards and nine Tejano Music Awards. In addition, his still-handsome face started popping up on magazine covers all over the Southwestern states.

"People began saying, 'Hey! René is back!' René exclaimed, "I guess I threw people off with reincarnations under other names but, I never quit. But I'm not back because I never left."

CHAPTER THIRTEEN

RENE THE ROMANTIC

In 1985, René René re-ignited his recording career with "Hoy Amanecí Pensando En Ti," because after experimenting with other musical ideas, he went back to being a romantic. René René said, "This song was born in Mexico City where I had gone to appear again on Raúl Velasco's TV show, 'Siempre En Domingo.' Before I left San Antonio, my wife Saundra sprayed her favorite perfume, 'Private Collection' by Estee Lauder, on my jacket. That perfume has tremendous staying power.

"After the TV show performance in Mexico City, I returned to my hotel room and hung my jacket on the back of a chair. The next morning, the perfume's aroma was still softly noticeable in the room. I was lonely for my wife, so I began to write a song just for her. 'Hoy Amanací Pensando En Tí' began to take shape and I couldn't wait to get home."

"VÁMONOS A COZUMEL"

The Hacienda-RCA connection was short-lived; but for reasons unknown, Hacienda released the next 10-song production by René René as a cassette instead of as a CD. This tape also included "Baby," which was originally recorded as "Nena," which René co-wrote with Jorge Ramírez.

The title song, "Vámonos A Cozumel" ("Let's Go to Cozumel,") painted a vivid image of the island of Cozumel and I told René that we ought to shoot a music video on the Caribbean Island. "What! ¿Estás loco?" ("Are you crazy?") René exclaimed. "It would cost us a fortune to fly there with a video crew – not to mention the hotel bill."

Despite that, he followed my suggestion. We went to see Jorge Gamboa and Rolando García at the Mexican government's Tourism Office in Houston where we gave them a good presentation for promotion of tourism to the island of Cozumel and they said they would get back to us.

The result was that they got Mexicana Airlines to provide free roundtrip air fare for René René, his wife, Saundra, for me, my wife Martha, and Carlos Carrillo, a videographer from UR Visión in Mexico City. In addition, the Mayan Plaza Hotel in Cozumel gave us three

116

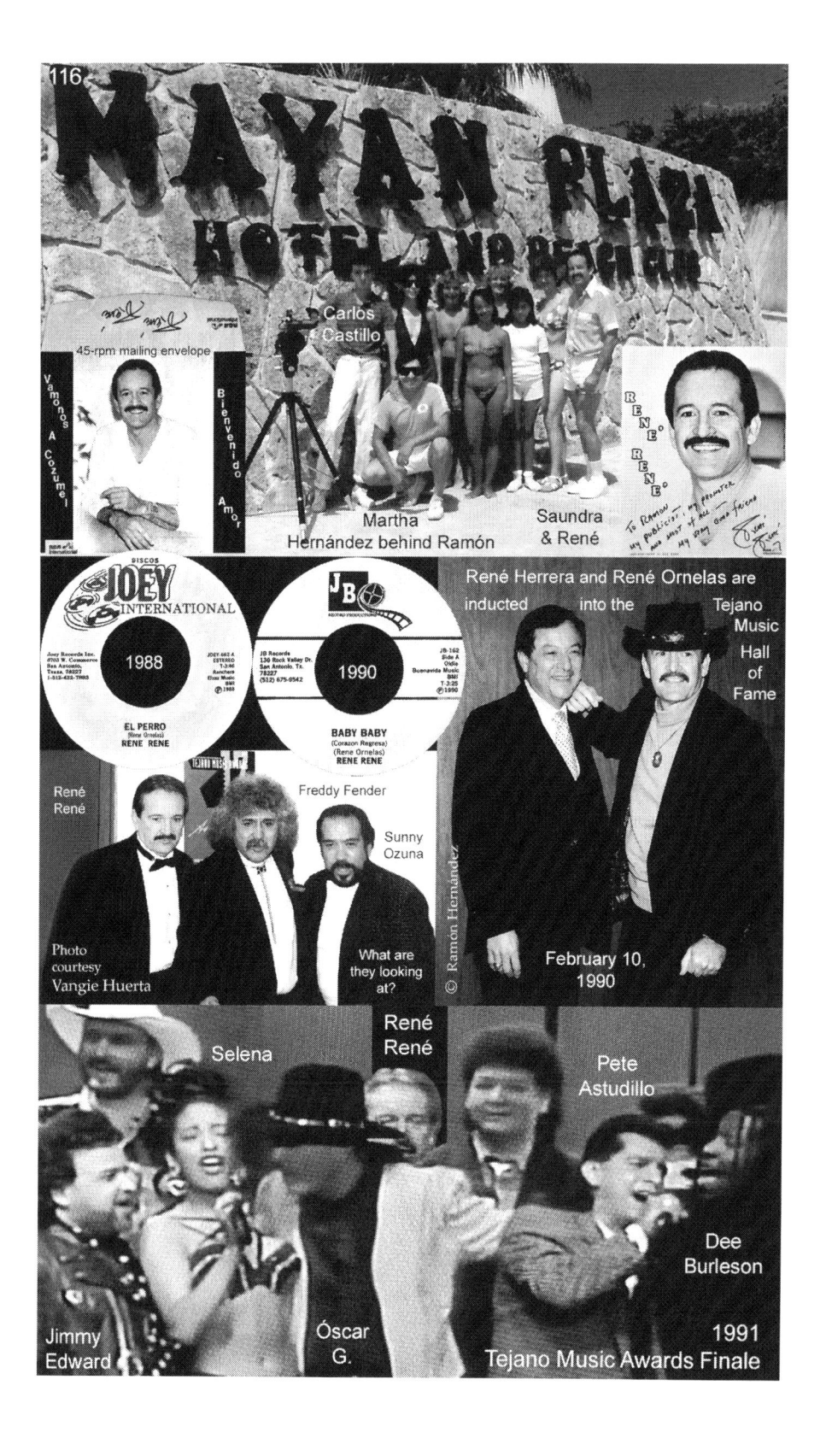

MAYAN PLAZA HOTEL AND BEACH CLUB

45-rpm mailing envelope
Vamonos A Cozumel · Bienvenido Amor

Carlos Castillo

Martha Hernández behind Ramón

Saundra & René

"Rene Rene" — To Ramón, my publicist, my promoter and most of all my very own friend

1988	1990
DISCOS JOEY INTERNATIONAL — Joey Records Inc. 4703 W. Commerce, San Antonio, Texas 78237 · JOEY-162 A ESTEREO · T-3:00 · Ranchera Elvas Music BMI · EL PERRO (Rene Ornelas) RENE RENE	JB Records, 136 Rock Valley Dr., San Antonio, Tx. 78227 (512) 675-0542 · JB-162 Side A Oldie Buenavida Music BMI T-3:25 · BABY BABY (Corazon Regresa) (Rene Ornelas) RENE RENE

René Herrera and René Ornelas are inducted into the Tejano Music Hall of Fame

René René · Freddy Fender · Sunny Ozuna

Photo courtesy Vangie Huerta

What are they looking at?

© Ramón Hernández

February 10, 1990

Selena · René René · Pete Astudillo · Dee Burleson · Jimmy Edward · Óscar G.

1991 Tejano Music Awards Finale

complementary suites for four nights. However, we had to insure them that Mexicana Airlines and the hotel would prominently appear on the video – no problem. See how we fulfilled those requirements at youtube.com/watch?v=6E5-CLKQVng.

I did a script and storyboard for three songs that René wrote – the title tune, "Vámonos A Cozumel," and also "Te Espero En La Playa" (I'll Wait For You on the Beach)(youtube.com/watch?v=ToEgZGapaLo) and the catchy "Hey Sayonara" (youtube.com/watch?v=7wkxyqwen7A). In fact, I wrote the entire script for Big O Video Productions' "René René – Mejor Que Nunca" ("Better Than Ever"), a one-hour television special where those Cozumel music videos were a part of that special.

The trip included an overnight layover in Mexico City, and that too was included in the deal. In gratitude, we would like to extend our special thanks to Carlos Castillo and Cristino Montoya at UR Visión, Jesse Castillo at Mexicana Airlines and Benjamin Villanueva, general manager of the Mayan Plaza Hotel in Cozumel – *muchísimas gracias*.

While in the Mexican state of Quintana Roo, we also went to radio station XERB AM-1170. René René shocked Manuel Jesús Castillo with the surprise visit; but Castillo lost no time in putting him on the air. During the interview, René René told the radio listeners about his new music video which would be filmed the following day. He extended an invitation for anyone desiring to be cast in the video, especially girls, to please be at the Mayan Plaza hotel lobby in a bikini, or other swimwear the next morning at 9 a.m.

Two island girls and two of the hotel's guests who were featured in the production were Gabriela Serrato and Suemi Pérez, both from San Miguel de Cozumel; Peggy Schmidt from Clarendon Hills, Illinois; and Vicki Caveness from Lake Stevens, Washington. Taking part in the video were our two wives, Saundra Ornelas, and Martha Hernández, plus some twenty girls in bikinis who were guests at the Mayan Plaza Hotel. They all formed a dancing conga line on the beach. This part of the video production was very effective and a lot of fun.

After we got back to San Antonio, I wrote a two-page article for the 'Travel' section of the *San Antonio Express-News*. I titled it "Let's go to Cozumel" and ended it with the lyrics to the song. That piece was published on January 25, 1987.

CHUCK RÍO, "TEQUILA" AND RENÉ RENÉ

How many people have heard "Tequila," a 1958 No. 1 hit instrumental written and recorded by Chuck Río, commonly known as the "Mexican Hillbilly" in the early 1950s? Yes, he was an American of Mexican descent and one of California's mid-50s rock and roll vocalists on a small Pasadena record label.

In 1957, he teamed up with songwriter/guitarist Dave Burgess and they performed as Danny and Dave. Danny because Río's real name was Daniel "Danny" Flores. Then, they recruited Buddy Bruce, on guitar; Cliff Hills, playing bass; Gene Alden, on drums; and Huelyn Duval, as a second vocalist and they became The Champs. On December 23, they recorded "Train to Nowhere," but 'side A' went nowhere. It was the instrumental that was highlighted by Flores's "dirty sax" arrangements and hollering of "Tequila" that caught the listener's attention and propelled the single to the 'number one' spot on *Billboard* magazine's Hot 100 in January 1958. And that's how they became so famous.

Being that Río and René were both on the oldies' concerts circuit, it was inevitable that they would meet; and they did, in 1987.

As René recalled, "Our trips to the west coast were always filled with surprises. On one of those trips, I met a young man named Chuck Río. He had written a huge, monster-hit song called, 'Tequila.' The song was all the rage, and it was one of the most popular songs at that time. I really loved it, but it was an instrumental song, and it had no lyrics – no words. So, when I got back to San Antonio, I went to Robert Ybarra's recording studio called Studio Cats. We got the best musicians available, and Robert helped me write the music arrangements."

Choosing not to use Lalo Guerrero's original lyrics (youtube.com/watch?v=tE87U0AebXI), René wrote new Spanish lyrics to "Tequila."

I wrote some lyrics in Spanish to the song 'Tequila' and I featured it in one of my latest CDs. It turned out to be awesome, and everybody loves it. You can see the video I made in Los Angeles by going to Jammin' Classics, youtube.com/watch?v=sHDesR_GlTg.

"FLASHBACK"

Inspired by "Tequila," in 1987, 23 years after "Angelito" and 19 years after "Lo Mucho Que Te Quiero," René decided to do an oldies hits album. And when you have two international mega-hits, as René René had with those two songs, they become hard to top. So, for him, the next best thing was to capitalize on the past as an oldies-but-goodies artist. With that in mind, I suggested he record an entire bilingual oldies album. The result was "Flashback."

The album included a Spanish-language version of Jimmy Clanton's "Just A Dream," bilingual versions of "I Only Have Eyes for You," "Deep Purple," "Little Bitty Pretty One," "Chantilly Lace" and many other classics.

The result was that René René was booked to do a concert with Little Anthony and the Imperials in a KONO radio-oldies show on Saturday, September 5, 1987. Radio personality Wild Bill Riley served as emcee. The opening acts were Sonny Ace, Rudy Tee, Jimmy Edward, Joe T. Campos, Mike and the Del-Rays, plus Patsy Torres.

René also performed in an oldies-but-goodies show where he, Sunny Ozuna, Sonny Ace, Rudy Tee of the Reno Bops, and Ray Liberto opened for Fats Domino at Fiesta Plaza aka The Pink Elephant in San Antonio.

L-R: Ramón Hernández, René René, Little Anthony, Jimmy Edward and Sonny Ace backstage at the Sunken Garden Theater
Photo by Saundra Ornelas

L-R: Ray Liberto, Héctor Saldaña (between him and) René René, Fats Domino, Rudy of The Reno Bops, Sonny Ace and Sunny of The Sunliners

© Ramón Hernández

What was interesting to watch was that the Anglos in the audience were singing along with the English lyrics, and older generation Mexican Americans were singing along with the Spanish lyrics. In simple terms, the bilingual lyrics united two countries, two cultures and two American ethnic groups.

For years, this writer has preached the importance of bilingualism in music so that anyone and everyone can enjoy Latin music to the fullest. It's a formula and musical style that René René was the first to create and use in his recordings. He is an extraordinary singer-songwriter and has perfected and capitalized on the formula for decades. René is a prolific song-writer, having written more than one hundred songs.

Tejano Roots Hall of Fame inductee Rick García
Jan. 7, 2012

© Ramón Hernández

If I were asked to describe the "Flashback" album, I would say, "Start with the voice of Tejano's best romantic singer. Season it with the keyboard master, foremost arranger, musical genius Fred Salas. Mix in the finest drums and percussion, and add the most experienced and talented musicians. Finish it with the recording engineer expertise of Rick García and Robert Ybarra, and presto, you'll get the undeniably best music, not only in the United States, but anywhere in the world.

RENÉ RENÉ GOES TEJANO

To expand his fan base and to appeal to what was now called "the Tejano market," René René began to write and record polkas, *rancheras,* and cumbias.

The result was "Quiero Pollo" ("I Want Chicken"), which really means, I want a chick, released by Joey International Records in 1988. On the menu in this album were other novelty titles, like "Menudo" (a spicy Mexican soup made from tripe [beef stomach] to cure hangovers. In San Antonio we call it "breakfast of champions"). Also, in the album was "Pico de Gallo" (a popular spicy salsa served at most Mexican restaurants). Next on the album was "Sácame De Aquí" ("Get Me Out of Here"). All of these songs were written by René René Ornelas.

The second Joey production, which was released on cassette that same year, was "El Perro" ("The Dog"). This cassette tape included "La Cerveza Está En Barata" ("The Beer's on Sale") and "La De La Mini Falda" ("The Girl in the Mini Skirt"). These songs were also written by René René.

This proves that René René is not one to just sit back and relax in past glories, for he is constantly charging ahead to carve out new innovative sounds and still has something new to say musically. That's one reason why René René was inducted into the Tejano Music Hall of Fame on February 10, 1990. That was one year after his father, Mike Ornelas, was honored by induction into the Tejano Music Hall of Fame. They were the first father-son pair to be inducted.

When Vilma Maldonado, a staff writer with *The Monitor* in McAllen, Texas, asked him how that felt, René answered, "Many artists have been recognized after they have died. So, it's good to still be alive and to feel the satisfaction of the recognition."

Shortly after René's induction, he switched to another record label. This time it was JB Records, owned by Javier Benavidez. The various styles of music that René writes is shown with "Baby Doll," which has an oldies-but-goodies flavor. Now, this song was as good as any old-school Chicano rock classic; and it quickly became a favorite with car clubs, *pachucos* and *cholos* from Texas to California. It remains so popular that you can find half a dozen posts on YouTube.com. Listen to it at youtube.com/watch?v=3Qv7foG_PKM and you will see what I mean.

Other songs on this album are "El Gallito Enamorado" ("The Rooster in Love") and "Te Gusta Chicotear" ("You Like to Mess Around"). A testimony to the songwriting talent of René Ornelas is the fact that he has written over 95% of the songs that he has recorded.

"In the song, 'El Gallito Enamorado' ('The Rooster in Love'), my wife, Saundra imitated a rooster crowing with a loud '*qui-qui-ri-qui*,' and she did a great job, too!" the green-eyed living legend said with pride.

Seeing his success with "Baby Doll," René René continued along the same line with "Baby, Baby" on the JB Records "Pachuco" album. The follow-up was "Sugar Baby," also on JB Records.

It was during that time that Benavidez re-introduced René to E.J. Ledesma, a very talented and prolific songwriter that René already had a good relationship with in writing some of the René René hits.

THE CHICANO OLDIES CARAVAN

In the early Fall of 1991, René René, Sunny Ozuna, Carlos Guzmán, Joe Bravo and Roy Montelongo embarked on a five-month national Chicano oldies caravan titled "The Legends of Tejano Music Tour" with this writer onboard as their biographer and official photographer.

In preparation, everyone rehearsed at the home of Joe Morales, a well-known general manager for radio stations in Austin, San Antonio, and the Rio Grande Valley.

"Each weekend we would meet in front of Rene's house and board an RV he purchased," Guzmán recalled.

"That's right," René answered. "However, the legends were supposed to share the cost and the expenses of the RV. But that didn't happen. So, I decided to get rid of the RV and sold it to Henry García the manager and co-owner of the Callaghan Ballroom after his brother Eddie was killed."

Next, The Legends leased a luxurious, greyhound-style-bus, changed the pick-up point to Sunny's house and from there, we would head out all over Texas, New Mexico, Arizona and Colorado. Needless to say, the five Tejano music pioneers packed them in. And sometimes, if in the audience, Rudy Tee of The Reno Bops , Jimmy Edward or Gilbert Rodríguez would get up and do a song or two. Thus, promoters and club owners were happy with big turnouts that filled their venues because this meant they also made a ton of money on the bar.

While each artist had a following, newspaper writers would single out René René in their print medium coverage as Vilma Maldonado wrote in McAllen, Texas: "The voice of René René endures, a sign that no matter how much time passes, a passion for music can keep you young."

(Maldonado, Vilma (1991, March 8) Scene. The Monitor, pp 1B.)

In a second article (Maldonado, Vilma (1991, March 14) Scene. *The Monitor*, pp 1B.) that she wrote six days later, the headline read, "Baby, Baby! René René still has it."

In that interview, René René explained why he felt that his latest two hits had struck a chord with his fans.

"I wrote 'Baby Doll' because everybody was watching 'The Fonz'

© Ramón Hernández

124   THE CHICANO OLDIES CARAVAN

on the popular TV show, 'Happy Days.' I was on a nostalgia kick. My song 'Baby Doll' was a big hit and I followed it up with 'Baby, Baby,' which made the most out of the '50s sound."

René

Mapping out the tour route at the home of Joe Morales

Joe Bravo, René René, Joe Morales and Sunny Ozuna

Roy Montelongo

co-writing last minute song with E.J. Ledesma

At the home of Joe Morales

All aboard!

Rehearsing with the band

Departing from René's house

CHICANO LEGENDS BAND

Robert "Quartermoon" Ortíz

William "Wild Bill" Perkins

Panchito Morales

Ricky Calderón

Jim Flores

René Hernández

© All photos by Ramón Hernández

JUSTICE OF THE PEACE — JUDGE ROY BEAN — LAW WEST OF
THE JERSEY LILLY

Sightseeing in Pecos, Texas on the way to New Mexico, Arizona and Colorado

Ramón
René
Sunny

Photo by Roy Montelongo

In a small town in northern Colorado where all the businesses were closed and there was one pay phone. In Arizona, we arrived in a tiny town where the only restaurant was closed, but we were able to buy cereal, bread, cold cuts and chips.

Women stormed stages to see René up close and personal and feel he's serenading them.

Glamorous life on the road

Carlos Guzmán

Clowning around backstage prior to going onstage where they'll be greeted with hugs and kisses from fans.

Juan Zertuche calls out "Showtime!"

Sunny and Carlos

Dancing with *The Monitor's* ace reporter

with fans in New Mexico

Rudy Tee Gonzales — René — Sunny Ozuna

Vilma Maldonado

At the end of a night, it's a quick bite and a lonely room

Thank God for 24-hour restaurants

Call it all joy.

© Photo: Ramón Hernández

At Johnny Herrera's 'House of Music' record shop in Corpus Christi, Texas

Joe Bravo — Sunny Ozuna — The singer-songwriter known as "El Suspiro de Las Damas" — Roy Montelongo — René René

Panchito Morales simultaneously plays the alto & tenor saxophones

Two of Beto Villa's former musicians at his home in Falfurrias — Mrs. Beto Villa — Roy

Roberto and Diana Pulido — Aurora and Raúl Hernández — Joe Bravo — René

© All photos by Ramón Hernández

As he explained, it is through his "Baby" themed songs that he tries to convey a romantic, positive message.

Now, René René had the best of two worlds; he was able to hang onto the oldies, and he was now a bona fide, genuine Tejano artist. However, he retained the famous René René uniqueness with sophisticated, classy self-produced polkas that he wrote and recorded.

THE FIRST COMPLETE TEJANO ALBUM BY RENÉ RENÉ

After 19 years of living in the city that is also known as the "Capitol of Tejano Music," in 1992 the world-renowned artist decided to record to the beat of this genre. And he not only dipped his toe in with a single song, but he emersed his whole foot in the water.

As René stated, "During most of my singing and recording career, I have recorded mostly my original compositions and many oldies-but-goodies songs that I made bilingual. I have also written and recorded some of my own Tejano numbers, but recently, I decided to go all-out, take the risk and I 'went for broke.' I wrote and recorded ten brand new super Tejano songs and came out with a great CD that is definitely top drawer, first rate and musically one of the best recordings I have ever produced. It is called – what else – 'El Tejano Man.'

"El Tejano Man" for Manuel Guerra's Manny Records marked his first compact disc and the title made it obvious that he wanted to be accepted as a Tejano artist. He was accepted, and that same year, Guerra featured René René, Sunny Ozuna, Jimmy Edward and Joe Bravo on the cassette called "4 Súper Estrellas" ("Four Super Stars") in which each artist re-recorded three of their most requested hit songs. I composed all the music and the lyrics to all ten songs. I wrote all the musical arrangements with the help of my good friend and recording engineer, Robert Ybarra. It took me about nine painful months to create that CD. So, after nine months, I gave birth to my first Tejano CD. Now I know the pain my mother felt during the nine months when she was creating me and I was being born.

"While I was at the studio, I re-recorded

Robert Ybarra

© Ramón Hernández

Photo session for the "4 Súper Estrellas" CD outakes

René René
Sunny
René
Joe
Joe Bravo
Jimmy Edward
Jimmy
Sunny Ozuna

"What's taking him so long?"
Joe Bravo
Sunny
Carlos Guzmán
Joe
René
Checking out the marquee

This was the photo chosen for the CD cover
Jimmy
Joe
René
Sunny

© All photos by Ramón Hernández

'Baby Doll,' a song that I had written a few years earlier. Because it had only been released on a cassette, it didn't have any chance of getting airplay on the radio. Therefore, I took the new recording and put it on a CD. It's one of the best songs that I have ever written, and I have a feeling that it could be another million-seller for me. It's a romantic bilingual song with a golden-oldies style that takes you back in time. I've got a 'Baby Doll' video on you tube under René René. Go and check it out. It's a winner!"

RENÉ RENÉ'S MUSIC IS INFLUENCED BY LA ISLA DEL COQUI

"On our 25th wedding anniversary, in 1999, my wife Saundra and I took a trip to Puerto Rico. Our friends from Oakdale, California, Dr. Martín Sandoval and his beautiful wife, Eva accompanied us because they were also celebrating their anniversary."

"I was born in Laredo, Texas, a small town 154 miles south of San Antonio. Here in south Texas, cactus grows everywhere, but in Puerto Rico, they have mango trees growing wild and the fruit grows everywhere. They also have great tropical music with a lot of Latin percussion rhythm."

Songs about fruit, like "El Coco Rayado," "La Papaya" and "Las Toronjas," have always worked for other singers and René joined the bandwagon to show his versatility with "Mango."

"I got hooked on that type of music and as soon as I got home to San Antonio, I started composing a song with the same style of rhythm. In a matter of days, I had written and recorded a song I titled 'Mango.'

"You can see my video at youtube.com/watch?v=WUMOAt02USE. Just look for my brand new "Mango" CD by René René. I promise that you will be astonished at how great it is!"

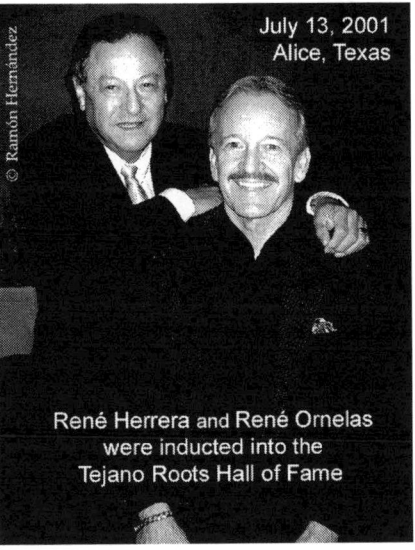

Best beef ribs at Ole Tyme Bar-B-Q in San Angelo on the way to KSJT
Catalina recording artist: Deya
Those are Ramón's beef ribs!

July 13, 2001 Alice, Texas
René Herrera and René Ornelas were inducted into the Tejano Roots Hall of Fame

CHAPTER FOURTEEN

RENÉ ORNELAS SIGNS WITH CATALINA RECORDS

From 1993 to 2000, René René had more than enough hits to take a break from recording and just tour. That is, until Arthur Cadena signed him to Catalina Records in 2001 and the first CD on this label was titled "Camino De La Música."

Asked about his last album, René René responded, "Last album? As of now, it's my latest, my most recent, but certainly not my last album because I'm already planning my next album! Besides, the 'last album' means exactly that, the last album of your musical career."

The first single from the album was "Babalú." René wrote it and it has a Santana-like sound. It's an international song that will make you move your *colita y lo de más* (booty and more). Another song from the album is "Te Necesito" ("I Need You") which starts out similar to "Tears on my Pillow" with a few bars that resemble "Baby Baby," another song that René wrote which is a beautiful, bilingual romantic ballad.

"Sangre Mexicana" is as good as any Julio Iglesias hit since he and René René both sing in the same style and the musical arrangement is one that can be enjoyed in any country on this planet. The romantic mood continues with "Quién Te Dijo" (Who Told You?)." However, this one is about heartbreak and the denial of how much the man loves a woman.

René said, "People often ask me where I get my ideas when writing a new song. I tell them that it's usually something that happened to me or to someone that I know. Let me give you an example about a song that I wrote and recorded. The song is about the mango fruit that grows abundantly in Latin America. It is also about love, romance and how to have a long and successful marriage.

As icing on the cake on July 13, 2001, he and René Herrera, the original other René were inducted into the Tejano Roots Hall of Fame in Alice, Texas.

RENÉ RENÉ CHANGES HIS TUNE

A few months later, toward the end of 2001, René began to change his tune. The old René never spoke about Jesus. Now he suddenly began writing new Christian songs and he also changed the lyrics to all his greatest hits. He replaced the secular messages of the original hits and put Christian words instead. Did he have a change of heart? Yes. Now, besides performing at secular shows, he began a Christian music ministry to glorify God.

Regarding criticism for continuing to sing in secular venues, René asked, "Where do you meet more sinners? In the churches or in the nightclubs? Jesus was known to associate with people who had sinned, like Mary Magdalene and Matthew, the hated tax collector, and other transgressors. Jesus is the Divine Physician and they needed Him to heal them. Healthy people don't need a doctor; sick people do."

While the titles of his two worldwide hits remain the same, they now have a Christian theme.

The opening line to "Angelito" became "*Me Encontré a Jesucristo, que bajó del cielo azul*" ("I met Jesus Christ, who came down from the blue heaven").

And the beginning of "Lo Mucho Que Te Quiero" is now "*Quisiera que supieras Jesucristo, lo mucho que te quiero y que te adoro*" ("Jesus Christ, I want you to know how much I love You and adore You"). "Hoy Amanecí

Pensando En Tí" became "The Greatest Love Affair" and "Baby Doll" is now titled "Jesus Christ."

However, the Christian song that most accurately describes the new René René reads in part: "I will tell everyone I see I'm a Christian. I'm a Christian and proud to be, praise the Lord. I'm at peace. God is in control ... I will follow the Master."

So, what brought about this change? Did it happen overnight, or was it a slow, gradual process?

"In the secular world, you travel with your band; and consequently, I never took my wife, Saundra, along. So, I was out there flirting with all the girls and doing all that you're not supposed to do, and I was not happy," René stated.

"As a recording artist, I was very successful selling millions of records and traveling all over the world, but I chose to go through life doing things my own way. I had money, success, bright lights and fame. My life revolved around fun, parties and booze. Still my life was empty.

"I needed something else. So, I started looking for the answer. To my advantage, I was born and educated in a Christian family environment and fortunately, some Christian seeds were planted around my life.

"Those seeds of Christianity lay dormant for many years while I searched for true happiness. Whether or not I realized it, God had a plan for me and slowly everything began to fall into place.

"Ángel Barrientos, a Denver promoter who was once into pot and drugs, used to book me in the secular world, but now he was a born-again Christian. During our trips, he would bear witness to me. One day he told me he was going to stop booking secular acts and start booking Christian acts. That remark started me thinking about my eventual transformation."

RENÉ RENÉ FINDS PEACE IN THE LORD

That conversation took place three weeks before René René was scheduled to do a New Year's Eve gig in Denver when Barrientos asked him to sing the next morning at his pastor's church on January 1, 2002.

"My wife Saundra and I had previously

discussed the possibility of my singing Christian music. For years, I was in a comfort zone singing secular music, making very good money. Agents were booking me all over the United States, so I found it hard to give up that income. What I didn't know is that when you follow God, the Lord not only provides, but multiplies your blessings," René explained.

"The Lord does not talk to you with a loud bullhorn. He doesn't yell at you. He speaks ever so gently. Sometimes you must be quiet and listen; but being quiet is the most difficult thing for me. So, I went to my music room, closed the door and just prayed for guidance. But the communication from God was not verbal. It was just a feeling. Eventually, I heard His voice calling out to me. It became clearer, and so did the calling.

"When I was an infant, I was baptized in the name of the Father, the Son and the Holy Spirit. But it took many decades for me to stir up the gifts of the Holy Spirit in me. I always believed in God, but I never had a personal relationship with Jesus Christ; so, I guess the Holy Spirit finally touched me. The answer had always been in my own heart. Those seeds of Christianity finally sprouted, and I realized that God was the answer.

"The day I made the decision to follow Jesus was truly the beginning of the rest of my life. I submitted and signed a lifetime contract with the biggest promoter, the promoter of life and salvation, Jesus Christ," René said with great joy.

So, in 2002, he started his Christian music ministry. It was then that René René the music minister was born. The Lord began to use René's talent and the Holy Spirit inspired him to begin writing song after Christian song. It seemed that every time he walked by the piano, he was drawn to it like a magnet. The songs that he was writing were inspired by the Holy Spirit. It was then that he began learning from the Master, Jesus Christ.

RENÉ WRITES CHRISTIAN SONGS

The first Christian songs René René wrote were "I'm A Christian," "Gracias," "Are You Making Room for Jesus?" "Capilla Blanca," "The Lord is Alive," plus other Christian inspirations to reflect his love and commitment to God. Then he went to Robert Ybarra's studio called

Studio Cats to record the music at his own expense. René said, "It is not easy to find someone who is willing to back and to promote a Christian artist who is just starting out.

"Even though I had a track record in the secular world, I had to prove myself as a Christian music artist. It was rough going, but I placed myself in the hands of the Lord. I wrote and recorded six Christian CDs: three in English and three in Spanish. I make them available at all my Christian concerts and online at renerenemusic@gmail.com or reneloveslucy@gmail.com."

René said, "During my first church presentation, I only sang, but the more I sang, the easier it became for me to talk between the songs, ministering to the people, as the Lord put His words into my mouth.

"What made it simpler is that I started reading the Bible, devouring countless Christian books, and telling people how God had changed my life." René René continues to do both secular and Christian performances. He thinks that by also doing secular performances, he can minister to the people who have stopped going to church and lead them back home to Jesus. He does this by always including a couple of Christian songs in all his secular concerts.

GOD HEALS RENÉ

While René continued to perform at countless venues and churches, what his audience didn't realize was that for years, René had to see a chiropractor at least three times a week; and he suffered increasing back pain, eventually reaching the point that he could hardly walk. More puzzling was the fact that no medical doctor had been able to diagnose, and therefore cure his worsening problem.

"I became very sick and didn't think I was going to last. Talk about being scared, I thought I was going to die because the pain was really excruciating," René said, twisting his face with anxiety, recalling a period when he thought he was headed for a wheel-chair existence or would become permanently

René praises the Lord

bed-ridden. "So, I turned to Jesus Christ, asking Him to heal me and to give me His favor and His blessings. His answer came swiftly."

René had now entered his Christian music ministry and it was evident the Lord had called him to spread His Word, and God takes care of his flock. After church one Sunday, René was visiting with his *compadres*, Deacon Frank, and Yvonne Martínez when he felt the pangs of pain and complained aloud about his painful back. Yvonne quickly advised him to go see Dr. John Abdo, ND (a naturopathic doctor).

Naturopathy is a system of treatment of disease that avoids drugs and surgery, and emphasizes the use of natural agents. Dr. John Abdo determined that for years René had been poisoning his body by eating the wrong foods for his blood type. He put him on a special diet consisting of a list of beneficial foods to eat and certain other foods to avoid eating. He also put him on several herbal remedies.

For example, instead of regular bread, sugar and coffee, he substituted these with 100 percent wheatless Ezekiel sprouted grain bread, spelt flour, Stevia sweetener and Cafix, a barley-based coffee substitute.

"After Dr. Abdo gave me a cleansing and I had followed his regimen for one month, I was back to normal," René said as he flashed a wide, happy grin. "Within weeks, I was walking perfectly and on my way to good health. Thanks be to God!

"I no longer had to see a chiropractor or take any medicines, and today I feel as though I'm 35 years old. It's really the power of God that healed me through this doctor because He wanted me to continue doing His work.

"I'm able to sing and to speak for up to two hours now, and I don't get tired because I have the Holy Spirit in me."

RENÉ'S CHRISTIAN MUSIC MINISTRY

"In 2002, when I started doing my Christian music ministry, I jumped in with both feet and all the faith and energy that I had. I contacted both Catholic and Protestant churches and they were very receptive. I realized that all the churches had something in common. They all needed money for repairs and upkeep of their church, and I wanted to help them raise some money with my concerts," René explained.

In addition, the attendance at many of the churches on Sunday had diminished due to the attraction of the football games on television.

"So, when I do my ministry, I tell the people, 'Let's put aside the secular things of the world. Let's quit idolizing the movie actors and other famous people. Let's stop glorifying the San Antonio Spurs and the Dallas Cowboys. Instead, let's start glorifying the real super star, the Son of God, Our Lord Jesus Christ.'

"I wanted to go out and tell the entire world that Our Lord Jesus Christ is alive and well. So, I wrote a glorious Christian song called 'The Lord Is Alive,' and everybody loves it."

RENÉ HERRERA JOINS GOD'S HEAVENLY CHOIR

Ornelas was saved and glorifying our Lord and Savior when in 2003, he learned René Herrera, his childhood friend and the original other half of René and René had already undergone open-heart surgery before he was diagnosed with cancer and he put him on his prayer list.

As Ornelas recalled, "Herrera had always been a heavy smoker and one day, after a routine physical exam, the doctor told him that there was something wrong with his lungs. He had already stopped smoking some time before, but it was too late. He was sent to the MD Anderson Cancer Center in Houston, where within days he was told that he had lung cancer. After months of treatment, the doctors removed one of his lungs. He could barely talk. His singing voice was gone but the doctor told him he was in remission. This lasted for almost a year.

"On one of the last examinations at the Houston hospital, the doctors gave him the bad news. The cancer had spread to his brain. Not long after, on December 20, 2005, René Herrera, my life-long friend and my original partner in René and René was dead. God bless him and may his soul rest in peace."

René now clings to every word in The Word

© Ramón Hernández

RENÉ BLESSES OTHERS

Today, René's biggest reward is to bring people to the Lord, as in the case when a young lady in California walked up to him after his Christian music concert and said, "God Bless you."

"Thank you. God bless you too," René replied. "What has God done for you?"

She answered, "My father would never come to church, but when he heard you were going to be singing and ministering here, he came to church for the first time and at the altar call, he gave himself to the Lord."

"That makes me feel that I'm doing something right," the Laredo native said. "I'm not a pastor. I'm not a preacher. I am a music minister, and my mission is to bring people to church and spread the Word of God by singing my Christian songs," René clarified.

Today, René and his wife, Saundra, serve the Lord by sharing their life ministry and their love for the Lord. Through his music ministry, they travel the road of their Christian walk together.

Elaine Ayala wrote a great piece that was published in the *San Antonio Express-News* and reprinted two days later in *Conexión* magazine. The article read in part:

"René Ornelas was the one with the melodious voice and dreamy looks ... of the pioneering '60s and '70s pop duo that was bilingual before bilingual was cool – or viewed commercially practical ...

"René Ornelas still has a quirky sense of humor. He's an animated speaker who breaks into song several times during an interview ... Today, at 70, he has a new partner ...and Supreme Promoter ... he still sings about love, but now it's of the spiritual kind."

Some quotes by Ornelas in this *Express News* article are:

"In many of my secular performances, people have been drinking and there is a lot of noise, but you get addicted to the spotlight and the

Luis and Holley Ramírez, Jane and Sunny Ozuna, Saundra and René Ornelas

availability of sin. My first church ministry was a different experience ... because everyone there was sober and paying attention."

He also said that since he gave himself to the Lord, he was no longer afraid of death. Then, after a short pause, he added, "Of course, I'm not looking forward to dying. but now I know what to expect." (Ayala, Elaine (2006, October 11) "From Angelito to Evangelist." *San Antonio Express-News*. Life section, pp 1G.)

This is a far cry from the days at the height of his popularity when Christian values were not exactly on his agenda. However, his wife, Saundra pointed out to him his many blessings and encouraged him to give back to God.

When Ayala asked him how he would like to be remembered, René responded with a frown as he asked, "Well, where am I going?"

In closing, Ornelas said, "When I was a young man, I wanted to make a million dollars. Now, I want to bring a million souls to our Lord Jesus Christ."

CHAPTER FIFTEEN

TEJANOS FOR CHRIST

In 2007, René formed "Tejanos for Christ" because he wanted to give back to the Lord for all the things God has given him.

"For five years, I was doing a Christian music ministry concert all by myself and even though it was a very successful two-hour concert, by the end of the evening, I was exhausted" René cited as his reason for expanding his ministry.

The first Tejano star that René invited to join "Tejanos for Christ" was Sunny Ozuna, who quickly accepted his invitation.

Sunny said, "In addition, many years ago I began to attend charismatic retreats with Freddie Martínez and Joe Revélez, Jimmy González (Mazz), Jesse Turner (Siggno) and Carlos Guzmán in Corpus Christi, Texas.

"I was brought up attending weekly Mass, going to Catechism classes, saying the rosary, and observing all Holy Days of obligation. So, the spiritual foundation had always been there for me. And as an adult, I have been able to get still closer to God," said Sunny, who is best known for "Talk to Me," an international hit he recorded with his own Sunliners Band.

"Taking our faith one step higher, for the last ten years, Freddie and I, along with the other charismatic retreat singers, have been inspired by God to write twenty new gospel tunes, which we perform at a concert during the Christmas season at Resurrection of the Lord Catholic Church in Corpus Christi, Texas. So, when René came up with the idea of helping churches in San Antonio, I was already on that *onda* (wavelength).

"René also noticed that Wednesday seemed to be the best evening for Christian concerts, since more people seem to be available to attend; so, the only thing I added was that I thought it would be a good idea to add a female to our group. René invited Patsy Torres and that's about as female as you can get!" Sunny said, laughing at his own joke.

Next, René invited Patsy Torres and Rudy Tee Gonzales of the Reno Bops to join him in his crusade to praise God in song and they joined him with enthusiasm.

Patsy in turn said, "In my case, my grandparents instilled religion in me and I went to Catholic school from the first to the fourth grade.

"But I became rebellious in my public high school years. Fortunately, though, I got more interested in what was going on in my music career. However, it was not until years later, when I was at my lowest point that I realized I had not prayed in a long time.

"My grandfather was very wise and gave me priceless advice on which I based the direction of my music career," Patsy continued. "I then let God guide me and I now praise His name.

"I was originally called by René René to fill in for another performer and I'm glad the group liked me so much because I'm now a part of 'Tejanos for Christ.' God made this possible and I'm now ready to use all my talents to bring others to Him," Patsy said.

Patsy also said that she is fortunate and blessed to have found her purpose in life, and now she has taken her show to the highest level by singing for God.

"My faith is my foundation and strength in all I do. I want to serve my God ... the more I strive to do the right thing, the easier and more natural it becomes. I just make sure I always do my very best, and God does the rest," Patsy declared.

In Rudy Tee's case, he said, "I attended and sang at my first Catholic retreat in September 2000 and for me, it's about feeling The Holy Spirit.

"I call myself a roaming Catholic because I've done about 200 A.C.T.S. retreats in many different churches, in so many cities, and in so many states. Now, I'm very proud that the Lord called me and I'm glad that I have brought a lot of men to God.

"I feel that the good Lord gave me a talent, and I use my talent not only to provide for my family, but also to help others," Rudy said.

These are testimonies from three fellow, nationally known, Chicano music artists, who in July 2007 did their first 'Tejanos for Christ' concert at St. Mary Magdalen Catholic Church.

"A few years later, I invited Javier Galván (formerly lead singer for the Tejano group called "Fama") to join us. Javier had traveled and ministered with Pastor Paulino Bernal for several years prior to joining "Tejanos for Christ." So, he was an asset to our group because he was already a seasoned Christian music minister," René stated.

A fourth artist who occasionally joined them was Santiago Eduardo Treviño, who was artistically known as Jimmy Edward. May he rest in peace.

René exclaimed, "It was payback time! Each one of us has a personal relationship with our Lord and Savior and each one of us has a different reason for joining 'Tejanos for Christ.'

"Most Tejano music fans are familiar with our hits, but they know very little about our personal and spiritual side. Now that we are all older, we thought it was important to open our hearts and share why we have been successful, realizing that we wouldn't be where we are without God," René explained.

Up to this point churches of all denominations had invited René René to minister. But as a group, it is mostly the Catholic churches that featured the five Chicano music artists known as "Tejanos for Christ."

René said with sadness, "Just now, as I am writing this chapter, Sunny Ozuna called me to let me know that our very good friend, singer Joe Bravo has just passed away (February 22, 2022). Joe had recently approached me to let me know that he also wanted to be a member of our 'Tejanos for Christ' group. We were in the process of arranging the details. God bless his soul and may he rest in peace. Joe, you will be truly missed. See you on the other side."

OLDIES-BUT-GOODIES CONCERTS

It was also circa 2007 when Rene entered the American oldies concert circuit and entered a new phase in his career.

"I began working with a booking agency called Pacific Concerts owned by a great guy named Alan Beck in California about 16 years ago," René explained. "They book concerts all over the west coast and have been very successful. They produce their shows at large venues attracting over 12,000 people per show. Most of the performers are stars from the 1960s and 1970s, the oldies-but-goodies era. Every performance has at least 10 to 12 headliners from that period. Some of

142 OLDIES BUT GOODIES CONCERTS

the super stars on stage include René René, Sunny Ozuna, Joe Bravo, Sly Slick & Wicked, Malo, Tierra, El Chicano, Richard Bean, Thee Midniters with Little Willie G (García), Los Lonely Boys and many others. All the shows are a sellout, and the crowds just can't seem to get enough.

Twenty Chicano living legends were honored at the West Side Legends Awards at San Antonio's Guadalupe Plaza on October 18, 2008. L-R (front row): Ralph Cortez, Little Henry Parilla, author Rubén Molina looks on, Rudy Palacios, Sunny Ozuna, Joe "Jama" Perales, Henry Hernández, Rudy Tee Gonzales, René René and Dimas Garza. Back row: Henry "Pepsi" Peña, Manuel "Red" Gonzales, Tommy "Gato" Luna, Jaimé Martínez, Sonny Ace, (can't see face), Rocky "OBG" Hernández Óscar Lawson and notably missing is Louie Escalante.

"I have been very satisfied working with this agency because they treat us like super stars. They pay us well and take care of all the expenses on the trip, including air fare, food and hotel room for me and my wife Saundra. They supply the band that will accompany all the performers and there is always a short rehearsal and a sound check before every show. We really enjoy being a part of these concerts because it gives us the opportunity to keep up with all our entertainer friends.

"When I started doing these concerts, I expected to see only the older people in the audience, but as time went by, I noticed that the crowds included many of the younger generation. I guess that for them, the oldies-but-goodies music sounds new, and they like it because they have never really been exposed to this type of good music."

To prove her husband's point, Saundra provided the following anecdote: "At one of the first concerts where René sang at the Honda Center in Anaheim, California, I was standing at the side of the stage during Rene's performance. Since I was behind a very large speaker, I was straining to see around it. A girl about 17 years old noticed that and pulled me toward her and said, 'Come over this way so you can see René René.' I said, "Oh, that's OK. I see him every day."

"Looking totally shocked, she screamed, 'You're his wife.? Wow'. "Then she turned quickly to the lady next to her and shouted, 'Mom! Mom! This is Rene's wife!' "That woman turned to the older lady next to her and said with excitement, 'Mother, this is Rene Rene's wife!' "Three generations of René René fans were together at that concert. I was really pleasantly surprised at how René's fan base is multi-generational."

One thing led to another and when Dale Berger, another booker in California, saw the success his friend, Alen Beck, was having with oldies artists, Berger took the same format and put it to work on cruise ships.

"That was in 2017 and since then, Sunny (Ozuna) and I have been doing cruise ship oldies concerts," René said with pride.

THE CLASS REUNIONS – A RUDE AWAKENING

Who doesn't have a class reunion tale? Here's Rene's story.

"Back in 1989, I received a letter from our class secretary informing

144 THE CLASS REUNIONS - A RUDE AWAKENING

me that the Laredo Martin High School class of 1954 was having its first reunion 35 years after my graduation. That was quite a pleasant surprise for me since I had never heard a word from our secretary in all those years. The Quarter Notes were asked to sing some of the old favorites. We happily agreed and we put on a tremendous performance. Everyone was thrilled to hear us sing again.

"We had a wonderful catered dinner at the beautiful La Posada hotel. At the reunion, I saw that most of my classmates had experienced change in their looks. After the initial shock, all of the former students got together in small groups, talked for hours and really had a ball.

"In 2004, once again I received a letter from our class secretary letting me know our class was having its 50-year class reunion. With great anticipation, I made plans to attend that great event. When I got there, I noticed that the changes in the looks of my classmates was now more drastic. I saw many faces that I could barely recognize.

"In the blink of an eye, the years had passed quickly, and it was now 2008 and this time around, it was a jolt for me when I realized that by now, we were all on Social Security. We spent most of the time telling each other all about how great things had turned out for us and talking about the good old days. We all hugged each other, laughed a lot and recounted wonderful memories. All-in-all, it was a great time and we had lots of fun.

"As we get older, it seems that time goes by faster and faster. You find out that once you're over the hill, you begin to pick up speed.

"Here comes that letter from Martin High School again letting me know that a reunion was being planned. It was to be the 55-year class reunion. I couldn't believe it.

"The class secretary told me that she had sent invitations to all the members of the pep squad, all the cheer leaders and to all the other school organizations. So, this time I was getting ready for heaven on earth. I could just see a parade of beauty queens and baby dolls swarming into the reunion. I should have known better, because even though I arrived a little bit early, I noticed that all the handicapped parking spaces were already taken. I had to park about two blocks away from the area. Since, by now, the number of classmates who were still around was rather small, the secretary had also invited members from all the classes of the 1950s.

When I was in high school, I made a lot of friends that I believed I would never forget. I thought their faces would be fixed firmly forever in my memory and that they would never change; but I was completely wrong. As I eagerly walked into our reunion, I saw many strange and older faces. There were wrinkles and gray hair everywhere I looked. I noticed that the changes in the looks of my classmates were extremely severe.

"On the men, I saw many huge bellies, bald spots with not a hair on top, and more hair coming out of their nose and out of their ears. A few of the women had round, matronly figures with a lot of makeup to cover the flaws of aging; but most of the ladies were still slender and very cute. For this I was extremely pleased. Some of the classmates had changed so much that I could not recognize them at all. I saw some of them using crutches, while others were in wheelchairs. ¿Que paso? (What happened?).

"It was a legendary homecoming. I talked to just about everybody at the reunion. I kept looking for a gorgeous beauty queen who, back in the 1950s, was everybody's dream sweetheart. I asked my good friend Chevo Contreras if he had seen that certain very beautiful girl that most of us had unsuccessfully tried to date. I thought that maybe she had not made it to the reunion. Chevo quickly told me, "René, do you see that plump little old lady sitting in the corner surrounded by plastic tubes and a small oxygen tank? – well, there she is. That's her." The impact of the shock hit me like a ton of bricks. I just couldn't recognize her at all. *Más triste* (How sad).

"Our 55th class reunion was at a beautiful patio area filled with classmates all with wallets full of pictures of their grandkids and photos of themselves when they were younger. Some of them were talking about how they experienced little pee-pee squirts or passed a little gas when they coughed or sneezed. The conversations were being discussed openly and without embarrassment and as my wife and I walked away, we could hear the laughter from that group.

"Back in high school, I used to be envious of all the football players because they were "stars" on the football field, and I was only a trumpet player sitting in the bleachers. At the reunion I saw some of the football players of the past. They used to be "hunks" and quite a catch for the girls. Now they were all overweight and abnormally huge. They had an outrageous hulking look as if they needed industrial-strength clippers to cut their toenails. What a sight! They were not the handsome football stars anymore.

"In those days, I was very shy. There were a lot of cute girls that I wanted to date, but I didn't have any confidence in my looks. I thought I was too skinny. At the reunion, all those cute girls told me that they thought I was very handsome and that they were all dying to go out with me. I just never asked them for a date. I had no belief in myself – what a dummy!

"On the final day of our last reunion, we all went to have dinner at a picturesque garden area near the Rio Grande River. It was the middle of summer and boy was it hot. I was asked to give the invocation and to welcome everybody. As soon as we started to eat a delicious meal, we were ambushed by a swarm of big, black, hungry mosquitos.

"After we got the situation under control, I was asked to sing a few songs. I thoroughly enjoyed singing for my friends. After a while, most of us were feeling sentimental and misty-eyed, because we knew that this would probably be our very last class reunion.

"One never knows though, because life is full of surprises; but one thing I do know, the older a man gets, the more he wants to live."

FLASHBACK TO 1962 – ANDREW DUNBAR

"Most of my adult life has been recording, performing, doing shows, and traveling. Around 1962, before Irene, my first wife, and I were married, I was on a concert tour. Some shows in Oklahoma were on my schedule of one-nighters. One evening, before my performance, I met a cute girl, and we made a date for later that night. To make a long story short, we had that date and the next morning, I was on my way to another town, another engagement, another encounter and maybe another rendezvous.

"About 55 years later, 2017 to be exact, I was living in San Antonio when I received a telephone call from a woman claiming that her brother-in-law, Dr. Andrew Dunbar, was my son. Thinking that it was a joke, I laughed. We talked for a little while and I told her I had my doubts about that. A few weeks later, I received a letter from an orthodontist in Colorado. He said that, according to Ancestry.com, I was his father. Right then, I decided that I would check my DNA through Ancestry.com just to be positive.

"My wife Saundra called his dental office in Colorado and she and I talked to Andrew for quite a while. We made plans to meet in San Antonio the following April. To my pleasant surprise, when we met, he looked and acted just like me and he had my same sense of humor. I could not have been happier. Now we talk to him and his wife, Jennifer, every week on the phone. And, as a bonus, I have two beautiful, ready-made blonde granddaughters, Sierra and Jane. As you can tell, I am definitely pro-life, and I thank God that my son's mother was also pro-life. She put him up for adoption as soon as he was born on August 13, 1963. Unfortunately, I knew nothing about the existence of my son. Andrew's adoptive parents did a great job of raising him.

He is so special!

"When my son Andrew and his awesome, beautiful wife Jennifer came to San Antonio to meet us for the first time and I had not yet received the results from Ancestry.com, I still wondered if Andrew was really my son. But anyway, we enjoyed giving them the San Antonio tourist attraction tour and tried to show them as much as possible in just two days. We took them to the Riverwalk downtown, the lightshow at San Fernando Cathedral, the Alamo, Hemisfair, The King William District, The Pearl shopping center, and to many of our great Mexican restaurants including Mi Tierra, Casa Rio, and Blanco Café which is famous for their unsurpassed enchilada plate with the best flour tortillas in town. All Andrew's life, he had thought that he was Scottish. We felt obligated to let him know that he was of Mexican descent. You can tell by the way he just craves Mexican food.

"We did not get my results from Ancestry.com until after Andrew and Jen had left, but as they were leaving, I said, 'Well, even if it turns out that you are not my son, we are still very happy to have made two wonderful new friends.'

"I was still a little bit skeptical; but when I received my results from Ancestry.com, I was overjoyed because sure enough, my DNA showed 99.9% positive that I was Andrew's father. I was simply ecstatic. I couldn't believe it. I had a son!

"My wife Saundra and I really do love our new and belated family. May God bless all of us."

CHAPTER SIXTEEN

RENÉ SHARES HIS SECRET
TO A LONG AND HAPPY MARRIAGE

"Because my wife Saundra is my right hand, she helps me with everything that I do, and she always travels with me wherever I go to do my shows.

"When people find out that we have been married for over 50 years, they ask me, 'What is your secret for a long and happy marriage?' I tell them that there is no secret. Every day, millions of people get married all over the world. Every couple makes a commitment. They vow that they will be married until 'death do us part.' But, according to statistics, around 60% of marriages wind up in divorce. What causes this breakdown in so many marriages?

"You need to have a real and true love for your spouse, not just a temporary type of physical attraction like what you see in the movies and on the television soap operas. You must also be grown up and mature enough to be making such an important and serious commitment. Next on the list is that you need to ask God to give you His favor and His blessings on your marriage.

"The trouble is that a lot of weddings follow this pattern, which is the wrong one:

"After a few weeks of dating, the couple starts 'going steady.' The young man thinks the girl is very beautiful. Everything is candy and flowers. A few months later, the girl gets an engagement ring. Now, things are formal, more serious, and the girl seems to be getting prettier as the young man gets more anxious.

Then, they set the date for the wedding. Ever so quickly, the wedding day arrives. Everything is perfect. All the flowers have been ordered and are now in place. The hall for the wedding reception is ready. The food has been catered from a top and popular restaurant. A band has been hired for the music. The invitations have been sent ... all but the most important one. Jesus Christ has not been invited. At a wedding, there has to be three people: the bride, the groom and Jesus.

"The bride in her white wedding dress looks gorgeous. Now, the groom is really anxious.

"After the reception, the couple goes on their honeymoon. They have reservations at a luxurious hotel in Acapulco, Mexico, and that night they are looking out from the balcony of their suite. They can see the ocean, hear the waves splashing on the shoreline and are captivated by the most romantic and glorious full moon.

"Wow! Everything is perfect. The bride is so beautiful, so gorgeous, she looks like a model from Victoria's Secret.

"After the honeymoon trip is over, the couple returns back home to the small apartment that they have rented. For a while, everything seems to be going ok. But, a few weeks later, things begin to change – welcome to reality. All the bills for the expenses of the wedding start to come in. In fact, they are all pouring in. *¡Más triste!* (How sad!).

"The honeymoon is over. Yesterday, her attempt at cooking chicken was a disaster. In fact, you could say, it was a massacre. This morning, her effort to make coffee was a sad catastrophe. She made and served her husband a flour tortilla that was so hard and crooked, it resembled the map of Texas.

"As her husband was leaving for work this morning, he took a good look at his wife. Her head was covered with rollers, her face had half a pound of gooey white cream all over it. She was wearing an awful bathrobe that looked like an old Indian blanket. He took a good look at her again and said, 'I wonder who that woman is – where is my model from Victoria's Secret?'

"When he gets to the office where he works, he is greeted by the new secretary. She is young and gorgeous; she is wearing sexy high heels and a tight mini-skirt that is so snug that you could swear that it was spray-painted on her shapely body. With a sweet, seductive voice she tells him, 'Mr. González, you look so downhearted. Let me help you. I can bring you some hot coffee and a couple of *chorizo con huevo* tacos. After work, let's go to happy hour and have some drinks. That will pick you up just fine.' He thought that was a great idea.

"Brother right here is where the troubles in your marriage begin. You are now a married man. You need to grow up. Your lack of maturity is beginning to show. Remember when you forgot to ask Jesus to your wedding? That was a fatal mistake. Without Jesus in your marriage, you don't have a protective, Christian defense against the attacks of Satan, the enemy of a long and happy marriage. Remember the devil's greatest desire is to destroy the family. Therefore, when you are making plans for your marriage, the first person you must invite is Our Lord, Jesus Christ.

"So, when somebody asks my advice for a long and happy marriage, you have just heard it."

RENÉ ON POLITICS VS. CHRISTIANITY

"Today, if you read a newspaper or watch TV, you find that they are loaded with politics and sports. During every election, we keep sending new politicians to govern our city, our state and our nation. They are supposed to be public servants. They are expected to be working for us, the public. But somehow, they ignore us and follow their party ideology. For them, the most important thing is to get re-elected and to make their political party look good. And to heck with the public," a concerned René said.

"Some of the politicians that we have sent to Washington, D.C. have been doing things that are against Christianity. They have taken Our Lord Jesus Christ out of the schools, legalized the abortion of millions of babies, and have removed the ten commandments from all the public places. Also, in church, the pastor is not allowed to preach from the Bible as it is written. Politicians have actually put a muzzle on the word of God. Those radical, bleeding-heart liberals have voted to weaken and water down everything that is connected to Christianity.

"During the Christmas season, we are pushed and prompted to say, 'Happy Holidays,' not the traditional, 'Merry Christmas.' The rationale is that Christmas contains the word 'Christ,' and some people might get insulted."

RENÉ ADDRESSES THE INEVITABLE

"All my life, I have been extremely fearful of death. Always on my mind has been the question of what is going to happen to me when I die. Is it all over? Where do I go? What will happen to me? Will I ever see my family and friends again? It seems that I have been searching forever for an answer to appease and satisfy my anxiety. I finally realized that in order to get rid of my terrifying fear of death, I would have to start doing a lot of investigative, fact-finding research. And that's exactly what I have done.

"We live in a society which denies death. This section of my book gives the reader an informative wake-up call by helping him to understand and accept death. Anyone who is not planning to live forever needs to slowly read this section of my book. Up to now, you probably have not given the matter of your departure from this world much thought. It has not been too pleasant or cheerful a topic to discuss and there seemed to be little that you could do about it.

"This part of my book is dedicated to all the people who, at this moment, are devastated and grief-stricken. It could be that one of your loved ones is terminally ill and is dying; or maybe you are approaching your own death with fear and anxiety.

"What if you knew positively, not just as a matter of belief, that you will survive death? No matter how strong your faith is, you are still just hoping that there is a life after death. You truly want to believe, but you are not positively sure. This uncertainty is preventing you from looking ahead in anticipation of the joining in heaven of the ones you love when your time comes to go. Now it is possible for you to have the assurance, the definite knowledge that life does not end at the graveyard. When you know the truth about death, it will set you free – there is no real death. Death is just a transition, and we will all survive.

"When people get together, the last thing they want to talk about is dying. What happens when we die? We just don't want to think about it, much less discuss it. Avoiding a discussion about our death, or the death of someone we love, is one of the biggest mistakes that we can make. Once you realize that there is no such thing as a real death, you will not be afraid of death anymore – you will be free!

"I have been trying to talk about death with all types of healthy people, but as much as I have tried, I have noticed that most of them have avoided any kind of conversation about how to understand and prepare for the inevitable – the death of your body. We just don't want to die. We don't want anybody we love to die. We don't want to think about it, talk about it, in fact, we want nothing to do with death.

"I believe that death is just a transformation. Your body passes away and the spirit, your soul, disconnects and separates away from your body, but you do survive, and you continue to live in spirit form for all eternity.

"There are so many outstanding and informative books written about life after death. Some of them have been written by medical doctors. I have read many of them and have gathered as much material about the subject of dying as I can. Here are some examples of what I have read.

"One day your telephone is ringing off the wall and as you answer it, you get the shock of your life. The call is from your doctor's office giving you the results of your physical exam and your biopsy. Then you hear what, to you, is a deadly diagnosis – your tumor is malignant. What comes out of your mouth is a cry of, 'Cancer, oh no, it's not fair. Why now, why me?' And the answer to your question is, 'Why not?'

"You have a lease on your apartment, and you might have a lease on your car, but as much as you search, you can't find the lease on your life. You are looking for that piece of paper that guarantees you a happy, long and healthy life. You look for it in the place where you keep your important papers, but sad to say – that document is not there because that document does not exist.

"Recently, I went to a funeral filled with grieving mourners, friends and relatives of the deceased. One of them said, 'I'm sure going to miss him. He was such a good friend. And you know something, I have already lost one half of my family in the last five years.' You will be tempted to say, 'Well, stick around, buddy, because soon you will get to lose the rest of them, or they will get to lose you. So, take your pick, because nobody gets out of this world alive.'

"There are two words in the dictionary that seem to confuse a lot of people. The two words are 'possibility' and 'probability.' A young couple and their baby were traveling north on Interstate Highway 35 heading towards San Antonio, Texas. They had bought a car and were on their way home. The reason they had chosen this particular car was because of the advertisement on the television ads. According to the ads, this European-made car was the #1 choice for safety. This car was designed to keep the occupants safe in case they were involved in a car wreck. Two idle young boys had found a rather heavy rock and were wondering what would happen if they dropped it from an overpass right onto the busy highway. They did drop it. The huge rock went right through the windshield of the supposedly super-safe European automobile, killing the wife in the car.

"The couple had done everything they could to keep themselves safe. They were using the seatbelts, they were not speeding, they were not drinking, and they were driving the #1 super-safe European car. The odds of dying by getting hit by a boulder on a busy highway were not too good. There was an extremely low <u>probability</u> that the wife would die this way; but the <u>possibility</u> that someday she would die was excellent. In fact, the <u>possibility</u> that someday she would die was 100%. Yes, someday, every one of us is going to die, but every one of us in this world is going to survive in spirit form.

"I have a library of hundreds of life-after-death books written by people who have done extensive research on psychic phenomena. There are many different forms of psychic phenomena through which messages have been received from discarnate souls (those who have died and have left this earth life). These books include thousands of letters from men and women describing experiences they have had which they feel have proven the continued existence of their departed loved ones.

"Everyone needs to be prepared and ready, but most healthy people do not want to learn any more about death than they absolutely have to know. And as far as being prepared, buying life insurance is about as far as most people want to go – that's it!

"The truth is that we don't want to die. We don't want anyone we love to die. In fact, we don't ever want to think about it, we don't want to talk about it or have anything to do with it – period! So, we sweep the discussion of death under the living room carpet or we jam-pack it into a closet and spend our time dancing around it, pretending that it's not there.

"In 1958, I got a letter from Uncle Sam. I was being drafted into the US Army. After serving in the military for three years, I was finally given an honorable discharge. I went back to my hometown – Laredo, Texas. One of the first things I did was to find an apartment. It was a very small one, but very inexpensive – only $35.00 a month and they paid for my utilities. So, I quickly signed a 3-year lease. That apartment was unconditionally mine for the next three years. Even though the landlord owned the property, he had no right to throw me out until the lease would expire – remember, I had a lease.

"However, we have no lease on the body that we are using to live on this earth. Our body can be reclaimed by its Maker at any time, for any reason, whether we are ready or not. We have to truly believe that we are not limited to our body and that we will still be around and alive in some form or fashion when our body dies.

"Around 1970, people all over the world started hearing more about near-death experiences. The research that was being done included case studies of people who had been pronounced dead by their doctor but before he could sign the death certificate, they were revived. Those people had been declared dead since they were found to have no vital signs – no heartbeat, no pulse and they were not breathing.

"Over fifteen million fellow Americans have had a near-death experience. When they were revived, they would tell everyone who would listen about their experiences, that there was life after death. They talked about leaving their bodies behind in the room and floating up to the ceiling. They kept rising so high that they levitated up from the earth traveling through a dark tunnel until they arrived at an incredible dominion, beautiful beyond imagination. They kept calling this magnificent domain – Heaven.

"Most of them were met by a friendly reception group. They talked about being greeted by friends and relatives who had died and groups of angels who were showing them around the many different areas in Heaven. During their visit to Heaven, they were told that it was not their time yet and that they had to return to their body on Earth. Heaven was so glorious that most of them did not want to leave, but reluctantly they did return to Earth."

"What happens when we die? It's the greatest of all questions. No question is more important. Whether we know it or not, all of us have been preparing for what will come after our life on earth is over. One day, our body will die and that will release our soul into a world that is extremely different. Yes, someday every one of us in this world is going to die, but every one of us is going to survive in spirit form.

CHAPTER SEVENTEEN

LIFE AFTER DEATH

"One of these days, you will be just a spiritual soul standing before God in Heaven and the way you will be judged might shock and surprise you. You might have been a multi-millionaire with a rich portfolio of stocks and bonds, or a queen crowned with gold and diamonds, or a handsome, famous actor from Hollywood or even a homeless, abandoned drug addict. At the end of our lives, we will all encounter God, and we will all face eternity. No human will escape that fate. Someday, we will all leave this planet, but we will keep on living forever in spirit form.

"There is a false belief that the human being is only a body and that when the body dies, you are eradicated, destroyed, demolished, wiped out and that you literally cease to exist. Those people think that you will be extinguished like a candle or snuffed out like an old cigarette butt. That's wrong! This mistaken theory causes you to suffer the fear of death. This erroneous belief is called The Annihilation Theory.

"Think of this: back in the middle of the fifteenth century, all the educated people were positive that the world was flat. All the maps showed a straight and flat world. This concept was taught in all the schools, universities, and places of learning. Can you imagine all the bookstores selling books that showed the dangers of going too far into the ocean and falling off the edge of the world? So, instead of traveling and sailing on long trips on the ocean, people were choosing to stay at home. Everyone was afraid. The people who held those beliefs were not unintelligent.

"All the best minds of the time believed that the world was flat. There was nothing unreasonable or improper about that. It was the accepted reality. When something that is false, but has always been believed to be true, intelligent people cannot be blamed for their beliefs. For example, people believed that the world was flat. But once the truth was known – that the world is round – there was no going back to their erroneous belief.

"Less than one hundred years ago, there was no proof that there was life after death. Today, however, millions of people have died, gone to Heaven and returned to Earth to talk about their experiences. When your time comes, you will discard that thing you call your body and you will exist only in a spiritual dimension.

"If you are prepared to meet God, it will be a glorious day beyond your wildest dreams. You could never wish for anything better. There is no fantasy that can have the heavenly and divine things that God has in store for you in Heaven. That is, if you are prepared, because if you are not prepared, eternity can be something of a predicament, because, in addition to Heaven, there is also Purgatory and Hell. Since you were born, you have been traveling on a road leading to one of these two places: Heaven or Hell, and probably with a temporary stay in Purgatory. In the *Holy Bible*, God has shown us how to get to Heaven. All you must do is to love God and to love your neighbor as yourself. Heaven is where God lives, and it is absolutely glorious. Hell is where Satan and all his devils live, and it is positively horrible. I don't have to define Heaven or Hell, but I do have to talk about Purgatory. It's a place where unclean souls go to be purged and purified before entering Heaven and facing the glory of God. No soul can be in front of God unless he is completely cleansed and free from the filth of sin.

"Even if God has already forgiven them for their sins, souls still have to make restitution to God for those sins that have greatly offended Him. Here is an anecdote that will help you to understand what I just told you about Purgatory.

"A little kid broke his neighbor's window playing baseball. He went over to apologize and to get his ball back. Mr. Jones, the neighbor, forgave him, gave the ball back and told him to be more careful and not to do it again. The kid went home and told his mother that Mr. Jones forgave him for breaking the window; but the kid's mother told him that even though he had been forgiven, he would still have to make restitution and pay for the repair of the window. This is my simple explanation about how Purgatory works. Even if God has already forgiven you, you still have to make restitution for your sins which have greatly insulted your Creator.

"One of my intentions for writing this chapter is to help you get rid of your fear of death. No one ever dies alone. Someone – whether it's Jesus Christ, the Blessed Virgin Mary, an angel, a deceased relative or a friend who has died or a combination of those beings – someone will come to comfort you when you are dying.

"I have not gone through this myself, but the hundreds of examples of life after death that I have read about, have all been very similar to the following: A man is dying and soon he hears the nurses and the doctors trying to revive him. He begins to hear a noise that makes him feel uncomfortable. It is usually a buzzing or a loud ringing noise. He suddenly feels that he is being transported through a long and bright tunnel. He has a sensation that he is now out of his physical body and he can see his own body from a distance. He is just a spectator and he is watching the resuscitation attempt. He feels that he still has a body but it is very different. His new body has incredible powers that he did not have before in the body that he has discarded.

"Other things begin to happen. He starts seeing the spirits of friends and relatives who have already died before him. They come to welcome him. He is also approached by a warm and loving spirit that he has never encountered before – it's a being of light. The strongest, most beautiful light in the universe. It's a bright, golden white light, the brightest you have ever seen, and yet it doesn't hurt your eyes. That being of light is God. The beings in Heaven communicate with each other, but they do it nonverbally. They exchange thoughts, not words. The man is then shown a panoramic movie-like film. It's a playback of all the things he did in his life – from the day he was born to the last moment of his life. It happens all at once, in a flash. I cannot tell you how long it takes because there is no time in eternity.

"At one point, the man finds himself coming close to a barrier that separates life in heaven from life on earth. Everything he has seen in heaven has been beautiful and glorious. He is overwhelmed by very strong and intense feelings of joy, love and peace. He does not want to return to live on earth. But the being of light tells him that he must go back to the earth, that the time for his death has not yet come.

"When he returns to life on earth, he tries to tell everyone about his near-death experience and about his visit to heaven. But he finds it very difficult. He can find no human words acceptable to explain all the glorious things that he found in heaven. Also, when he talks about it, people make fun of him and tell him that he is losing his mind. So, most of the time, he just keeps it to himself.

"That man who died and had a near-death experience, but was revived by a doctor said, 'Death is just a transformation. When your soul leaves your body, there is no pain. It's as pleasant and peaceful and as easy as just stepping into another room of your house. I will never again be afraid to die. I know that when your body dies, you are not being wiped out. You will continue to exist because you are more than just your body. There is a soul inside your body, and that is the real you. I know that I will always be alive because nobody can kill the soul. Only the body can die. The soul, which is really you, is eternal and it will live forever.' That person who died and came back, as well as millions of others who have had that experience, has given us proof that there is life after death.

"Another person who had a near-death experience wrote this story in one of the books that I have been reading. That woman said, 'Death has always been my earthly companion. It has been watching me since the day I was born. One day, death just tapped me on the shoulder and said that it was time to go. I passed through death to the other side, but I returned to talk about it. After I was shown all the glorious things in heaven, I wanted to stay there forever. I did not want to return to earth.

"But I was sent back when a being of light told me that it was not my time, that I still had some important things to do. He said that my mission on earth had not been completed. So, in a flash, I started descending rapidly and returned to my physical body. I was back. Ever since it happened, I have not been the same. How could I be? Now I know what death is all about. I have taken a look at the mysterious secrets of death and now my concept of life has been extremely changed.'

"In the dictionary, the definition of death is 'to die; to expire; to cease to exist; the permanent stopping of all the vital functions in your body;' but, there is another definition for death. In the Bible, we are told that Jesus, our Lord, spoke Aramaic, and from that language, death is translated as 'not being here, and being present elsewhere.'

"When we face depression, misery, anguish, and despair, we feel as if it is never going to end. Well, the one thing that is certain is that, it is going to end. If you believe in God, there is no such thing as everlasting hardship. Jesus gave us His astonishing promise on the night before He was crucified. When Jesus was in the upper room with His disciples, He told them, 'Do not let your heart be troubled. Believe in God and also believe in Me.

"One of these days, your life on Earth is going to be over. I want

160   LIFE AFTER DEATH

Lord, I'm ready when you call me home

© Ramón Hernández

to assure you that when it's over, I have prepared a place for you in Heaven.' That is His glorious promise to all His believers.

"I pray that this conversation about death is the one you were hoping to discover. And may you find out that only your body can die. Your soul, which is really you, will live on for all eternity.

So, apply these simple, uncomplicated thoughts and words and use them in your own life right now. May peace and tranquility take the place of your fear of death when you find out the truth and realize that there is life after death."

Susie Hernández
Ramon's beautiful daughter

Emmy winning Spectrum TV reporter José Arredondo interviews René

© Ramón Hernández

Mario Montez interviews René at the the Ramón Hernández Archives

© Ramón Hernández

Brothers in Christ

CHAPTER EIGHTTEEN

ART LABOE

According to articles by Esmeralda Bermúdez, Russell Contreras, author Harvey Kubernik and the Associated Press, Art Laboe is credited with helping end segregation in Southern California by organizing integrated shows that attracted white, Blacks and Latinos who danced to rock-n-roll and shocked an older generation still listening to Frank Sinatra and Big Band music. In doing so, Laboe gave birth to a new youth subculture.

Most importantly in the history of American music, Laboe is credited with coining the "oldies, but goodies" phrase when he was a disc jockey at KPOP in Los Angeles.

Born Arthur Kezerian Egnoian in Salt Lake City to an Armenian-American family, Laboe grew up during the Great Depression in a Mormon household run by a single mom. His sister gave him his first radio when he was eight years old; and the voices and stories that came from it enveloped him.

"And I haven't let go since," Laboe said in an interview when he was 97 and still doing his show.

"Drawn by the anonymity of radio, it was 1938 when a 13-year-old kid started his own amateur station out of his bedroom. His name was Art Laboe, and he went on to become the most popular radio personality in California where crowds followed him wherever the top entertainment promoter held his dances," René said of the radio genius who made it a point to book him on every Chicano Soul Legends tour throughout the Southwestern states.

After moving to California and attending Stanford University where he studied radio engineering and obtained his FCC first-class radio telephone license, he served in the U.S. Navy during World War II. After getting stationed at Treasure Island, he landed a job at KSAN in San Francisco, and it was there where he shortened his name to Art and adopted Laboe after one of his bosses suggested the baritone-voiced radio announcer take the last name of one of the secretaries to sound more American. Hence, the entire world would come to know him by that name.

He was also on radio when in the early 1950s, Laboe formed Original Sound and not one to be left behind, Laboe also wrote songs

162

ART LABOE
August 7, 1925 - October 7, 2022
The radio personality that coined the phrase "Oldies but Goodies," integrated three cultures and made Chicano rock popular all over the USA

19-year-old Art Laboe — 1945 — René lauds Laboe — 96-year-old Art Laboe

HONDA CENTER WELCOMES BACK

CHICANO Soul Legends

DECEMBER 3, 2016

TIERRA — SUNNY OZUNA — JOE BRAVO — MAD LADS — MALO — RENÉ RENÉ — THE NOTATIONS

René Reyes — with Tony Reyes, owner of Jammin' Classics — Art Laboe and Joanna Morones

Saundra Ornelas

Photos courtesy of Joanna Morones executive assistant Dart Entertainment

for some of the groups on his small label that specialized in compiling and re-releasing oldies.

By 1956, his afternoon show became Los Angeles' top radio program. He was so popular that when Elvis Presley came to Hollywood with Colonel Tom Parker, their only interview granted was with Laboe.

Next, in 1962, he turned the tables around when he recorded "Mexican Midnight b/w "Pickwick Twist," two instrumentals on his own label. However, there are no musician credits to know what instrument he played.

"If he maintained a strong following among Mexican Americans for generations, it was because he always played Latino, white and Black artists together on his shows," said Lalo Alcaraz, a television writer and syndicated cartoonist, who credits Laboe for opening the door for Chicano Rock when he played The Premiers' "Farmer John" in 1964. He also began to host numerous dances at the El Monte Legion Stadium because that's where all the Chicanos live; and that's where the Latino connection came in with stars such as Rosie and the Originals of "Angel Baby" fame along with Chuck Berry, Ray Charles, and Jerry Lee Lewis. As a result, he is the only non-Latino selected as grand marshal of the East L.A. Christmas parade and is a favored award recipient among Latino organizations.

In 1960, Laboe teamed with Dick Clark to stage an unprecedented rock'n'roll show at the Hollywood Bowl that sold 18,000 tickets.

On Laboe's playlist in 1963 was "Angelito" and in 1967 was "Lo Mucho Que Te Quiero" because those two million sellers were among his radio audience's favorites, especially after René and René's appearance on Dick Clark's "American Bandstand." It's no secret that Laboe was one of Rene's biggest fans.

"Throughout the years, Laboe was responsible for many, many concerts featuring scores of super stars including René and René.

"That's because he is more Chicano than some Chicanos," added comedian Paul Rodríguez, who grew up listening to Laboe. "And everyone from the toughest *vato* to the wimpiest guy would say the same."

Laboe never retired and in later years he transformed himself into a promoter of aging Black and Latino rock'n'roll acts 'who never faded from Mexican American fans of oldies.'

Today, at 87, René is still an oldie, but a goodie. Therefore, Laboe kept on booking René René, Sunny Ozuna and sometimes Joe Bravo on his Chicano Soul Legends concerts for *firme* homies until developing pneumonia that claimed his life on October 7, 2022.

RENÉ RENÉ MAKES VIDEOS IN CALIFORNIA

After having written and recorded hundreds of songs, René Ornelas needed to make some music videos. One of his very good friends, Tony Reyes from Whittier, California, was one of the top video producers in the area. He used to work in production at KTTV in Hollywood and at KABC News. He also worked as a government photographer and video director. Tony worked in video production on the popular TV show "Soul Train" with Don Cornelius. He later started Jammin' Classics, producing documentaries and music videos for many recording artists. René René was the first to do music videos with Tony Reyes at Jammin' Classics doing his million-selling songs "Angelito," "Lo Mucho Que Te Quiero," "Baby Doll," "Mango," "Babalú," "Tequila" and some of his other hit songs.

Working side by side with Tony, is a cute and talented Italian girl, Cynthia Cecena, who used to work in production at ABC studios on the popular TV show "General Hospital." Tony and Cynthia are both very gifted and have a God-given talent in producing all types of videos. If you need to make some good professional videos, Tony can be reached by going to JamminClassics@gmail.com or by calling him at (562) 305-1199 in Whittier.

I mentioned the video "Tequila" earlier and there is a bit of trivia I want to add. If you watch the video, you can see a polka dot handkerchief in my coat pocket. I have always liked polka dots, so I started looking for a black and white polka dot handkerchief. I couldn't find one at any store, so my wife suggested that I make one from a piece of cloth; but I just couldn't find what I wanted. I even went to some resale shops and bought some polka dot blouses and dresses to cut up into handkerchief-size squares. The problem was that the dots were either too far apart, too close together or they were just too small to make the right statement. After searching for months, I finally found just the right thing. When I brought it home, my wife started laughing hysterically. I had taken a piece of cardboard, slipped it into the material to give it some shape and put it into my brand-new coat pocket. My new handkerchief was made from a beautiful black and white polka dot *calzetín* (sock). It was perfect! For years now, that sock/handkerchief has been my signature piece. When I'm performing, other artists ask me where I bought that beautiful polka dot pocket handkerchief. If they only knew that it was a sock!"

"Another bit of trivia from the "Tequila" video is that since I forgot to take my hat to California, I had to borrow Frank Álvarez's Fedora with a feather. The car I am riding in belongs to Frank and you can see the name of the car club --- Bomb Heaven --- in the back window. The other members of the car club drove their classic cars all down the streets of East LA as Tony was making the video. You can see several of the members waving and dancing in the video.

"One of them was brother Rich, who has since passed away. May he rest in peace. Members in the club are Frank Álvarez, president; Richard Reyes, Cindy and Rudy Zepeda, Rudy Campos, Sergio Ocampo, Anthony Rodríguez, Eddie Rodríguez, Timmy Rodríguez, Sergio Vásquez and Robert Del Guesaval. It was such a pleasure working with these car club members.Thanks to everyone. You go, Bomb Heaven!"

TODAY

Today, René Ornelas, the healthy, energetic singer/songwriter/composer continues to write and record new songs. René, like Sunny Ozuna, also continues to tour nationally as an Oldies But Goodies artist with several booking agencies. He performs at various large venues attracting thousands of people and he also entertains in gambling casinos in Nevada and all over the west coast. René has also been performing on the Carnival Cruise Lines based out of Long Beach, California. These cruises are arranged by Dale Berger, another top booker from California.

As a little bit of trivia, on the last cruise, René and his wife Saundra were mistakenly assigned to a cabin the size of a closet. Because René is very humble, he would not complain. His friend, Sal Rodríguez, who has played drums with War, Tierra, Malo and Santana for many years, was appalled when he saw the size of the tiny room. So, he jumped right in and ran down to speak to management about the situation. He said to her, "Do you know who René René is? He is a super star who has sold millions of records and has appeared with Dick Clark on "American Bandstand." He deserves better accommodations!" She immediately changed their tiny room to a much more spacious cabin with a large balcony that had a perfect view of the ocean.

Besides performing at all these concerts, René René is still doing the "Tejanos for Christ" concert tours in Texas.

As for Sal, besides being René's friend, he is also a fan whose bucket list includes doing a duet with him. This wish came true during a visit to San Antonio on January 8, 2023 when they entered Marvin Palacios' studio to re-record "Angelito" and "Lo Mucho Que Te Quiero."

Best of all, this writer was present at the recording session when the former lead vocalist for Malo, Pastor Martín Cantú, plus his brother Michael walked in with a bag of goodies. Then, after laying the bag on a table, the minister yelled out, "It's Miller Time." Then, he proceeded to pull out an assortment of barbecued meat from Bill Miller's BBQ for everyone to enjoy during a recording break.

Sal is also a Christian brother. Thus we had a brief fellowship during which Martín prayed and Rene's wife, Saundra, laid hands on David Tello of Los Hermanos Tello. Then it was back to business.

There's no stopping this in-demand 87-year-old performer. Today, René Ornelas continues to be a favorite interview subject. His most recent television appearance - along with Rudy Tee Gonzales of the Reno Bops and veteran radio personality Lee Woods - was on George Rivas' "Tejano Legends TV Show" which can be seen on the Roger Hernández-

René and Saundra Ornelas with Madeline and Sal Rodríguez of War following a Latin Legends Cruise gig onboard the Carnival Radiance.
Photo courtesy Sal Rodríguez

Rudy of the Reno Bops, Ramón Hernández and René (back row) Roger Hernández, host George Rivas, and Lee Woods following an interview on the "Tejano Legends TV" program, which can be seen on the Totally Tejano Television network on Roku TV
Photo by Mary Ann Rodríguez Hernández

owned Totally Tejano Television Network on Roku TV.

"Above all, he is always ready to greet the public," said fellow living legend, Carlos Guzmán.

On hearing this, René's wife, Saundra said, "René will not walk out the door of his house to go outside and pick up the newspaper, take out, or bring in the trash can if he does not shower, shave, spray his hair and put on some nice, clean clothes because he always wants to look his best."

"That's right, because there's always the chance someone will see you," René confirmed.

"Sure enough, there was one day when someone drove by and when the driver recognized me, he stopped, turned to his kids, and said, 'That's René René. He appeared on "American Bandstand," et cetera, et cetera. Then, they got out, took pictures, got my autograph and were on their way. That's why I always have to be clean and nicely dressed," the always dapperly attired entertainer said with a smile.

RECAPPING "ANGELITO" AND "LO MUCHO QUE TE QUIERO" POPULARITY

It is interesting to note that regardless of which company René Ornelas recorded for, all the label owners asked him to re-record "Angelito" and "Lo Mucho Que Te Quiero" for their company because they knew those songs would make good money for them. That was mandatory of ARV, White Whale (a division of Falcón Records in Los Angeles), Arriba Records (Los Angeles, CA), East Bend, Certron, Epic, Joey, JB Records, Hacienda, RCA, Manny Records and Catalina record company.

Although some people claim that they want to hear only the original recordings, we would like to explain why they have been re-recorded. To satisfy the nostalgic craving for the two greatest hits by René and René, he recorded brand new versions of "Angelito" and "Lo Mucho Que Te Quiero." So, if you have old 45 rpms, vinyl singles or 33 1/3 rpm vinyl albums and they are scratched, warped, broken, misplaced, lost, or now in the possession of your ex, here's your chance to enjoy these golden oldie classics, as you've never heard them before. They have now been recorded with the latest technology, and digitally remastered for a new and better listening experience. Enjoy!

Joe Quezada, the upright bass player and fifth member of the Casa Blanca Quintet supposedly left Laredo and was never heard from again.

Jorge "Tito" Sánchez preceded all of the Quarter Notes' members in death.

Lizandro Héctor "Chando" Guerra, who preceded Sánchez. passed on December 13, 2013.

René Ede Herrera joined God's Heavenly choir on December 20, 2005. A week later, Ornelas, the sole surviving vocalist and Ramón Hernández attended his viewing and burial in Laredo.

Juan Garza-Góngora went to be with our Lord and Savior on October 12, 2016, and was buried in San Antonio. He is survived by his wife, Alma, his children, and grandchildren.

John Eugene "Juan" Orfila died on Sunday, November 1, 2020. A proud Laredoan, Orfila dedicated 28 years of his life working for the City of Laredo's Community Development Agency. He was also happy to oblige his community by reuniting The Quarter Notes for nostalgic musical shows. But since René Ornelas had relocated to San Antonio, Orfila would enlist his dearest friend, "Tito" Sánchez to complete the quartet.

Orfila was survived by his wife Laura née Martínez, his children: John Jr., Robert J., Dr. James E. Orfila, Laura O'Conner and their spouses.

René Ornelas continues to write and record more of his unique bilingual compositions. He has recorded over forty LPs and CDs in his extensive career. His latest release, "Mango," is sure to be another million-seller hit. Check out his new video on utube. René Ornelas, who turned 87 on August 26, 2023, is still going as strong as the Energizer Bunny performing in concerts all over the Southwest.

Jorge Ramírez was inducted into the Tejano Roots Hall of Fame in January 2023 and turned 79 in

November. He is now retired but continues to write new songs.

Marvin Palacios, now 69, continues to write, publish songs, is a music consultant, was chosen for induction into the Tejano Roots Hall of Fame and plays guitar at St. Thomas More Catholic Church. Furthermore, he recently reunited with René Ornelas as the other René to embark on a tour as "René and René."

Mario Rivera moved to Layton, Utah after eight years of singing with René Ornelas.

"It's a city about 30 miles north of Salt Lake City and once I got here, I joined a regional Mexican group and recorded an album as a backup vocalist and guitarist for that group. And I also sang at restaurants with a computer for a while," Mario said.

Now 68, Rivera says, "*Ahora no tengo pelo* (I now have no hair), but I'm singing with Grupo Ilusión, which features Elaine Gallegos on lead vocals." Moreover, he and Gallegos also sing as a duet. As a soloist, Rivera loves to perform much of René and René's repertoire.

Richard Noriega, the former KGNS-TV anchor in Laredo now 73, showed off his journalist style by summarizing his up-to-date information in one sentence, "I still play music on the side, but my main gig now is doing 'Rich in the Morning, a Sunday morning show from 6:30 a.m. to 9 a.m. on KHOY radio." However, he occasionally performs with the Ramiro Cervera Orchestra. In addition, he is often asked to sing the National Anthem at various events and functions in Laredo.

On the personal side, Noriega is extremely proud of his four sons, Jason and Aaron Noriega, Tito and Benjamin "Ben" Montiel, who have blessed him and his wife, Ophelia née Falcón, with 13 beautiful grandchildren. As for the headliners of the Chicano Oldies Tour, here's their latest information.

Raúl, best known as Roy Montelongo went to be with our Heavenly Father on June 14, 2001 at age 62.

Joe Bravo (r.n. José Jasso) went to be with our Lord on February 21, 2022. He was 76.

Sunny Ozuna, now 80 continues to tour on the oldies circuit along with René and other internationally known American music pioneers.

Carlos Guzmán, now 83, continues to perform and make personal appearances, but not as often.

SELECTED DISCOGRAPHY

MIKE ORNELAS Y SU ORQUESTA
1949   Bonita (Luis Alcaraz) Panchito Rodriguez con la orq. de MO   IDEAL   201
https://frontera.library.ucla.edu/recordings/bonita-13
Side B: Así Lo Quisiste (Tomas Vogel Moralez)
https://frontera.library.ucla.edu/recordings/asi-lo-quisiste-5
1949   Side A: Los Tres Sabinos (A. Ballardo) vals instrumental   IDEAL   331
https://frontera.library.ucla.edu/recordings/los-tres-sabinos-10
Side B: Tengo Un Amor polka instrumental
https://frontera.library.ucla.edu/recordings/tengo-un-amor-15
Side A: Carmen Mi Amor (Mike Ornelas)   IDEAL   343
https://frontera.library.ucla.edu/recordings/carmen-mi-amor-0
Side B: Plenilubio (Jesús Reyes Limón) Vals
https://frontera.library.ucla.edu/recordings/plenilubio-0
Side A: Raquel vas instrumental   IDEAL   620
https://frontera.library.ucla.edu/recordings/raquel-1
Side B: La Coquena (Mike Ornelas) polka instrumental
https://frontera.library.ucla.edu/recordings/la-coquena-2
No Te Me Retires polka instrumental   IDEAL   627
https://frontera.library.ucla.edu/recordings/no-te-me-retires-0
Blanca Estela danzón instrumental
https://frontera.library.ucla.edu/recordings/blanca-estrella
Side A: La Niña Popaff (Pérez Prado) instrumental   IDEAL   678
https://frontera.library.ucla.edu/recordings/la-ni%C3%B1a-popaff-0
Side B: Nidito De Amor (instrumental)
https://frontera.library.ucla.edu/recordings/nidito-de-amor-7
1951   Carmencita polka   IDEAL   954
https://frontera.library.ucla.edu/recordings/carmencita-6
Rico, Caliente Y Sabroso
https://frontera.library.ucla.edu/recordings/rico-caliente-y-sabroso-6
1951   Sylvia (D. Pérez Prado) vals instrumental   IDEAL   958
https://frontera.library.ucla.edu/recordings/sylvia-14
Side B: Suby A La Mangano (Mike Ornelas) suby instrumental
1951   Tres Dilemas (V. Garrido) Canta Pepe Morales   IDEAL   964
https://frontera.library.ucla.edu/recordings/tres-dilemas-2
Side B: Por Pasar El Rato (M.A. Vallsdares) Canta Pepe Morales
https://frontera.library.ucla.edu/recordings/por-pasar-el-rato-4
Side A: No Te Tardes (Raul Gracia) polka   IDEAL   1176
https://frontera.library.ucla.edu/recordings/no-te-tardes-2
Side B: Raton Macias danzón instrumental
https://frontera.library.ucla.edu/recordings/raton-macias-4
Side 1: El Gallo Giro polka instrumental   FALCÓN   A49
https://frontera.library.ucla.edu/recordings/el-gallo-giro-4
Side 2: Canción Mixteca vals instrumental
https://frontera.library.ucla.edu/recordings/cancion-mixteca-70
Side 1: El Tacuachi Ito (Manuel Compeán) polka instrumental   FALCÓN   A62
https://frontera.library.ucla.edu/recordings/el-tacuach-ito-0
Side 2: Rag Mop (Wills, Lee-Anderson, Deacon) instrumental
https://frontera.library.ucla.edu/recordings/rag-mop-0
Side 1: Sueño (Arturo Vásquez) vals instrumental   FALCÓN   A64
https://frontera.library.ucla.edu/recordings/sueno-10
Side 2: Donde Estas Corazón (Luis Martínez Serrano) danzón
https://frontera.library.ucla.edu/recordings/donde-estas-corazon-10
Side 1: Quinto Patio (Luis Arcaraz) Canta Pepe Morales   FALCÓN   A87
https://frontera.library.ucla.edu/recordings/quinto-patio-5
Side 2: Amor Y Mas Amor (Bobby Capo) bolero mambo
https://frontera.library.ucla.edu/recordings/amor-y-mas-amor-2
Side A: Amigo (Hilario Duarte) Canta Chris Sandoval   TORERO   TO-112
Side B: Su Mama Tuvo La Culpa cha cha cha instrumental

RENÉ ORNELAS' DISCOGRAPHY with MIKE ORNELAS Y SU ORQUESTA
1950   Recuerdo Mi Pasado (Arturo Vásquez) (Canción Fox) as Víctor René
      https://frontera.library.ucla.edu/recordings/recuerdo-mi-pasado-1
      La Chinguenguenchona (Raúl García)   TORERO   TO-110
1970   … Canta René (Long-Play 33 1/3 rpm vinyl album)   EL TORO   ETLP-8006

Once René and René became world known, this record company capitalized on their popularity, dug out long-lost obscure recordings, and released them as an album.

RENÉ'S 45 RPM 7" VINYL SINGLES
DISCOGRAPHY with THE QUARTER NOTES: (… denotes songwriter credits)

1954   Side 1: Pretty Pretty Eyes (René Ornelas)   GUYDEN   G-TQN 1
youtube.com/watch?v=MHEKNjIi2OM
Side 2: I Don't Wanna Go Home (Jimmy O. Duncan) Only available on Amazon Music
1956   Loneliness (O-Toole/Herrera) / Come De Night   DE LUXE   6116
Loneliness: youtube.com/watch?v=Z0amAgdM4qA   re-released as   KING   5028
Come De Night: youtube.com/watch?v=4LzsLUY4mTE
1957   My Fantasy / Ten Minutes to Midnight (…/England)   DE LUXE   6129
My Fantasy: youtube.com/watch?v=Sil7eZsnICA
Ten Minutes to Midnight: youtube.com/watch?v=zzwQqXXP0Y0
Side 2-A   Who Am I   youtube.com/watch?v=5qOy8VvWjj8   FOX   2
1957 René Herrera wrote both sides of this single and sings lead on "Who Am I"
Side 2-B   Teen Age Blues youtube.com/watch?v=ccG82iZtvgM
    Remastered and re-released in 2015 by Bacci Bros Records music.apple.com
Dec. 1957   Like You Bug Me (E. René - R. Ornales) / Please Come Home (Ornales)
They misspelled Ornelas' last name on both sides of the record.
Like You Bug Me: youtube.com/watch?v=5yR7fUtw0rE   DOT   15685
Please Come Home: youtube.com/watch?v=ybCKGFj13oQ

LONG-PLAY 33 1/3 RPM VINYL ALBUMS with THE QUARTER NOTES

1959 Army Entertainment Program Album produced by the Special Services Division for the Sixth Annual   Ed Sullivan Show. Side 4 contains "Who Am I" by the Quarter Notes.
1960 "Rolling Along" All-Army Entertainment contest album features the Quarter Notes on its 10-record-set cover.
Side 6 contains "Mobile," "The End" and "Lazy River" by the Laredo foursome.
Most of the songs in the following discographies may be heard on YouTube.

DISCOGRAPHY AS RENÉ AND RENÉ – WITH RENÉ HERRERA
45 RPM VINYL SINGLES

Some YouTube links are provided so the reader can hear the actual early recordings that made René and René a household name. However, and "*" indicates there is 'no video' for that tune.

11-63   Angelito (Ornelas-Herrera) youtube.com/watch?v=hqOvBrw3MjM   JOX   JO#017
Write Me Soon (Herrera) youtube.com/watch?v=CsIexAveF_k
Released with yellow, green and white label
Angelito / It's Impossible ("Somos Novios") (Wayne, Manzanero)   EAST BEND   EB-501
It's Impossible (youtube.com/watch?v=Gv3lmKcx2Lw)
1964   Yo Te Lo Dije (I Could Have Told You) (C. Sigman-J. VanHeusen)   JOX   JO-025
youtube.com/watch?v=l44PJOpRMDs
Pretty Flowers Fade Away (Herrera) youtube.com/watch?v=G2uCa7qJsjY
4-28-64   Angelito / Angelito (radio station copies on red vinyl)   COLUMBIA   4-43045
9-22-64   Yo Te Lo Dije (I Could Have Told You) (C. Sigman-J. VanHeusen)
Side 2: Pretty Flower Fade Away (R. Herrera) Red label   COLUMBIA   4-43140
1964   Indeciso (Undecided) (S. Robin-C. Shavers) released in Mexico   CBS   5583
youtube.com/watch?v=bHIrht7hBUw
Side 2: Yo Te Lo Dije (C. Sigmen-J. Van Heusen)
11-9-64   Please Don't Bother (No Te Enojes) (R. Herrera)   COLUMBIA   4-43163
youtube.com/watch?v=pjJsQDD6PNM
Undecided (S. Robin, C. Shavers) Picture sleeve
1964   Angelito / Love Is for The Two of Us (Picture sleeve) (BELGIUM) SUPREME   S. 117
01-65   Chantilly Lace (J.P. Richardson)   JOX   JO-032
features The Dreamliners on backup vocals
youtube.com/watch?v=DROA5lfXEpE&list=RDDROA5lfXEpE&start_radio=1
I'm Not the Only One ("No Soy El Unico") (Milt Lance)   youtube.com/watch?v=6SChlFa1sOI
2-15-65   Angelito / Write Me Soon (Picture sleeve) (NETHERLANDS)   CBS   1.539
1965   Escribeme Pronto (Write Me Soon) (Herrera) / Angelito (COLOMBIA) CBS   45-2070
1965   Little Vagabond (Ornelas, Herrera) youtube.com/watch?v=01cjZ6l-c60   JOX   JO-041
Features Sylvia "Sol" Salas on background vocals
Little Peanuts (Guerrero, Ornelas, Lance)
1965   No Soy El Unico ("I'm Not the Only One") (Milt Lance)   COBRA   CO-212
youtube.com/watch?v=8SheSK_3aDY released on both a blue and a yellow label
Side 2: Creí ("My Dream") (Chucho Monge / Ornelas-Herrera)
youtube.com/watch?v=JKkvrc9ZNjo features Fred Salas on saxophone
1965   Miénteme (Every Day I Only Live to Love You) (Armando Domínguez / Ornelas-Herrera)

	youtube.com/watch?v=Y2w5e9gjNc8		
	Side 2: El Perro Bravo (Ornelas, Herrera) (written for Flaco Jiménez) COBRA		229
	youtube.com/watch?v=KaMtGVoG27c Special arrangement by Fred Salas		
1965	Miénteme / El Perro Bravo	VIVA	VV-103
06-65	Chantilly Lace (J,P,Richarson) vocal acc: The Dreamliners	ABC-	
	I'm Not the Only One (No Soy El Unico) (Milt Lance)	PARAMOUNT	15 10699
9-10-65	Chantilly Lace / I'm Not the Only One (UNITED KINGDOM) H.M.V. POP		1468
10-25-65	Chantilly Lace / I'm Not the Only One (NETHERLANDS) CBS		1.942
12-65	Side A: Loving You Could Hurt Me So (Ornelas-Herrera)	JOX	JO-050
	youtube.com/watch?v=sM__xHaT5PE (Picture sleeve)		
	features musical backup of The Dell Tones, was arranged by Fred Salas		
	Side B: Little Diamonds (Ornelas-Herrera) youtube.com/watch?v=y7hGCU-yKh8		
	Both sides: Special arrangement by Fred Salas Musical assistance: The Dell Tones		
1966	Loving You Could Hurt Me So / Little Diamonds (UK)	ISLAND	WIP 6001
1968	Enchilada José (Ornelas-Herrera) ARV INTERNATIONAL		ARV 5007
	Hiding In the Shadows (Ornelas-Herrera)		
1967	El Amor Es Para Los Dos (Lee-Izumi) (MÉXICO)	FALCÓN	116
	Sally Tosis (Ornelas-Herrera) youtube.com/watch?v=UAlgALwrPUM		
1968	Mornin'/ Lo Mucho Que Te Quiero	ARV INT'L	5011
	released on orange label and turquoise label orange label		
1968	Las Cosas (Think of The Moments) (Ornelas-Herrera)	ARV INT'L	5015
	Lloraras (Lawrence, Harold-Ramirez, Rafael)		
1968	Love Is for the Two of Us (Sydnes Lee Toku-?)	ARV INT'L	5019
	youtube.com/watch?v=0V1e_YPBGXc / Sally Tosis (Ornelas-Herrera)		
1968	Que Me Castigue Dios (Herrera-Ornelas) (MEXICO)	ARV INT'L	5024
	Side B: Mi Corazón Está Llorando (Rohr)		
1968	Side 1: Amor No Fumes En La Cama (Adolfo Salas)	FALCÓN	1742
	https://frontera.library.ucla.edu/recordings/amor-no-fumes-en-la-cama		
	Side 2: Cuando Llegue a Phoenix (Jim Webb-RenéOrnelas) as René/Mike Ornelas, Su Piano y		
	Ritmos https://frontera.library.ucla.edu/recordings/cuando-llegue-phoenix-0		
1968	Side 1: Enchilada José (Herrera-Ornelas)	FALCÓN	1747
	youtube.com/watch?v=EhEGSPt4jfc		
	Hiding in The Shadows (Ornelas-Herrera) youtube.com/watch?v=ls20BODP_E		
1968	Mornin' (George Ramírez) youtube.com/watch?v=AN6eEYiNPQ8 FALCÓN		1774
	Lo Mucho Que Te Quiero youtube.com/watch?v=F6p1XIdM6Ks		
1968	Lo Mucho Que Te Quiero / Las Cosas (Ornelas-Herrera)(MEXICO)	FALCÓN	1774
1968	Las Cosas youtube.com/watch?v=v1RSsygzhDE	FALCÓN	1801
	Relampago (Martínez Gil) youtube.com/watch?v=Pe9j6eJLOKU		
1968	Creí / Angelito	FALCÓN	1843
1968	Angelito	ISELA	IS-100
	Lloraras ("You Will Cry") (Harold Lawrence-Rafael Ramírez)		
1968	Side A: Lo Mucho Que Te Quiero	EAST BEND	EB-503
	Side B: Hablame (Michel) youtube.com/watch?v=73J1kuN3Ah4		
1968	He Sabido Que Te Amaba (DAR)	EAST BEND	EB-505
	youtube.com/watch?v=Tp3LwbXP-5s		
	Y Volvere (A. Barriere) youtube.com/watch?v=j_PKDxqbg7A		
1968	Crei (Monge, Herrera, Ornelas)	EAST BEND	EB-507
	Yo Vivo Mi Vida (DAR) youtube.com/watch?v=x-vkNnY6Ad4		
1968	Mienteme (Ornelas-Herrera) youtube.com/watch?v=JR6tJWdxaVU	E. BEND	EB-509
	El Amor Es Para Los Dos ("Love Is for the Two of Us") (Lee- Izumi)		
	youtube.com/watch?v=Nl7UY8X_-2o		
1968	El Amor Es Para Nosotros Dos ("Love Is for the Two of Us") (Sydney Lee-Taku-Izumi)		
	youtube.com/watch?v=fRljqy2mgNI	FALCÓN	1855
	La Mentira (Yellow Days) (Alvaro Carrillo) youtube.com/watch?v=Y2w5e9gjNc8		
1968	Lo Mucho Que Te Quiero / Mornin' El Salvador release	FALCÓN	AEF-612
1968	Lo Mucho Que Te Quiero / Las Cosas	FALCÓN	68086
1968	Lo Mucho Que Te Quiero (The More I Love You)	WHITE WHALE	WW 281
	youtube.com/watch?v=XDfEEWoUgSo Side 2: Mornin'		
	Made No. 14 on *Billboard*'s Top 40 Hits on Dec. 14, 1968, and stayed on the charts 9 weeks		
11-68	Lo Mucho Que Te Quiero / Mornin'(George A. Ramirez)	WHITE WHALE	WW 287
	Lloraras (Rafael Ramírez) youtube.com/watch?v=S16Di9wqzCw		
	WW 287 was RELEASED TWICE WITH TWO DIFFERENT B SIDES		
11-68	Lo Mucho Que Te Quiero / Lo Mucho (Radio Copy) WHITE WHALE		WW 287
1968	El Amor Es Para Nosotros Dos / Creí (Picture sleeve) (SPAIN)	MAFER	MF 20-101
1968	Lo Mucho Que Te Quiero / Lloraras (ITALY)	CBS	3881
1968	Lo Mucho Que Te Quiero	MCA	D2572
1968	Lo Mucho Que Te Quiero / Mornin' (CANADA)	WHITE WHALE	WW287X
1968	Lo Mucho Que Te Quiero / Mornin' (Pic sleeve) (NEDERLANDS) PRESIDENT		PTF 213

1968	Lo Mucho Que Te Quiero / Lloraras (UNITED KINGDOM)	MAJOR MINOR	MM 589
1968	Lo Mucho Que Te Quiero / Mornin' (Picture sleeve) (BELGUIM)	FRANKIE	141
1968	Lo Mucho Que Te … / Lloraras (Pic sleeve)(NORWAY/SWEDEN)	POLAR	1065
1969	Lo Mucho Que Te Quiero / Angelito (Picture sleeve) (SPAIN)	MARFER	MF 20-073
1969	Lo Mucho Que Te Quiero / Las Cosas (AUSTRALIA)	STATESIDE	OSS-8816
1969	La Capilla (Ornelas-Herrera) / Peleas (D.A.R.)	EAST BEND	EB-511
1969	Las Cosas (Ornelas-Herrera) / Mendocino (Doug Sahm)	EAST BEND	EB-511

NOTE: Two East Bend singles were accidentally released as EB-511

03-69	Las Cosas / Las Cosas (DJ Copy)	WHITE WHALE	WW-298
04-69	Enchilada José (Ornelas-Herrera) / Lloraras (Rafael Ramírez)	WHITE WHALE	WW-303
04-69	Enchilada José / Enchilada José (Promotion copy)	WHITE WHALE	WW-303
09-69	Love Is for the Two of Us / Sally Tosis	WHITE WHALE	WW327
1969	Should You Ever Leave Me (Cuando Tu Te Me Vayas)	ARV INT'L	A-5022
	(Ledesma, Herrera, Ornelas) youtube.com/watch?v=EQ9jsXXCe-A		
	Kiss Me One More Time (Herrera, Ornelas) youtube.com/watch?v=9ffEyaqMwx4		
1-31-69	Muchachita (Herrera–Ornelas) youtube.com/watch?v=ae6PS6rFu38	EPIC	5-10443
	Our Day Will Come (Nuestra Dia Vendra) (M. Garson – B. Hilliard)		
	youtube.com/watch?v=wwINUAbVlw0		
1970	Touch My Heart (B. Austin, J. Paycheck)	CERTRON	C-10007
	Apartment #9 (A. Mayhew, J. Paycheck) as Tommy Pharr		
08-70	My Amigo José (R. Ornelas, R. Herrera) (D.J. Copy)	CERTRON	C-10011
	Side B: Good Ole Days (R. Ornelas, R. Herrera Renato Correa, Raynaldo Rayol)		
	youtube.com/watch?v=Ot3QKfRk9lc		
1973	Lo Mucho Que Te Quiero / Mornin' (re-release)	GOLDIES 45	D-2572
1975	Angelito / Lo Mucho Que Te Quiero	ARRIBA	AR-102
1976	Miénteme (Ornelas-Herrera) / Creí (Chucho Monge)	ARRIBA	AR-111

45 RPM EXTENDED PLAY (EP) VINYL ALBUMS

1969	Side A: Lo Mucho Que Te Quiero / Mornin'	FALCÓN	FEP-35
	Side B: Angelito / Enchilada José		
1969	MUCHO RENÉ & RENÉ (MEXICO)	EPIC	EC-55011
	Side A: Angelito / Indeciso (Undecided) (S. Robin-C. Shavers)		
	Side B: Muchachita / Te Deseo Amor (I Wish You Love) (A. Beach-C. Trenét)		
	RENÉ & RENÉ	ARV INT'L	FEP-36
	Side 1: Las Cosas / Cuando Llegue A Phoenix		
	Side 2: Lloraras / Hand Me Down		
	EL AMOR ES PARA LOS DOS	ARV INT'L	FEP-38
	Side 1: El Amor Es Para Los Dos / Sally Tois		
	Side 2: Creí / La Mentira		
	RENÉ & RENÉ	FALCÓN	FEP-177
	Side 1: Angelito / Las Cosas		
	Side 2: Relampago (Hnos. Martínez Gil) / Lloraras (Rafael Ramírez)		

DISCOGRAPHY AS RENÉ & RENÉ – WITH JORGE RAMÍREZ:

1970	El Doctor Jeringa (Ornelas-Herrera)	FALCÓN	1875
	youtube.com/watch?v=fMHyq9tVex8		
	Cuando Tu Te Me Vayas (Ledesma, Ornelas, Herrera)		
	youtube.com/watch?v=jT6KhaTRgFU		
1971	La Perrita (David Curiel-R. Ornelas-J. Ramírez)	ORFEÓN	45-15058
	youtube.com/watch?v=ye30KOlovng		
	Side B; Tres Dias y Tres Noches (David Curiel-R. Ornelas-J. Ramírez)		
	youtube.com/watch?v=qt7S46cU1RY features Steven Jordán on both sides		
1971	Pasan Los Dias (R. Ornelas-J. Ramírez) /	ORFEÓN	45-15066
	youtube.com/watch?v=7yzBKiO6WGg		
	Se Está Haciendo Tarde (René Ornelas) youtube.com/watch?v=qntjpqpaeU4		
1971	Lado A: Yo Soy Chicano (N. Gómez)	ORFEÓN	45-15080
	youtube.com/watch?v=X3MVvWsV3cY		
	Lado B: Where Is The Love (Di Que Pasó) (Ralph McDonald • William Salter)		
	youtube.com/watch?v=-UFgz9bD1rI		
1971	RENÉ Y RENÉ (Extended-Play album)	ORFEÓN	EP-1204
	Side 1: Tres Dias Y Tres Noches / La Perrita / Side 2: La Diablita / Un Engaño Más		
1971	Side A: He Sabido Que Te Amaba (Luigi Tenco)	EAST BEND	EB-105
	Side B: Hablame (Paco Michel) as Fermín Dos Santos		
1971	Que Me Castigue Dios (Ornelas-Herrera)	EAST BEND	EB-205
	youtube.com/watch?v=04ocT-a954M		
	Mi Corazón Está Llorando (Rohr) youtube.com/watch?v=ewPAtrvm_dE Chicano funk		
1971	Dices Que Me Dejas youtube.com/watch?v=mzqpZPnrbWo	EAST BEND	EB-207
	Ya Volví youtube.com/watch?v=XRJceqaw6g0		

Year	Title	Label	Cat. #
1971	El Mexicano (Ornelas-Herrera) Described by some as Latin funk youtube.com/watch?v=WLQXt2yPy2A Really Hurtin' This Guy both (Ornelas-Herrera) youtube.com/watch?v=Bpy9gKcAt4o	EAST BEND	EB-209
1972	La Capilla (Ornelas-Herrera) youtube.com/watch?v=NZ1RRUD5KSA Peleas (DAR) youtube.com/watch?v=3eNozfFIqjA	EAST BEND	EB-211
1972	Put Me in Jail (Castiguame Ya) (Sunny Ozuna) youtube.com/watch?v=hxwpZ_IqrYE El Bandito (R. Buzzeo) youtube.com/watch?v=Uv81FLMu7Oc country	EAST BEND	EB-213
1972	Side A: Para Que Me Enseñaste (Ramírez, Ornelas) youtube.com/watch?v=xuq5BUuXPww Side B: Deja Que Murmuren (Ornelas, Herrera) youtube.com/watch?v=o7qMT9yfP2A	EAST BEND	EB-215
1972	Mira! (Ramírez-Ornelas) youtube.com/watch?v=ju3nOE4e8N0 Verdad Amarga (C. Veláquez) youtube.com/watch?v=S7VUjSyRUqo	EAST BEND	EB-217
1972	Cómo Has Combiado Mujer (Ramírez, Ornelas) youtube.com/watch?v=_cGRldoSG9U Cambiado was mispelled on label Contigo Aprendí (Armando Manzanero) youtube.com/watch?v=QlXAvdc-bfI	EAST BEND	EB-219
1972	Ingrata Mujer (Rosado) youtube.com/watch?v=BLnqts46GzE Poquito A Poquito (J. Ramírez, Ornelas) youtube.com/watch?v=tpn47vEqAAk	EAST BEND	EB-221
1973	* Te Vi Por Primera Vez / * The First Time I Saw You Girl Recorded by Ornelas and Ramírez / Both sides written by Palacios	ORFEÓN	45-15084
1976	No Puedo Darte Mas (Que Mi Amor) (Can't Give Anything But My Love) Toma Mi Corazón (Ketelboy-Creatore) as Rene	ARV INT'L	A-5109
1977	* Libre Cómo El Sol / * Mis Amiguitos as René	ARV INT'L	A-5136
1977	Side A: Ya Se Va (Jorge Ramírez) Side B: Cuando Vuelva A México (José Barrientos-René Ornelas)	ARV INT'L	A-5145
1977	* Cuando Vuelva A México / * Ya Se Va (J. Ramírez)	ARV INT'L	ARV-5145
1978	Side A: Estrellitas De Amor (Encarnación Fuentes) youtube.com/watch?v=Q1KTWVR4qaA Female vocalist unknown Side B: Que Pasaría (Marvin Palacios) youtube.com/watch?v=Zdva7w5taj4	ARV INT'L	5156
1978	Side A: Quisiera Ser (David Curiel) youtube.com/watch?v=g_Y-ZQtd_hg Side B: Corazón Corazoncito (Ramírez-Herrera) youtube.com/watch?v=73Z5xBzvBz8	ARV INT'L	5169
1979	Nena / Ya Me Voy Para Acapulco	ARV INT'L	5178
1980	Angelito / Lo Mucho Que Te Quiero	EAST BEND	EB-405
1980	Miénteme / Creí	EAST BEND	EB 407
	Till Then by The Classics / Angelito	GOOD OLD GOLD	018
	Mountain of Love by Harold Dorman / Lo Mucho Que Te Quiero	GOOD OLD GOLD	032
2011	Ingrata Mujer youtube.com/watch?v=VopDl0t9Ols Poquito A Poquito (J. Ramírez-Ornelas) youtube.com/watch?v=tpn47vEqAAk	PHOTOMASTER	CD

DISCOGRAPHY AS RENÉ ORNELAS

Year	Title	Label	Cat. #
1974	Lado A: Esperando A Mi Hijo (P. Anka-G. Antunez) youtube.com/watch?v=hHHNiOHglAE Lado B: Ya Volví (René Ornelas) w/SA sound organ as René Ornelas youtube.com/watch?v=vTQMD5JREDo	LADO A	5016
1974	Un Momento (Roberto Cantoral) youtube.com/watch?v=P_fTr8EQNQQ Una Carta De Cuba (G. Antúnez) is actually "Guantanamera" youtube.com/watch?v=teN0dQNFNPU	LADO A	5021
1975	Hey Baby (DAR) w/Spanish lyrics as René Ornelas youtube.com/watch?v=WLEUbVi9VUI Bajo Un Cielo Azul (M. Palacios-R. Ornelas) youtube.com/watch?v=ebCeN6zx_40	LADO A	5023
1975	Lado A: La Llevo En La Mente (René Ornelas-Marvin Palacios) Music: Marvin Palacios as René Ornelas youtube.com/watch?v=yn32q9lFdag Lado B: No Vivo Un Dia Sin Ti (Paul Williams) youtube.com/watch?v=_T4LZb8pwYQ	CARA	CA-120

DISCOGRAPHY AS RENÉ RENÉ

Year	Title	Label	Cat. #
1976	I'm Sorry Sir (M. Palacios-R. Ornelas) as René/René 180youtube.com/watch?v=BE-TZ6eNIvw Lado B: Try Me Again Tomorrow (R. Ornelas-M. Palacios) youtube.com/watch?v=MDqjzuuM7IQ	LADO A	5038
1976	Los Mucho Que Te Quiero / I'm Sorry Sir (Palacios-Ornelas) As René/René	LADO A	5042
1979	Nena (Ramírez-Ornelas) youtube.com/watch?v=MBKtqAthIxc Ya Me Voy Para Acapulco (David Curiel) René & René youtube.com/watch?v=funvOC0Luuc	ARV INT'L	5178
1979	*El Telephone (Andres Ríos) / *La Del Moñito Blanco (Ornelas)	ARV INT'L	5193
1980	Lado A: Dos Mujeres En La Misma (E.J. Ledesma)	ARV INT'L	5216

youtube.com/watch?v=TM8h94CixQ0
Lado B: Split Personality (E.J. Ledesma) English-language version of "Dos Mujeres"
youtube.com/watch?v=ln-aOZ7P6qU

1980	Dos Mujeres En La Misma / Split Personality (E.J. Ledesma)	ARV INT'L	AC-ARV-3671
1980	Dos Mujeres En La Misma / Split Personality (E.J. Ledesma)	FALCÓN	3671
1980	Dos Mujeres En La Misma / Split Personality (E.J. Ledesma)	FALCÓN	AC-ARV-3671

DISCOGRAPHY AS RENÉ or RENÉ ORNELAS

1982 Hoy Amanecí Pensando En Ti (Ornelas) as René   HACIENDA   HAC 285
youtube.com/watch?v=LC1FDDy80po
Dímelo (Ornelas) youtube.com/watch?v=54lrRfF8_o4
1983 Voy A Descubrir Un Paraiso (Love Is the Answer) (Ornelas-E.J. Ledesma)
youtube.com/watch?v=qdEv501VZ8I   as René   HACIENDA   HAC 306
Hay Cariño En Este Amor ("Because I Have You")
youtube.com/watch?v=nEseOtRCzDw
(Ornelas –Spanish lyrics / Palacios–English lyrics)
1984 Let's Turn Out the Lights (René Ornelas)   HACIENDA   HAC 314
youtube.com/watch?v=N6fmXzWP3rc   as René
Hoy Amanecí Pensando En Ti
1984 Quiero Dormir (Ornelas-Rick García)   as René   HACIENDA   HAC 318
youtube.com/watch?v=YyjpxDh1W84
Se Fué Mi Vida (Ornelas-Héctor Saldaña-David Saldaña) BUV: The Krayolas
youtube.com/watch?v=YomJKbmmNcQ
1985 Side A: Let's Turn Out the Lights (Ornelas)   HACIENDA   HAC 714
Side B: Hoy Amaneci Pensando En Ti (Ornelas)

DISCOGRAPHY AS RENÉ RENÉ

1985 Love Is the Answer (Un Paraiso) (Ornelas-Ledesma)   RCA INT'L   IP1-7895
youtube.com/watch?v=Gwt1Q71iyVA
Let's Turn Out the Lights (Ornelas)
1986 Vámonos A Cozumel (Ornelas)   HACIENDA   HAC-354
youtube.com/watch?v=6E5-CLKQVng music video featuring his wife and my wife Martha
Bienvenido Amor (Ornelas)   youtube.com/watch?v=ffE1R6lM1GA
Mailed out in collector's photo envelope
1986 Baby (Ornelas-Ramírez) available on "Topic"   HACIENDA   HAC-359
Ando Necio Por Tu Amor (R.O.)   youtube.com/watch?v=NRRtDxKTa2A
1987 Tequila (Chuck Rio) youtube.com/watch?v=sHDesR_GlTg   DISCOS CBS   ZSS-14008
René wrote lyrics to The Champs 1960s Grammy Award winner which was a monster hit
* Angel Dream (R. Ornelas)
1988 Quiero Pollo   youtube.com/watch?v=0blIsC9IYXQ   JOEY INT'L   646
Ando Necio Por Tu Amor   youtube.com/watch?v=KMONTvwu_9s   as René & René
1988 Menudo   youtube.com/watch?v=-6n_dwxWCMY   JOEY INT'L   653
Cuando Vuelva A México   youtube.com/watch?v=CPUzFluYWk8
1988 El Perro (Ornelas)   youtube.com/watch?v=mwY0fMvBvhs   JOEY INT'L   662
No Te Vayas (Soy Tu Amante) (Ornelas)   youtube.com/watch?v=MoLQT3OEtRY
1989 Yo Quiero Que Vivas Conmigo ("I Want You to Be My Lover") (Ornelas)
youtube.com/watch?v=RODqv7hAAGo   JOEY INT'L   675
Side B: Llorar (Cry) (Ornelas: Spanish lyrics.)   youtube.com/watch?v=9QyxBd6qtrw
1989 El Gallito Enamorado (Ornelas) youtube.com/watch?v=q2tInMzz0Z4   JB   JB-140
Las Cosas (Ornelas-Herrera)   youtube.com/watch?v=yD_l5hb3QYk
1990 Baby Baby (Corazán Regresa) (René Ornelas)   JB   JB-162
Embrujado (René Ornelas) youtube.com/watch?v=_R-x4ZkPIt4
1992 * El Ganador (Richard Allen) / * El Hombre Lobo (Salvador Tornel)   MANNY   MS-508
1992 El Tejano Man (Herbie Hancock)   MANNY   MS-519
La Ultima Canción (René Ornelas) youtube.com/watch?v=9uoIfTRT_EY

LONG-PLAY (LP) 33 1/3 RPM VINYL ALBUMS AS RENÉ & RENÉ

1968 **LO MUCHO QUE TE QUIERO, ANGELITO +**   ARV INT'L   ARVLP-1002
Contains "Far Away"   youtube.com/watch?v=8ccyAjIseQU
and "Hand Me Down"   youtube.com/watch?v=iXD6ySbAEm8
1968 **EL AMOR ES PARA LOS DOS**   ARV INT'L   ARV-105
Contains: "Besame Una Vez Más," "Crei," "My Cherie Amour," "Sally Tosis,"
"No No," "Cuando Tu Te Me Vayas," "Ya Volví," "La Mentira," "Haciendo Lo Mio,"
"El Doctor Jeringa" and "Muy Lejos"
1968 **"LO MUCHO QUE TE QUIERO, ANGELITO,**
ALL I NEED IS TIME AND MORE"   FALCÓN   FLP2085
re-released with same photo and tunes as ARVLP-1002
1969 **CUANDO TU TE ME VAYAS**   FALCÓN/PALACIO   LP 7697

1969	**LO MUCHO QUE TE QUIERO** national reléase	WHITE WHALE	WWS-7119

1969 **MUCHO RENÉ & RENÉ** (USA/Canada)   EPIC   BN 26459
The rarity and beauty of this album is that it contains five tunes that were 'never released' as a single. They are "Quizás, Quizás, Quizás" (J, Davis-O. Farres) youtube.com/watch?v=gTQRMlcTNck, "How Can I Tell Her" ("Cómo Puedo Decirselo") (R. Herrera-R. Ornelas) only available by subscribling to YouTube, "Raining My In Heart" ("Lloviendo En Mi Corazón") (B. Bryant-F. Bryant) youtube.com/watch?v=pM9gGVY1nn4, "I Wish You Love" ("Te Deseo Amor")("Que Reste-T-Il De Nos Amours")(Charles TRenét-Léo Chauliac) youtube.com/watch?v=jjkfXwI9aHg, and "More" ("Más") (N. Newell-R. Ortolani-N. Oliviero) youtube.com/watch?v=oEm5TR18do0&list=OLAK5uy_nhWQAYhDH2PJrpekaLpMh5-wTm-QyUZwA performed bossa nova style.

1969 **MUCHO RENÉ & RENÉ** (México)   EPIC   LNS-17008
1969 **MUCHO RENÉ & RENÉ** (Colombia)   CBS   DCA 867
1969 **CUANDO AMANEZCA**–By the Time I Get to Phx   FALCÓN SERIE 3000 FLP 3004
Compilation of East Bend recordings and what made this album seem to contain two new songs were that they retitled "Cuando Llegue A Phoenix" as "Cuando Amanezca" and "El Doctor Jeringa" to "Saquenme De Agui"

1970 **BESAME OTRA VEZ" – "KISS ME ONE MORE TIME**   CERTON   CIS-4001
Contains three songs never released as a 45-rpm single. They are "My Cherie Amour" (Wonder-Cosby-May) (youtube.com/watch?v=Yl6it1jAiks), "No No No" (Ornelas-Herrera) is not available on YouTube and "Doing My Own Thing" (Ornelas-Herrera) (youtube.com/watch?v=L-s7Zo2jYn4).

1970 **THE MAGIC OF RENÉ & RENÉ**   CERTON   CS-7008
Contains six songs never released as a 45-rpm single "Yesterday, Today and Tomorrow" (R. Ornelas-R. Herrera) (youtube.com/watch?v=TCSY4KB9FdM), "Padre" (P. Webster-A. Román) youtube.com/watch?v=eARxpKaJOHk&list=OLAK5uy_kifrigyU0Lp7Vzz2vg35LhnMd1dkSWELg&index=6), "Everybody's Talking" (F. Neal), "Take A Letter María" (R. B. Greaves), "All I Have To Do Is Dream" (youtube.com/watch?v=6cx222iRsMM), "Breaking Up Is Hard to Do" (N. Sedada-H. Greenfield) (youtube.com/watch?v=DkhKZMk6phI) and "Loving You Could Hurt Me So" (R. Ornelas-R. Herrera) youtube.com/watch?v=0IeaT_i8yCM) new version.

1971 René & René: **BIG TEN** compilation album   OVACION   LP-1105
1971 **ÉXITOS DE ORO** vol. 1 compilation album   EAST BEND   EB-1005

1971 René & René: **EL MEXICANO – PUT ME IN JAIL**   EAST BEND   EBLP-1010
Engineered by Paul Butts Mastered by Jeff Locket. "Ingrata Mujer" by Carmelo Rosado Photography and cover layout by César Agusto Martínez

1972 **BOSS OLDIES** compilation album   CBS   CS9359
1972 René & René: **¡MIRA!** w/Jorge Ramírez   EAST BEND   EBSLP 1015

1974 **RENÉ & RENÉ** aka "The Brown Album" (with Ramírez)   ORFEON   EP-12-38020
Side A was arranged and produced by Fred Salas; recorded at Amen Studios with Manuel "Manny" Guerra serving as technical advisor.
Side B was arranged and produced by Esteban "Steve" Jordán. It was recorded at Jones Studios in Houston, and is also unique in that it features accordionist Steve Jordán on half of the cuts

1976 **LA EPOCA DE ORO** De René & René – The Golden Era   ARRIBA   ARS-1005
1976 **MIÉNTEME - Y VOLVERÉ** - El Mexicano   ARRIBA   ARS-1010
   is a re-release of East Bend EBLP-1010 therefore featuring Ornelas and Herrera
1978 René & René: **"CREÍ"**   ARV INT'L   LP-1005
   Contains "Muy Lejos"

1978 René Y René: **CUANDO VUELVA A MÉXICO**–Ya Se Va   ARV INT'L   LP-1045
Contains six tunes never released as singles. They are "Alli En Laredo" (youtube.com/watch?v=hAfhC05G5zU), "Conozco A Los Dos" (Pablo Valdés Hernández) (youtube.com/watch?v=yo-QXOibkA0), "Esta Canción Es Para Ti" (Jorge Ramírez), "Te Espero En La Playa" (Jorge Ramírez-René Ornelas)(later versión) (youtube.com/watch?v=ToEgZGapaLo), "Nuestro Amor" (Rafael Ramírez), and "Sentimiento De Papel" (René Ornelas).

1978 René & René **"QUISIERA SER"** (David Curiel)   ARV INT'L   LP-1050
"Tengo Ganas De Tu Amor" and "Promesas Sin Cumplir" were written by Ramírez-Palacios. This album also contains "Nena," written by Ramírez and later re-recorded as "Baby," by Ornelas as René René.

1980 René René **"SOY TU AMANTE"** aka "No Te Vayas"   ARV INT'L   LP-1059

Contains a new versión of "Amor No Fumes En La Cama," "El Mismo Cuento" (Ornelas-Palacios), "El Telephone" (Andrés Ríos), "Eres Casado" (Carlos Landin), "Este Amor De Los Dos" (Marvin Palacios) (youtube.com/watch?v=N_SZyngEJmM), "La Del Monito Blanco" (René Ornelas), "La Movida" (Andrés Ríos), and "Soy Tu Amante (René Ornelas) (youtube.com/watch?v=piY2wMVe_vA&list=PLll4YKsPsotE6mPV5JjCY8RmjpFaRec5C).

1980 **RENÉ ORNELAS** LADO A LP-113

1983 **RENÉ RENÉ ORNELAS** HACIENDA LP-7002
Features Rick and Patricia García on background vocals; plus, The Krayolas (Héctor and David Saldaña) doing harmonies on "Dímelo," "Mafioso," and "Se Fué Mi Vida." The musicians on this album are Mike Gregory, keyboards; John Santos, harmonica; Cindy Engle, Christine Klosterman and Bob Zidicky on strings; Johnny Davis, guitar; Lewis Garing, bass; Tom Robinson, sax; and David "Poco" Falcón on drums.

1985 René René: **LOVE IS THE ANSWER** (Un Paraíso) RCA IL6-7417
Produced and arranged by Fred Salas. Recorded at Salasound Studios in San Antonio. Background voices by Rick and Patricia García.
Musicians in this production are Mike Gregory, keyboards; Cindy Engle, strings; Johnny Davis, guitar; Lewis Garing, bass; Tom Robinson, sax; John Santos, harmonica; and David "Poco" Falcón on drums. Furthermore, "Amor Escondido" features Fred Salas on keyboards and bass;
Sebastian Campesi, strings; and David González on electric guitar.

1985 René René: **HITS** compilation album RCA IL6-7476
1986 **LO MEJOR DE TEXAS** compilation album RCA IL6-7537

1987 René' René': **"FLASHBACK"** CBS ZML-14325
This album leased to Discos CBS International under license from Hacienda Records marked the return to his forte, bilingual oldies. This album contains:"Angel Dream," "Baby Doll" (R. Ornelas), "Chantilly Lace" (J.P. Richardson), "Deep Purple" (DeRosa/Pariah), "I Only Have Eyes For You" (Warren/Dublin), "Just A Dream" Jimmy Clanton/C. Matassa), "Little Bitty Pretty One" (R. Bryd), "Lo Mucho Que Te Quiero," "Please Come Home" (R. Ornelas) and "Tequila" (Chuck Río).
All vocals and Spanish lyrics by Ornelas. Milton Lance, publisher; Rick García and Joe De Los Santos, recording engineers; and Ricky, Joe and Ornelas mixed the album. Musicians on this album are Paul Valero, keyboards/synthesizers/bass; and David "Poco" Falcón on drums and percussion. Other credits include Ornelas' wife, Saundra Ornelas, as associate producer and this writer, Ramón Hernández, as personal and business manager, photographer also created the art and graphics.

1988 René' René': **QUIERO POLLO** JOEY INT'L 3132
Contains the title song plus "El Dia Que Regrese," "Menudo," "Ando Necio Por Tu Amor," "Sacame De Aquí," "El Aguila Va A Volar" (R. Ornelas/Ledesma), "Pico De Gallo" (R. Ornelas) and "Prisionero De Tu Amor" R. Ornelas).
Recorded at ZAZ Recording Studio with guitarist Gilbert Velásquez, engineer, mix down and guitar. Arrangements by Velásquez and Ornelas. Musical credits: Luvine Elías and Paul Valero, keyboards; Pete Ojeda and Paul Valero, bass; Donald Garza, trumpet; and Steve Solís on timbales.
Other credits include yours truly, Ramón Hernández, for photography

1989 René' René': **BABY DOLL** JB JB-1049-LP
René Ornelas wrote every single tune on this album which contains "Baby Doll" youtube.com/watch?v=e-ZB8GUbSWM, "Damelo Cosita" youtube.com/watch?v=AQ39umoovCA "Dices Que Me Dejas" youtube.com/watch?v=RbmH4LW6gdo, "El Gallito Enamorado" youtube.com/watch?v=q2tInMzz0Z4, "Las Cosas," "Tequila," "Se Esta Haciendo Tarde" youtube.com/watch?v=qntjpqpaeU4, "Se Le Vio" youtube.com/watch?v=XgW2SQ5mvAs, "Te Gusta Chicotear" youtube.com/watch?v=HwSFTo_t_Jw, "Tequila," and "Yo Quiero Estar Contigo" youtube.com/watch?v=bQc2_mPdzIE.
This album was recorded at Emerald Studios in San Antonio with Mitchel Markham, recording engineer; Ornelas, musical arrangements, Roland 626 drum machine and percussion; Luvine Elías, keyboards; Panchito Morales, saxophone; Saundra Ornelas, special sound effects
(She's the rooster you hear on "El Gallito Enamorado"). Photography by Ramón Hernández.

1990 René René: **PACHUCO** JB JB-1062-LP
All but two songs on this album were written by René Ornelas. They are "Que Casualidad" (Carlos Cardenas) and "No Tengas Miedo" (E.J. Ledesma) (youtube.com/watch?v=uxLDJ4EF5yM&list=OLAK5uy_mw5BbaH07GkOiHUhsTCVdeXLXgiWkA6t8&index=7) (youtube.com/watch?v=uxLDJ4EF5yM), plus "Estos Días" (René Ornelas/E.J. Ledesma) (youtube.com/watch?v=U5WvaOFrRhk). "Baby, Baby (Corazón Regresa)," "Bienvenido Amor," "Como Todo Un Caballero," "Ojitos Caprichosos" "Pachuco," " (youtube.com/watch?v=DiahzipZcHo&list=OLAK5uy_mw5BbaH07GkOiHUhsTCVdeXLXgiWkA6t8&index=3), "Embrujado,", "La Virgen Morena," and "Te Gusta El Chisme" made up the rest of this album.
Recorded at Hacienda Studios with Rick García for JB Records. The entire album was done with

Ornelas, vocals and 626 Roland drum machine and Luvine Elías on keyboards and bass. Photography by Ramón Hernández.

CASSETTES (Photography on all cassettes by Ramón Hernández)
1986 **VÁMONOS A COZUMEL**   HACIENDA   7054
Contains "Ando Necio Por Tu Amor" (youtube.com/watch?v=NRRtDXK1a2A&list=OLAK5uy_nPSQ5pv1zZOBIzaxphYH6RqyWv6ihtp2U), "Baby" (youtube.com/watch?v=GTKL8_peKj8&list=OLAK5uy_nPSQ5pv1zZOBIzaxphYH6RqyWv6ihtp2U&index=9), "Bienvenido Amor" (youtube.com/watch?v=ffE1R6lM1GA&list=OLAK5uy_nPSQ5pv1zZOBIzaxphYH6RqyWv6ihtp2U&index=5), "Chica-Chica" (youtube.com/watch?v=SGSDOciEMGw&list=OLAK5uy_nPSQ5pv1zZOBIzaxphYH6RqyWv6ihtp2U&index=4), "Donde Naci" (youtube.com/watch?v=MFb07Bz59dU&list=OLAK5uy_nPSQ5pv1zZOBIzaxphYH6RqyWv6ihtp2U&index=7), "El Dia Que Regrese" (Ramírez-Ornelas) (youtube.com/watch?v=5jqoaymFF8s), "Hey Sayonara" (youtube.com/watch?v=7wkxyqwen7A&list=OLAK5uy_nPSQ5pv1zZOBIzaxphYH6RqyWv6ihtp2U&index=10), "Los Celos" (youtube.com/watch?v=qoWsWoFcgME&list=OLAK5uy_nPSQ5pv1zZOBIzaxphYH6RqyWv6ihtp2U&index=8), and "Te Espero En La Playa" (Ramírez-Ornelas) (youtube.com/watch?v=5jqoaymFF8s).

1988 **EL PERRO** (BRAVO) all songs by René Ornelas   JOEY INT'L 3156
"La Cerveza Esta En Barata" youtube.com/watch?v=8RitcB8Oueg, "La De La Mini-Falda" youtube.com/watch?v=Zj2OP8AeyYM, "Llego Mi Amor" youtube.com/watch?v=g-olfgvBAWM

1989 René' René': **EL GALLITO ENAMORADO**   JB   JB-1049-LP
This cassette is actually the "Baby Doll" vinyl album, but renamed to "El Gallito Enamorado," the first song on that album. Thus, just refer to the information listed in the vinyl album.

1990 **15 ÉXITOS** compilation album   HACIENDA   SC-163

1990 **PACHUCO**   JB   1075
"La Virgen Morena," "Embrujado," "Ojitos Caprichosos," "Estos Días," "Te Gusta El Chisme," "Pachuco," "Que Casualidad," "Bienvenido Amor," "No Tengas Miedo," "Baby Baby (Corazón Regresa)"

1991 **SUGAR BABY** youtube.com/watch?v=1yZ2DNT_bEI   JB   1090
Contains new songs: "Ay Palomita" "Dame Un Besito" youtube.com/watch?v=yr3YQkkP2Ys, "El Bebito" youtube.com/watch?v=XqfU-nTm9Ic
and "Puras Mentiras" youtube.com/watch?v=k2xbGHLyqAk   All songs by René Ornelas

COMPACT DISCS
1992 El Ganador - René René - El Tejano Man   MANNY   MCD-3013
Contains "El Ganador" (Richard Allen), "El Hombre Lobo" (Salvador Tornel), "El Tejano Man" (Herbie Hancock), "La Ultima Canción" (René Ornelas), "Let Me Let Go" (Richard Allen) (youtube.com/watch?v=yXjqyFWxU_I), "Lo Siento Por Ti" (Agustin Lara), Más Cerca De Ti" (Richard Allen) (youtube.com/watch?v=W-mj97fzpAk), "Muñequita De Seda" (Dimas Garza), "Perdon" (Gabriel Ruiz Galindo), and "Voy A Volar" (Richard Allen) (youtube.com/watch?v=l2rz4Oy-rdo).

1992 **4 SÚPER ESTRELLAS**   MANNY   MCD-3019
features Sunny Ozuna, Jimmy Edward, Joe Bravo and René Ornelas singing new versions of "Angelito," "Lo Mucho Que Te Quiero" and "Hoy Amanecí Pensando En Ti"

1992 **NAVIDAD MUSICAL** contains "Triste Diciembre"   MANNY   MCD-3020

1993 **THE QUARTER NOTES – THE REUNION**   no label   no #
Contains: "Please Come Home," "Gigolo," "La Hiedra," "Lazy River," "Lo Mucho Que Te Quiero," "Te Estuve Esperando," "Bono Sera," "Loneliness," "The Great Pretender" and "Angelito." Recorded by all four original Quarter Notes singers.

1994 **AMOR AJENO**   JB   JBCD 1186
Includes new songs: Amor Ajeno youtube.com/watch?v=4xApA9-_F2s, "Embrujado" youtube.com/watch?v=sJqsvwe8ddA, "Estos Dias" youtube.com/watch?v=U5WvaOFrRhk "No Le Pongas Ajo" youtube.com/watch?v=Lmg-Ef6qN0M, "Tu Color Es Natural" youtube.com/watch?v=j-LQLc_r-Jk, and "Vigilante De Tu Amor" youtube.com/watch?v=soIRGFud0eg

1994 **15 GOLDEN HITS** – Éxitos De Oro – Orig. Hits Vol. I   PHONOMASTER PMD-001
       Contains "La Hiedra" and "Hijo De Su"
1995 **15 GOLDEN HITS** – Éxitos De Oro– Orig. Hits Vol. 2   PHONOMASTER PMD-013
1997 **GREATEST HITS** compilation album   THUMP   TH 9966
1998 **31 GOLDEN HITS** – Éxitos De Oro (2-CD set)   PHONOMASTER PMD-068

2000   **15 ÉXITOS** compilation álbum + six new tunes   JB   JBCD-5012
They are "Brindo Por Ella," "El Merengue," and "La Calentura" – all written by René Ornelas. Plus "Go Away" (Louis C. Cate) (youtube.com/watch?v=TYTEo1_wL3M) and "Tu Color Es Natural" (Alejandro G. Pérez) (youtube.com/watch?v=j-LQLc_r-Jk), Special thanks to Luvine Élias, keyboards; Panchito Morales, tenor saxophone; René Gasca, trumpet; and Armando Crespo. This album was recorded at Custom, Emerald, and Hacienda studios for Javier Benavides's JB Records. It was engineered by Toby Torres, Rick García, David González, Roberto Ybarra, and M. Markham. Art & graphics: Pixel Point Studios. Photography by Ramón Hernández

2001   **CAMINO DE LA MÚSICA**   CATALINA   5829 00012
New songs are "El Babalu" (René Ornelas) (youtube.com/watch?v=3bMRkbWLknU), "Mango" (René Ornelas), "Quien Te Dijo" (René Ornelas), "Sangre Mexicana" (René Gasca) (youtube.com/watch?v=6oRvjJ6gSMI), and "Te Necesito (I Need Your Loving)" (René Ornelas) (youtube.com/watch?v=dKu6z5rANmg). This CD also includes Marcos Orozco on "A Mis Padres" (Marcos Orozco) and "Amor Has Nacido Libre" (Blanez Cortez Camilo), plus Deya on "Amor Chiquito" (Ramiro Villalpondo) and, "Hoy Escribí Tu Nombre" (René Ornelas), Then, Orozco and Deya pair up to do a duet on "Para Decir Adios" (Roberto Figueroa) (youtube.com/watch?v=wbGDLYrYBiQ). CREDITS: Arthur Cadena, executive producer. Recorded, mixed and edited by Gilbert Velásquez. In addition, it was mastered by Kurt Wipfli at Wiptrax Studios. Art design and photography by Jorge Flores/The Graphic Studio. Musicians (by instrument) on this álbum were: Keyboards and programming: Óscar Cruz, Gabriel Zavala. Guitars: Gilbert Velásquez, Robert Ybarra, and David González. Bass: Richard López. Trumpets: René Gasca (plus programming and musical arrangements) and David Villarreal.
Gilbert Garza, trombone, Chente Barrera, drums; and Henry Brun on percussion.

2001   **GRANDES ÉXITOS** – Flashback   compilation album   HACIENDA HAC-7557
2002   **ANGELITO … y muchos éxitos más** compilation album   JOEY INT'L   3699

2003   **I'M A CHRISTIAN** (Soy Cristiano)   R&R   RRO-CD01
    René changed the lyrics to "Lo Mucho" to make it a Christian tune and did his own version of Gene Maclellan's "Put Your Hand in the Hand." This album contains eight new compositions by René. They are the title tune, "Are You Making Room for Jesus," "I Will Work for Food," "Jesus Christ," "Little Chapel," "Thank You," The Greatest Love Affair," and "The King Is Back." Robert Ybarra engineered this session at Studio Cats. Al Gómez played trumpet on all tunes and
yours truly did the photography and graphics.

2003   **LO MUCHO QUE TE QUIERO** (Christian album)   RENÉ RENÉ   RR-1001
Same as "I'm A Christian," but with photos and packaged as a regular CD.

2003   **SOY CRISTIANO** (I'm A Christian)   R&R   RRO-CD02
Godly songs with a deep heartfelt – sometimes bilingual lyrics. They are "Gracias" ("Thank You"), "Po Tu Mano" ("Put Your Hand"), "Oh Mi Dios" to the tune of "Baby Doll", "Sangre De Mi Cristo", "Capilla Blanca" ("Little Chapel"), the salsa-flavored "Yo Tengo Un Amigo," "Me Encontre JesuCristo" to the tune of "Angelito." The Christian hits continue with "Jesús Resucitó" to the tune of "Babalu," "Lo Mucho Que Te Quiero."

2005   **THE LORD IS ALIVE** (Jesús Revivió)   R&R   RRO-CD03
"There Is Favor In My Life," "Buenos Dias" to the tune of "Quiero Pollo, "Jesus Went to Work On Me," "The Power of The Spirit" to the tune of "Sangre Mexicana," "To Move A Mountain" to the tune of "Quiero Pollo," "I've Got A Friend in Jesus," "Surrender," "The King Is Back" to the tune of "Babalu" and "Celebrate," which is by far one of the catchiest, additive praise and worship song this writer has heard in years. Most importantly, every single song was written
by René Ornelas.

2005   **ANGELITO** (Christian album)   RENÉ RENÉ   RR-1002
Same as "The Lord Is Alive," but with photos and packaged as a regular CD

2005   **JESÚS REVIVIÓ** (The Lord Is Alive)   R&R   RRO-CD04
"Tengo Gracia," "Buenos Dias," "Yo Quiero Ser Libre," "La Sangre De Mi Cristo" to the tune of "Sangre Mexicana," "The Power of God" to the tune of "Babalu," "Yo Tengo Un Amigo," the awesome praise and worship "Celebrar," "Yo Me Entrego," and Jesús Resucitó."
Again, each tune was written by René Ornelas.

2005   **DON'T BE TALKING GOSSIP, TALK ABOUT MY JESUS**   R&R   RRO-CD05
"Christians We Must Unite," "The Mount of Olives," "Make A Stand for Jesus," "Come and Follow Me," "Jesus Will Reach Out to You," "The Day of Pentecost," "He Wrote My Name
in Heaven," "Now We're Singing to the Lord," and "Twelve Disciples of Jesus."

2005	**EL HIJO DE DIOS**	RENÉ RENÉ	RR-1003

Same as "Don't Be Talking Gossip," but with photos and packaged as a regular CD

2005	No Me Traigas Chisme … Háblame De Cristo	R&R	RRO-CD06

"Hay Que Juntarmos Mas," "En Un Jardin de Olivos," "Hay Que Hacer Batalla," "Encontre A Jesús," "El Hijo De Dios," "Llego Pentecostés," "Dios Escribio Mi Nombre," "Le Cantamos Al Señor," and "Pescadores de Cristo."

2006	**MIRA** re-release of East Bend EBSLP 101	GOLDEN EAGLE	GECD 7072
2007	**25 GOLDEN HITS** compilation album	HACIENDA	HAC-7874
2008	**ANGELITO** compilation album	RENÉ RENÉ	RRO-CD-001
2008	**LO MUCHO QUE TE QUIERO** (Secular álbum)	R&R	RRO-CD-002

Erroneously released with "same number" as 2003 "Soy Cristiano" Christian CD

2008	**MÉXICO** contains "Comprometida" (René Ornelas)	RENÉ RENÉ	RRO-CD-003
2009	**TEJANO** contains "Llego Mi Amor" (René Ornelas)	R&R	no #

2010	**EL TEJANO** – all songs on this CD by René Ornelas	Q-VO	QVO-013

'Estoy Durmiendo Solo" (youtube.com/watch?v=TTAsnB6r-o4), "La Cama Está Vacía," "La Flecha Me Pegó," "Presumida," "Que Lindos Ojos Tienes" (youtube.com/watch?v=B0L85FgiC_w), "¿Que Pasó?" (youtube.com/watch?v=TABe23dpa7c), "Yo Quiero Que Vivas Conmigo," and "Yo Soy Tu Gavilán." This album features producer/engineer and co-arranger Robert Ybarra on keyboards, guitar, synthesizer bass, David Farís, accordion; Max Baca, bajo sexto; Al Gómez, trumpet; and co-executive producer Chente Barrera on drums. It was recorded at Studio Cats Productions. Every single image was shot by ace photographer/graphics designer Jorge Flores. thegraphicsstudio.com.

2010	**ANGELITO** secular music compilation album	R&R	RRO- CD001
2010	**LO MUCHO QUE TE QUIERO** (Jesucristo) Spanish version	R&R	RRO-CD002
2012	**LO MUCHO QUE TE QUIERO** (Christian) English version	R&R	RR-1001
2012	**ANGELITO** (Subject changed to Jesucristo) (Christian) English	R&R	RR-1002
2012	**EL HIJO DE DIOS** (Christian)	R&R	RR-1003

Photography, art and graphics on all Christian CDs by Ramón Hernández
Some discography obtained at 45cat.com, discogs.com, youtube.com, frontera.library.ucla.edu, ebay.com and google.com.

2012	**THE QUARTER NOTES – ULTIMATE COLLECTION VOL. 2**	no ID	no #

René Herrera had passed in 2005 and René Ornelas was unable to attend and Jorge Ramírez went in his place. This CD contains "What A Difference A Day Makes," "Can't Help Falling in Love," "Love Is A Many Splendored Thing," "Love Me Forever," "the Naughty Lady of Shady Lane," "Nevertheless," "Perdón," "Sincerely," "You Always Hurt the One You Love," "You're Nobody Till Somebody Loves You," and "Ave María No Morro."

VIDEOS
01-87   Vámonos A Cozumel – One hour TV special   BIG "O" Video Productions

AWARDS and CAREER HIGHLIGHTS
11-27-57	Arthur Godfrey's Talent Scouts Contest: The Quarter Notes won 1st Place singing "Quien Será"
1958	Received the key to the city of Laredo, Texas
1960	USAREUR All-Army Entertainment Finals: The Quarter Notes won 1st Place with "Who Am I"
1960	Appeared on the Ed Sullivan Show
1960	All-Army Entertainment Grand Finalists Contest: won Vocal Group
1960	Appreciation plaque from Round the World With "Rolling Along of 1960" La Estrella De Plata, Mexico City Disco De Oro in Los Angeles
8-8-64	René and René sang "Angelito" on Dick Clark's "American Bandstand"
1969	Broadcast Music Inc. (BMI) Radio Airplay Achievement Award to René Ornelas and René Herrera for "Lo Mucho Que Te Quiero"
1969	"Lo Mucho Que Te Quiero" earned Ornelas and Herrera a Gold Record.
1973	KCOR 21st Anniversary trophy to René & René (Ornelas & Ramírez)
1976	Appreciation plaque from Pan AM Hillside in Austin
1977-78	Falcon Records' "Best Comeback Artist Award"
1978-79	El Globo De Oro: Golden Globe award to René & René (Ornelas & Ramírez) for "Dueto Internacional"
01-79	KUKA, Radio Fiesta award to René & René for "Corazón Corazoncito"
1979	La Estrella De Oro Award to Ornelas and Ramírez
1983	KIWW 3rd Annual Music Awards: Song of the Year - "Hoy Amanecí Pensando En Ti"
1983	KIWW 3rd Annual Music Runner-up: Male vocalist of the Year

Bonus Photos

"I've earned many awards. But my favorite award my children."

© Ramón Hernández

Rene's daughter and her husband

Denise   Louis Villarreal

Courtesy Denise Villarreal

Andrew's wife Jennifer Dunbar

Andrew Dunbar (Rene's son)

René and Saundra Ornelas

René gives much of his time to fundraisers and telethons

René checks out Ramón Hernández's exhibit at the Institute of Texan Cultures.

© Ramón Hernández

AWARDS and CAREER HIGHLIGHTS continued

1983	KIWW 3rd Annual Music Runner-up: Songwriter of the Year
1983	KIWW 3rd Annual Music Runner-up: Album of the Year
1983	KFLZ 4th Annual Music Awards: Song of the Year - "Hoy Amanecí Pensando En Ti"
10-14 83	TASA's El Zenzontli Award: Most Promising Solo Artist
10-14-83	TASA's El Zenzontli Award: Most Requested/Most Popular Song "Hoy Amanecí Pensando En Ti"
	TASA: Texas Association of Spanish Announcers
1983	Tejano Music Awards: René & René nominated "Vocal Duo of the Year"
1984	Tejano Music Awards: René Ornelas nominated "Male Vocalist of the Year"
1984	Tejano Music Awards: 'Hoy Amanecí Pensando En Ti' nominated "Song of the Year"
1984	Tejano Music Awards: 'Hoy Amanecí Pensando En Ti' nominated "Single of the Year"
1984	KFLZ: "Que Feliz" Music Awards: "Hoy Amanecí Pensando En Ti" won "Song of the Year"
1984	KFLZ: René Ornelas nominated "Male Vocalist of the Year"
2-26-84	Mike Ornelas (René Ornelas father) was posthumously inducted into the Tejano Music Awards Hall of Fame
1985	Tejano Music Awards: René Ornelas nominated "Male vocalist of the Year"
1985	Tejano Music Awards: René Ornelas nominated "Songwriter of the Year"
1987	Tejano Music Awards: René Ornelas nominated "Songwriter of the Year"
1988	Tejano Music Awards: René Ornelas nominated "Songwriter of the Year"
1989	Tejano Music Awards: "Flash Back" nominated "Album of the Year"
2-10-90	Ornelas and Herrera were inducted into the Tejano Music Hall of Fame
3-12-93	Ornelas presented Selena with the "Best Entertainment of the Year" award at the 13th Annual Tejano Music Awards. Also present were Freddy Fender and Sunny Ozuna
3-31-93	Ornelas was inducted into the Hispanic Entertainment Hall of Fame
7-13-2001	Ornelas and Herrera were inducted into the Tejano Roots Hall of Fame in Alice, Texas
5-15-2014	Rene Ornelas was inducted into the Rocky Mountain Promoters Association Music Hall of Fame in Denver, Colorado
5-8-2015	Rene Ornelas received a Lifetime Achievement Award from Radio Aztlan

TELEVISION APPEARANCES
Ed Sullivan Show
Arthur Godfrey Show
Dick Clark's "American Bandstand
Domingo Peña Show   "
Val De La O
Raul Velásco's "Siempre En Domingo
Johnny Canales Show   "
Video Estelar
Artistas Tejanos
Dr. Zeko show
Mundo Musical
Noche De Estrellas
Estrellas De Tejas
Pepsi Peña Show
Cita con Carlos
La Onda En Tejas
En Caliente
Rincón Bohemio
Está Con Placido
En San Antonio
Óscar Zamora Y Don Chema
Festival OTI
MEJOR QUE NUNCA TV Special
Tejano Legends TV

To contact Ornelas, one may email René
at reneloveslucy@gmail.com
To contact the author, email him at
ramon.photog.hernandez@gmail.com

This book is dedicated to my
handsome son, author, photographer, pro ice skater,
Antonio Hernández Conte, MD, MBA, FASA
and Daddy's beautiful little girl
Susanna Simona Conte "Susie" Hernández

ABOUT THE AUTHOR

Ramón Roberto Hernández is a recognized musicologist, Latin American contemporary historian, archivist, writer, photographer, ghost writer, author, co-author, and researcher; plus, author, of *Redneck Meskin Boy: The Little Joe Story*, and publisher of five *Hispanic Entertainment Directory* reference books (1990, 1992, 1995, 2000 and 2005).

After serving 23 years in the United States Navy during which he served in Europe, Africa, the Caribbean and the Orient, he retired as a Radioman Chief Petty Officer on May 31, 1983. Since then, he has dedicated his life to documenting and preserving Texas' Chicano/Tex-Mex music history. To sustain himself, he was a contributing writer to the *San Antonio Express-News*, *Billboard* magazine and *La Prensa*. Also *Latino Star*, *Streettalk* and *Nuestra Música* magazines, plus many other Latino publications.

As a photographer, his work has appeared in *Time*, *Newsweek* and other national magazines He also was a publicist for Patsy Torres, Selena, Ram Herrera, and Emilio Navaira to name a few. He also worked as a Latin music promoter for Ralph Mercado's RMM label on the road with Celia Cruz, Tito Puente and other artists.

Acknowledged as a walking encyclopedia of Latin American music, this native Texan's prominence is nationwide as a collections specialist and curator. His expertise is also acknowledged by curators the Smithsonian Institute, the proposed National Museum for the American Latino and other historical preservation entities in the U.S.

As an archivist, he has assisted the Bob Bullock Museum, the Institute of Texan Cultures and others with artifacts/memorabilia. Furthermore, the Ramón Hernández Collection, which is available for research by students, professors, and the general public, was acquired by the Wittliff Collections in San Marcos, Texas in 2018.

This proud native American is also a consultant to several PBS Latin music documentaries and has been the subject of several newspaper articles and television programs. As an example: "Texas Country Reporter."

Hernández also serves as a consultant, advisor and panelist at symposiums and conferences and as a featured speaker at libraries, colleges, and universities.

As an author, this octogenarian is concurrently writing *Sunny and the Sunglows/Sunliners, Texas Chicanos in Doo Wop and Rock 'n' Roll Music*, *The San Antonio Westside Sound,* and *The Latinization of American Music*; plus, a five-volume *Tejanopedia*.

For more information, google Ramón Hernández Collection or email him at ramon.hispentpublishing@gmail.com.

Made in the USA
Columbia, SC
21 January 2025